KU-028-700

ECONOMIC BEHAVIOUR

ECONOMICS AND SOCIETY SERIES
General Editor: Professor Colin Harbury

1 ECONOMICS IN SOCIETY: A BASIC COURSE
by D. T. King and G. D. Hamilton

2 SOCIAL AND BUSINESS ENTERPRISES
An Introduction to Organisational Economics
by J. S. Boswell

3 PROBLEMS OF ECONOMIC POLICY
by Keith Hartley

4 AN INTRODUCTION TO QUANTITATIVE ECONOMICS
by Brian Haines

5 PRICE DETERMINATION AND PRICES POLICY
by Joan Mitchell

6 MACROECONOMIC POLICY IN THEORY AND PRACTICE
by John Brooks and Robert W. Evans

7 LAW AND ECONOMICS
by J. M. Oliver

Economic Behaviour

An Introduction

COLIN HARBURY
Professor of Economics, The City University, London

London
GEORGE ALLEN & UNWIN
Boston Sydney

First published in 1980

GEORGE ALLEN & UNWIN LTD
40 Museum Street, London WC1A 1LU

British Library Cataloguing in Publication Data

Harbury, Colin Desmond
Economic behaviour. – (Economics and society series).
1. Economics
I. Title II. Series
330 HB171 80–40515

ISBN 0-04-330305-6
ISBN 0-04-330306-4 Pbk

Set in 10 on 11 point Press Roman by the Alden Press and
Printed and bound in Great Britain by
William Clowes (Beccles) Limited, Beccles and London

Contents

PART THREE NATIONAL INCOME OUTPUT AND THE PRICE LEVEL

PART FOUR ECONOMIC POLICY

PART FIVE THE NATURE OF ECONOMICS

Preface

Every teacher of an introductory course in economics knows that his first problem is where to begin. Economics is not a subject with a natural starting point and logical development. You can begin almost anywhere, but wherever you do begin you cannot get far without wishing you had already dealt with something else to clarify the point you are making.

I have experimented with countless orderings but never managed to overcome the problem. The solution I have favoured has been to try to get students to skip quickly through their main text. 'Don't bother to master the details', I tell them, 'just get a feel for what the subject is all about and then go and start your serious study.' I do not know why I delude myself this is good advice. I admit that very few people take it. I can't say I blame them. The excellent texts I recommend for the course are just too long. It is not realistic to expect anyone to 'skip through' over 800 pages of Lipsey, Samuelson or Baumol and Blinder.[1] The result is perennially predictable. Too many students are overwhelmed by the detailed analysis they are required to study. They go around in a kind of haze, examining the structure of the bark of trees without any idea what sort of a wood they are in. It usually seems to take many months before the first glimmer dawns of the nature of economics and why they have been learning the technicalities of elasticity and marginal revenue or, if they started with macroeconomics, the multiplier and the quantity theory of money.

The solution to the problem of how to start the beginner off is, I believe, obvious. You get him or her to read a book which is a lot shorter than his main text, but which will put the subject into context. This is the book I have tried to write.

There is, of course, no shortage of brief introductory books on economics, but I have yet to find one that fits my bill. They seem to be either too simple, too discursive, too problem-oriented, too limited in scope or too 'popular'. The need is for a book which makes economics relevant and at the same time approaches major economic issues in a professional manner. It calls for some acquaintance with theory, with techniques, with applications and with policy. It must honestly set out major controversies about how the economy functions and about policy alternatives. In brief, it must speed up the 'settling in' process for beginners and provide a rudimentary framework into which they can fit abstract ideas and theories as they meet them.

This book is offered as an introduction to economics for students about to embark on a serious study of the subject, who want a quick appreciation of the nature of economics. I hope it will provide an adequate base for GCE A level. But it will certainly need supplementing for degree courses, even in the first year. I have expressly tried to write in a manner which will make the translation to one of the standard major theory texts as smooth as possible. When the reader turns to one of these, he or she should already be familiar with most of the important concepts in economics. He should be ready to study them in greater detail. Most important, he ought to have some idea about why he is doing so and where the various bits and pieces fit into the body of the subject.

The general reader interested in current affairs may also find this book of value. It is emphatically not a *vade mecum* guide to the pros and cons of different economic policies. I happen to believe that they are useless, if not positively dangerous. Economics is not a subject which is capable of giving easy guides to the best economic policies. This book does, however, have two quite long chapters on economic policy. They contain no simple solutions to economic policy problems. There are none. But they provide a framework within which issues of current economic policy can be seriously debated.

The origins of this book are to be found in an earlier one of mine with a similar title. It has, however, a different purpose. *An Introduction to Economic Behaviour* was written ten years ago as one of a series of half a dozen short volumes which, together, comprised an introductory set of readings. The present book is self-contained. It tries to fulfil the objective described earlier of acquainting the beginner with the whole range of thinking that underlies modern economics.

After the opening remarks of this preface the reader may perhaps wonder how I have been able to begin the book at all! I confess it was a bit of a problem, but the ordering here reflects the special purpose the book is designed to fulfil. It starts at the shallow end by making the subject as relevant as possible to the student's experience. Chapter 1 considers the family budget – the consumer's view of the economy. Chapter 2 switches to the supply side and looks at business decision-taking. The next chapter launches into what is the starting point for many conventional texts – resource allocation, opportunity cost, and all that. The following two chapters deal with the analysis of supply and demand in goods and in factor markets. We turn then to macroeconomics. Chapters 6, 7 and 8 are on the national income and its determination and money – giving, I hope, Keynesian and Monetarist approaches a fair airing. Then follow two chapters on economic policy, one on micro and the other on macro. The last chapter is on methods of economics and describes basic tools and techniques. Many texts put this at the very beginning. My experience suggests that students find the detail of 'scope and methods' largely meaningless and boring when they are asked to study it before they have the remotest idea what economics is all about. There is an appendix on how to use and interpret graphs, which should be read early on by any student who is not very confident about them.

Finally, I should say that my desire to keep the book as short as possible has forced me to restrict descriptive and institutional material to a minimum. The reader will need to supplement this book with others such as the National Institute of Economic Research's *The UK Economy* (Heinemann) and A. R. Prest and D. J. Coppock (eds), *The United Kingdom Economy: A Manual of Applied Economics* (Weidenfeld & Nicolson). There is also my own *Descriptive Economics* (Pitman). Dates and editions have been omitted deliberately because all three books are frequently revised.

It is quite impossible to thank everyone who helped me directly and indirectly with this book. I owe debts of gratitude to many colleagues and students on whom I have tried out much of the material. The factual background comes from both public and private sources and I must acknowledge in particular a debt to the Central Statistical Office for making available a detailed breakdown of one of the input-output tables for the United Kingdom which has been used in the construction of Table 2.2.

NOTES: PREFACE

1 Lipsey, R. G., *An Introduction to Positive Economics* (Weidenfeld & Nicolson, 5th edn, 1979); Samuelson, P. A., *Economics* (McGraw-Hill, 11th edn, 1980); Baumol, W. J., and Blinder, A. S., *Economics, Principles and Policy* (Harcourt Brace, 1979).

To Jan

Part One

INTRODUCTION: CONSUMER AND PRODUCER BEHAVIOUR

Chapter 1

The Family Budget

The average London family spends almost twice as much on housing as does a family living in Wales.

This may not seem perhaps to be the most inspiring piece of information with which to begin a book on economics. Yet it is one which is full of exciting implications for an economist.

Why, one wonders, does the Londoner spend nearly £15 a week putting a roof over his head, while the Welshman spends only a little more than half that amount?[1] What reasons lie behind this rather startling difference?

The explanation is unlikely to be a simple one. High housing expenditure in London certainly has something to do with the price of houses there compared to those in Wales. But that is not, in a real sense, a basic cause, for it begs the important question as to *why* house prices are high in the capital. Not everything is dearer in London, by any means.

It is not difficult to think of possible explanations. Does it have anything to do with costs of production? Are building costs higher in London and is the land itself more expensive? Alternatively, is it perhaps because Londoners are richer and can afford to spend more on housing? Or do Londoners just happen to enjoy being well housed relatively more than being well fed or well dressed, so that their larger housing expenditure is a reflection of their tastes? Is it perhaps even that housing needs are lower in Wales because the weather is milder and high standards of insulation are less necessary there? Or is the difference the result of government policies, such as rent control, which keep average housing costs lower in Wales than in London?

Whatever the full explanation we can be fairly sure that it is likely to involve many complex factors including some of those already mentioned as well as others. The unravelling of interrelationships of this kind, identifying the important causal links, is a part of the job of the economist, though he may often profit from drawing on the work of other social scientists, such as sociologists, psychologists, and political scientists.

TOTAL FAMILY EXPENDITURE

Family expenditure on housing is only one kind of economic behaviour that the economist tries to analyse. Attention was focused on housing because it happened to show some rather dramatic regional variations. Let us for a moment take a wider view and look at the pattern of total household expenditure in Britain.

Figure 1.1 is based on information obtained from more than 10,000 families and shows how total spending was divided between various goods and services in 1977. Average weekly expenditure in that year was over £70. Income was about a third more than this, but deductions for income tax and national insurance took more than half the difference between income and expenditure while the remainder largely consisted of savings of one sort or another, including life assurance and mortgage repayments by persons buying their own houses.

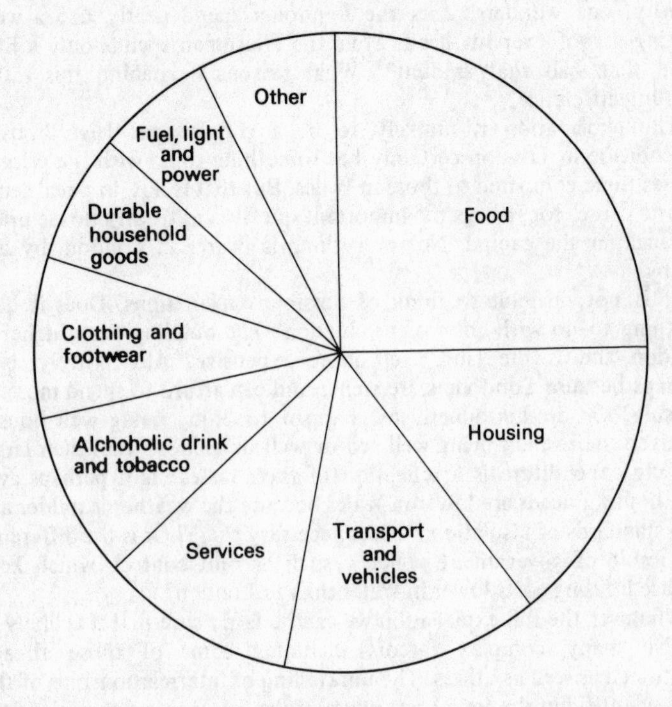

Figure 1.1 *Family expenditure, 1977 (average weekly expenditure of all households).*

Source: Department of Employment, *Family Expenditure Survey, 1977* (HMSO, 1978).

The diagram shows the way in which the population as a whole allocated its spending on goods and services. About a quarter went on food, and a trifle more on the combined categories of housing and transport. The next most important class of expenditure is described as 'services' and requires a word of explanation. This is the name given to spending which is made not to acquire tangible goods but for the performing of services. We obtain a service when, for example, someone cuts our hair, entertains us at a theatre, repairs our old alarm clock, cures us of a disease or even tries to teach us economics. The remaining categories are largely self-explanatory. Durable household goods are articles like furniture and electrical appliances. 'Other goods' comprise all products not previously covered and include such things as sports goods, newspapers, toys, medicines and toiletries.

EXPLAINING CONSUMER BEHAVIOUR

The pattern of household expenditure outlined in the last paragraph throws no light on the causes of consumer behaviour, which are a concern of economists. At this stage of our study of economics we are not going to be able to identify all the reasons why people spend their income in the way that they do. We can, however, suggest what some of these reasons may be.

Two determinants are, in fact, of such great importance that they must be mentioned immediately. They are the prices of goods and services and the incomes that people have available to spend. The role of prices in determining consumption will be dealt with in Chapter 3, but we may straight away observe the influence of income.

INCOME AND CONSUMPTION

Table 1.1 shows the way in which households with different incomes allocate their expenditure over the categories of goods and services shown in Figure 1.1. It is a simplified version of the full survey which separates sixteen income size classes. Four categories only are used here; each relates to a quarter of the total number of households from the richest to the poorest.

Study of Table 1.1 reveals a number of different kinds of relationship between income and consumption. It is useful to classify goods and services on the basis of these relationships. Two main categories may be distinguished: (1) goods where income and expenditure are inversely correlated, that is, where consumption is low at high incomes and vice versa; (2) goods and services where income and expenditure are positively correlated, that is, consumption is high at high incomes and low at low incomes.

Table 1.1 *Family expenditure by household income, 1977* (per cent of total weekly expenditure on goods and services)

	Weekly income of household			
	Bottom quarter	*Third lowest quarter*	*Second highest quarter*	*Highest quarter*
	%	%	%	%
Housing	20·1	15·2	14·2	12·4
Fuel, light and power	10·8	7·2	5·7	4·5
Food	30·5	27·3	24·4	22·0
Alcoholic drink and tobacco	6·4	8·9	8·6	8·9
Clothing and footwear	5·7	7·1	7·9	9·2
Durable household goods	4·7	6·4	7·4	7·5
Transport and vehicles	6·8	11·7	14·9	15·4
Services	7·6	8·3	8·7	11·5
Other	7·4	7·9	8·2	8·6
Total	100·0	100·0	100·0	100·0

Source: Department of Employment, *Family Expenditure Survey, 1977* (HMSO, 1978).
Note: Totals may not add to exactly 100% because of rounding. The median (average) household income in 1977 was £85 per week. Households in the top and bottom quarters had incomes greater than £123 and less than £46 respectively.

(1) Goods and services where income and expenditure are inversely correlated

The most common of the products where expenditure tends to decline as income rises is food. As can be seen from Table 1.1, expenditure on food accounts for nearly a third of total spending of the poorest group, but closer to a fifth of that of the highest income class. The German statistician Ernst Engel drew attention in the last century to the tendency for expenditure on food to fall proportionately as income rises, and it is sometimes known as Engel's law. Expenditure on housing and on fuel, light and power are in the same category. These are goods that are sometimes loosely described as 'necessities'. But it would be wise to resist the temptation to call them all necessities. The word has, unfortunately, no unambiguous meaning for all people. This is partly because what is absolutely essential to life forms only a very small part of the whole – the bare minimum of food and shelter to avoid death.

In current usage the term necessities includes items which are necessary not to sustain life itself, but to maintain it at a socially acceptable level. Once this view is admitted, it becomes hard to find an objective standard by which to judge whether any particular good should or should not be classed as a 'necessity'. It becomes a question of personal opinion, and it seems reasonable to expect individuals to differ in their views on the matter. A middle-class white-collar worker might consider it necessary for him to have two suits, a colour television set and perhaps even a car. On the other hand, to a student, or even a teacher, these may not even be desirable possessions. There are no universally accepted standards. Even if there were, they would certainly change over time. As societies get richer what are deemed the 'basic necessities' of life, without which a person might feel he did not approach a 'decent' standard of living, are rising almost continuously.

It is important to understand that although expenditure on a commodity may fall *as a proportion* of the total as income rises, this does not necessarily imply that absolutely smaller quantities of the goods are bought at higher income levels. It may or it may not be the case. But if the proportionate fall in expenditure is great enough to offset the rise in income, then consumption does indeed fall as income rises. Goods which qualify on this account happen to be given a special name in economics – *inferior goods.*[2] By this is meant no more than that they behave in the manner described – larger quantities being bought at low incomes than at high. Inferior does not imply anything in an absolute sense, but the sort of goods which qualify are those which people find less desirable than others as they get richer.

It is likely that some goods start to become inferior after a certain income level is reached rather than throughout all ranges of income. For example, a family living close to the poverty line probably buys mainly cheap cuts of meat, margarine, potatoes and bread. As its income rises it may pass through a phase of buying more of all these things until at various points it starts to substitute butter for margarine, choicer for cheaper cuts of meat and, eventually perhaps, more meat for bread and potatoes. One example taken from the *Family Expenditure Survey* of a good on which expenditure at some higher incomes is absolutely less than at lower levels is coal. This is presumably, at least in part, a reflection of the fact that people who can afford more modern and expensive forms of heating, such as gas, electricity and oil, prefer it to solid fuel.

(2) Goods and services where income and expenditure are positively correlated

This is probably the most normally expected kind of relationship – that is, one where rising incomes lead to rising expenditure on a commodity. Goods and services consumption of which increases when incomes rise are, in fact, called normal in contrast to inferior. Table 1.1 suggests that clothing and footwear and transport and vehicles are in this category, as are durable household goods. Services are among the most widely recognised in this group since expenditure on them rises quite substantially with income. As people become richer they tend to spend more on holidays, dining out, entertainments, and so on.

Many things commonly and loosely described as luxuries are properly included in this class. However, for reasons similar to those which were advanced in discussing necessities, it would again be wise to resist the temptation to describe all these goods and services as luxuries, for one man's luxury is another man's necessity, to twist a cliché. It is better to stick to an objective definition of goods and services such as that based upon whether expenditure on them rises or falls as income increases.

Two exclusions

The twofold division of ways of disposing of income used so far conceals two omissions. One is major and must not be ignored. The other is minor.

(a) Saving. One of the most important ways of disposing of income does not appear here at all, namely, saving, that is, not spending on any goods or services. Saving does not show up in the figures presented in Table 1.1 and Figure 1.1 because these are confined to expenditure. However, there is a pronounced tendency for the proportion of income saved to be greater among the rich than among the poor, for the obvious reason that the former need to spend most, if not all, of their income to cover everyday living costs. We shall return to consider the implications of this matter in Chapter 7. A major part of economic theory is closely related to it.

(b) Goods on which consumption expenditure is proportional to income. The second and less important omission concerns goods expenditure on which tends to remain a fairly constant proportion of income. Table 1.1 does not throw much light by way of illustration on this category, mainly because it compresses hundreds of items into a mere nine classes. Alcoholic drink and tobacco and the miscellaneous 'other' category come closest to it (especially for the top three-quarters of households) but expenditure statistics containing more detail are needed to identify particular goods and services which qualify.

CONSUMPTION DETERMINANTS OTHER THAN INCOME

Attention has been concentrated so far on the relationship that exists between level of income and family expenditure. It has also been stated that the prices of goods and services influence expenditure patterns. It is clear that there are many other determinants of consumption

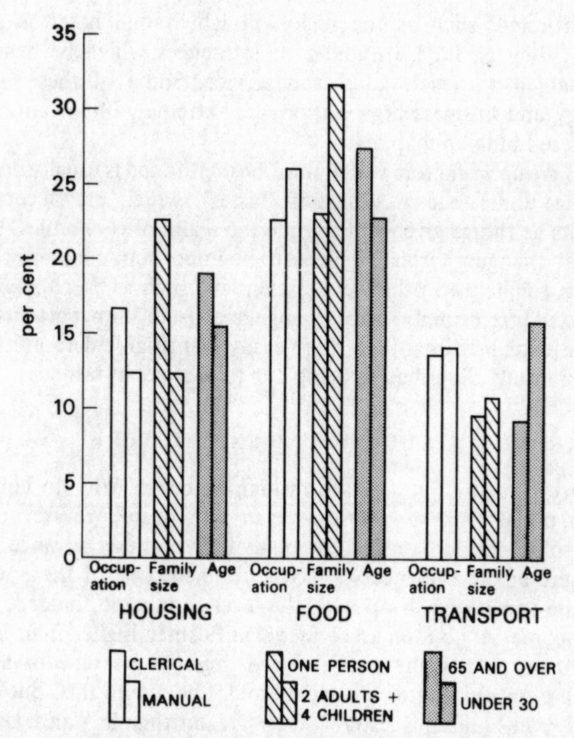

Figure 1.2 *Family expenditure by occupation, family size and age, 1976 (per cent of total weekly expenditure on selected goods and services; age and occupation refer to the head of the household).*

Source: as for Figure 1.1.

expenditure and Figure 1.2 has been drawn to illustrate some of them. It portrays the percentages of total weekly household expenditure that go on housing, food and transport for certain occupational, family size and age groups. The diagram shows, for example, that large families tend to spend relatively less on housing than do small ones. If this tendency seems surprising, it may be less so when it is realised that large families almost certainly need to spend relatively more on food and clothing.

Occupation also influences consumption patterns. Families whose head has a clerical job spend, on average, relatively more on housing and less on food then do those whose head is in manual work. Age is a third determinant. Households with young heads tend to spend relatively less on food and housing and more on transport than older families. The factors listed in Figure 1.2 are illustrative only and are far from complete. They do not include some determinants that have already been mentioned, such as the region in which one happens to live. Moreover, they exclude a number of influences which lie behind the prices charged for each good and service. Some of these, such as technology and business organisation, are extremely important and will be considered in later chapters.

A final group of factors which must be mentioned is usually described as coming under the heading of 'tastes', which are accepted by economists as things given and outside the realm of economics. When it seems that changing tastes are likely to be important, economists sometimes turn for help to other social scientists, such as psychologists and sociologists. Interestingly, also, changing consumption patterns which cannot be explained by other, more easily identifiable determinants are not uncommonly described as being due to changes in taste.

THE DETERMINANTS OF HOUSING EXPENDITURE

Let us return to the question with which we began. Why do Londoners spend so much more on housing than the Welsh? We are now in a position to reconsider some of the possible hypotheses advanced earlier in the light of the evidence we have examined. One of these was that it might be something to do with the level of income. Indeed, average family income in London is in fact significantly higher than in Wales (about 20 per cent higher, in fact) and thus the greater *absolute* level of spending on housing in the capital might be due to this. But housing expenditure in London is also *relatively* greater than in Wales. Given the conclusion drawn from Table 1.1 on the relationship between income and housing expenditure, therefore, we might doubt that we have identified the primary cause.

What else can the data we have looked at suggest? Referring to Figure 1.2 it will be seen that relatively large housing expenditure seems to be associated with three household characteristics other than income: clerical rather than manual occupations, small rather than large families and older rather than younger households. Since there are indeed relatively more clerks than manual workers living in London and households are on average smaller there, these facts may help explain the differential behaviour. On the other hand, the proportion of the population over 65 living in the metropolis is very similar to that in Wales. Hence the age structure of the population is a weaker candidate for providing the answer to our question.

These suggestions can be no more than tentative. It would be entirely unwarranted to pretend that we have provided even part of the solution to our particular puzzle. However, higher housing expenditure by Londoners is probably related to most of the factors mentioned – higher incomes, smaller families, more white-collar workers and higher house prices in the capital. It is likely too that other factors are involved, such as the influence of government policy, including rent control and the extent to which council house rents are subsidised. It may also reflect regional differences in tastes. But we cannot be sure that these are true causes, let alone estimate their quantitative importance.

The entire business of identifying the causes of economic behaviour is a very complex one. It involves the use of advanced statistical techniques, which do not always lead to definite conclusions. Because of this, some economists might consider it dangerous and misleading to suggest that light can be thrown on the subject by the simple kind of analysis which we have been able to perform at this stage of our study of the subject.

There is some truth in this argument. The reason we have not been greatly influenced by it is that we are not primarily concerned here with the question of explaining any particular aspects of consumer behaviour. Our concern with housing expenditure has been simply because it illustrates the kind of problem that interests economists and shows something of the way in which economists go about solving such problems. The method used here, highly oversimplified though it is, is not too far removed from that often employed. The economist typically hypothesises about the causes of economic behaviour and then tests his theories by confronting them with evidence, often statistical, taken from the real world. In this manner advances may be made in understanding answers to a whole range of questions – from 'why do expenditure patterns vary?' to 'what causes inflation?'.

One final point needs to be made. Expenditure on a commodity depends not only on how much people want it but also on how much is available. Goods and services that interest economists do not fall from the skies like rain. They have to be produced – a costly business in terms of the resources that are needed for it. Our next task is to consider how resources are organised for production.

NOTES: CHAPTER 1

1 The figures here relate to the year 1977; these were the most recent available at the time of writing. Statistics on this subject are published annually. The source is given at the foot of Table 1.1 so that you can bring those in the text up to date.

2 See below, Chapter 4, page 59, for a further discussion of inferior goods. Note that we cannot use the information in Table 1.1 to identify inferior goods because the figures there are proportions of total expenditure, not absolute quantities purchased.

Chapter 2

The Business of Production

In the last chapter we discussed the question of how families spend their income on different goods and services. We were looking then at the economy from the viewpoint of the consumer. We now have to turn to consider the different question of how all the food, clothing and household goods that consumers choose are there for them to buy. In other words we must now examine the production side of the economy.

PRODUCTION DECISIONS

There are two common features about the kind of decisions that consumers and producers have to make. Both need to choose (1) *what* goods and services to buy or to sell and (2) *how much* of each of them. We must now look further into the ways in which these decisions are made on the production side.

It is, however, important to point out first that production, which is undertaken by what we shall call businesses, does not necessarily result in goods and services for direct or immediate consumption by individuals or households. Figure 2.1 portrays the composition of domestic production in the UK, revealing, for example, that roughly a quarter of all output takes place in the manufacturing sector, about 5 per cent in agriculture and mining, and so on.

It may be useful to compare the picture of production in the diagram with that of household consumption in Table 1.1 in the previous chapter. The two do not tell exactly the same story, and it is important to understand why. There are two major reasons.

(1) *Capital goods*. In the first place, some categories of output in Figure 2.1 are of a kind which would not be of interest to consumers at all. Chief among these are items of capital equipment such as machinery and factory buildings. The production of these goods naturally reduces the resources which are available for

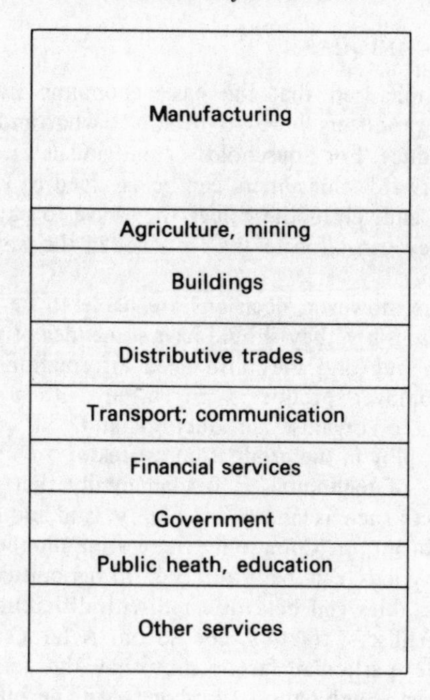

Figure 2.1 *Domestic production, United Kingdom, 1978.*

consumption in the short run. But once they are in existence they eventually benefit consumers because they tend to raise productivity. Building machines to make components for transistor radios, for example, lowers production costs in the long run in the radio industry. Economies like Britain typically devote between 10 and 20 per cent of their resources to the production of capital rather than consumer goods and this helps to keep up the rate of ecomonic growth. The great importance of the distinction will become clear as we proceed.

(2) *Imports and exports*. The second reason why the total value of domestic production is not the same as that of consumption arises from the fact that we do not live in isolation from the rest of the world. Some of the goods and services that we produce are exported to foreign countries and other goods are imported from them. For example, some of the bread we eat is made from North American wheat, which we pay for by selling home-produced manufactured products. International trade is of particular importance to Britain and about a quarter of our economy is directly linked through foreign trade to those of many other countries in Europe, the Middle East, Asia, Australasia and elsewhere.

CHOICE OF TECHNIQUES

It has been emphasised that the basic economic issue which both consumers and producers have to decide is what and how much to consume or produce. For households or individuals these questions are fairly straightforward. Consumers can be assumed to know what they like and dislike and, given the prices they have to pay for goods and and services, they can allocate their budget in the way that gives the most satisfaction.

For producers, however, decisions are liable to be more complex. In order to act sensibly they should have some idea of what consumers are prepared to buy and they also need information about costs of production. Moreover producers are faced with a supplementary question – *how* to organise production and, in particular, what techniques to employ in the production process.

The question of techniques is fundamentally that of how best to combine resources such as labour, machinery, land and raw materials to achieve a certain output. Commonly there are a number of alternative ways in which goods can be produced. In agriculture, for instance, cereals and vegetables can be cultivated with different proportions of land, labour, fertilisers, tractors, and so on. A farm's efficiency may well reflect the particular factor mix that the farmer selects. In choosing the best combination, producers will be influenced by the relative cost of labour, capital and other resources as well as by the technical efficiency of each. The question of costs will be examined again later in this and other chapters, but there are three further important factors which influence decisions about output to be mentioned first. These are the institutional organisations which engage in the production of goods and services, the goals or objectives which motivate decision-makers and the market environment within which businesses operate.

BUSINESS ORGANISATION

There are several forms of business organisation, distinguished principally by whether they are owned by private individuals or by the state. Private businesses, often known as firms, are of very different sizes. A great many are small one-man concerns or partnerships, and some are operated as co-operatives. However, the most important form of business organisation is the joint stock company, or corporation.

Most large and medium and many small firms in Britain are organised as companies, mainly because this structure makes it much easier to borrow large sums of money to run the business. A joint stock company raises capital by issuing, or selling, shares in the business, which carry the right to receive future profits in return for cash.

Persons buying shares become shareholders, and are the true owners of the business. However, shareholders do not control the detailed policy of the company. Instead, they appoint directors who they hope will act in their interests. In theory, shareholders can sack unsatisfactory directors. But, in practice, in very large companies there are thousands of individual small shareholders and it may be very difficult for enough of them to get together to do this. In such cases the business is effectively controlled by the directors. Giant multinational corporations operating across national boundaries are probably the extreme example of where the director-managers have the most power.

Enterprises in the public sector are generally owned by the state and act, in principle, on behalf of the general public. Again, there is more than one form of organisation. In some cases a department of the central or local government directly takes charge of operations, as in the case of roads and defence. In others, independent public corporations like the National Coal Board and British Airways are set up to make the production decisions of what, how much and how to operate.

BUSINESS GOALS

The importance of the form of business organisation outlined in the previous section is seen when we come to consider the goals at which a business is aiming. Much economic theory is based on the assumption that the principle objective, at least of private enterprise, is the maximisation of profits. The assumption does not imply that firms necessarily try to earn as much profit as possible in the short run, though they may well have to do so in the long run if they are not to be forced out of business.

There are, however, other targets at which a business may aim. These include maximising the growth of the firm or of its sales, philanthropy, prestige or securing a quiet life for the owners or managers at a lower satisfactory level of profits. These alternative objectives may be particularly relevant in the case of certain large joint stock companies, where, as was pointed out, the owner-shareholders have little control over the director-managers. While the interests of the former are mainly in the profits of the firm, the managers, whose salaries tend to rise with the size of the organisation, may be more concerned with its growth. In such circumstances the main pressure on the managers to seek large profits may be the fear that their company will be bought up, lock, stock and barrel, by a larger company and that they may then lose their jobs.

Public sector businesses are less likely than private ones to seek to maximise profits, though they are often set commercial targets of profitability. This may be partly a political matter in some cases.

Moreover, several industries in the public sector possess a degree of monopoly which makes the objective of profit maximisation inappropriate. The matter is pursued later.

MARKET CONSIDERATIONS

The final set of factors which influence a firm's production decisions relate to characteristics of the market in which it operates.

Economists find it useful to distinguish between market situations according to their competitiveness and the extent to which an individual firm has power to control the price at which it sells its product. This power depends on such matters as the number of firms in the industry and their size relative to total consumer demand for the product, how far each firm sells a product which is individualistic (described as *differentiated* from those of its competitors) and whether there are any barriers to the entry of new firms into the industry.

All these matters clearly affect a firm's room for manoeuvre. Moreover, competitive forces in a market may be relevant to the goals of a firm – in particular as to whether its objective really is to try to maximise its profits. Indeed, the extent to which a business has a choice between profit maximisation and seeking a more modest return may depend heavily on its power to influence the market for its product. For example, a director-dominated company, concerned more with sales growth than with profits, may be forced into bankruptcy if competition is strong and the level of profits generally low in the industry. A strong firm in a monopolistic position, however, may be able to sit back and earn a comfortable level of profits with relatively little effort.

There is one final point to be added. Market considerations are important not only for the market in which a firm sells its product (which has been discussed in the previous paragraph) but also for the market in which it buys its labour and other resources used in the production process. This may have implications for its choice of techniques and factor combinations.

FACTORS OF PRODUCTION

Mention has been made above of the resources used by businesses, particularly in connection with the decision about choice of techniques. These resources, or inputs, are known as the factors of production. There are several ways of classifying them, but it is common to group them according to certain characteristics that they possess. The traditional division of factors of production distinguishes labour, land

and capital, with a fourth factor, enterprise, sometimes separated from the rest.

(1) LABOUR

The distinctive feature of the production factor, labour, is that it provides a human service. The term covers clerical, managerial and administrative functions as well as skilled and unskilled manual work. The reward, or price, that is paid to labour in return for the services it performs is known as a wage or salary. A man's wages are associated with his productivity or efficiency and this depends on a variety of factors including the education and job training he has received, his innate skill and the extent to which he is motivated to give of his best effort in the work he is doing. In making decisions about the employment of labour, a business man considers rates of pay and the various kinds of skilled workers that are available to him.

Over a long period of time the size of the labour force is affected by the total population and its age, sex and geographical distribution. Changes in birth, death and marriage rates are therefore key influences. So are rates of emigration and immigration.

(2) LAND AND NATURAL RESOURCES

This group of inputs represents what might be called the gifts of nature, the naturally fertile land in the world, the fish in the sea, the heat of the sun that helps to dry grapes and change them into raisins, the rain that helps farmers everywhere grow their crops, the mineral wealth below the surface of the earth, and so on. One characteristic of this set of productive factors is that they cannot, as a rule, be increased in supply very quickly and, in the case of physical land itself, virtually not at all. In consequence, their prices tend to be extremely sensitive to changes in consumer demand, rising sharply if they become more desirable. Witness the phenomenal growth since the war of the cost of a piece of building land in London. However, new discoveries are often stimulated by high prices and, like that of oil in the North Sea, tend to moderate price increases.

The income received by land is known as rent. It should be noted that rent is commonly paid for something more than the use of land or another natural resource, but includes also an element of payment for another factor which is involved in making the resource available in a useful form. The labour which assists in the process of bringing minerals to the surface is a fair example. Iron ore is of no use while it is still in the ground. Land, too, increases in productivity and value if it is improved with fertilisers, irrigation, and the erection of fences and buildings. So 'rent' paid for this kind of fertile land is rather a mixed sort of factor reward.

(3) CAPITAL

The third major factor of production, capital, consists of outputs of man-made goods such as machinery, factory and office equipment, industrial buildings, lorries, and so on, the presence of which raises the productivity of other factors. Increases in the amount of capital are referred to as *investment* and it is not always easy to draw a clear distinction between changes in the quantity of capital and in that of other factors of production. For instance, expenditure on education may be considered as capital investment, since it tends to raise the productivity of labour. Hence, when a firm hires a skilled worker, it is really buying some human capital as well as pure brawn. Capital is, however, traditionally distinguished, in principle, from both labour and land (which are sometimes referred to as primary factors) because it is an output of one industry and an input of another.

The productivity of a business is related to the quality of its capital as well as to the quantity. Old machines are often replaced by new larger and better ones. It is of great interest to know how much an increase in efficiency depends upon a rise in the quantity of capital employed, and how much on the technical progress implied in the development of an improved machine. In practice this turns out to be difficult to measure at all precisely.

The earnings of capital, the price that has to be paid for it, are known as interest, which is usually stated as a rate per cent, representing the sum paid by a borrower who needs finance to purchase a piece of capital equipment.

(4) ENTERPRISE

A fourth factor of production, enterprise, is sometimes distinguished in economics. This is a rather artificial concept, introduced in order to be able to give a name to a single factor which might be said to receive the residual profits of a business after all costs of production have been covered. Profit is said to be the reward for bearing the risk of organising production of a novel kind. When a totally new product, such as a three-dimensional encyclopaedia, for example, is being contemplated, or a company wants to start drilling for oil in an area where none has been found before, someone, or a group of persons, has to put up the finance before the operation can get off the ground. If there is no way of estimating the probable success of the project except by intuition or guesswork, then any financial return on the investment is pure profit.

The risk involved in some large capital investments may be so great that no private individuals are prepared to undertake it. Governments sometimes then step in if it is thought to be in the national interest as was the case with the Concorde airliner. In other cases, the hope of high profit may secure the necessary investment, especially since there have grown over the years ways and means of reducing business risks, such as by pooling them. But if the risks are reduced, the return on investment begins to assume the nature of interest rather than of profit. This illustrates one of the greatest difficulties of trying to pretend that there is a single separate factor of production which undertakes the risks of new investments. We cannot, in practice, identify any actual persons whose entire income is 'pure' profit. The problem is, however, a general one and is not confined to the factor enterprise. Only on rare occasions can a person be associated with a single type of factor income. It is often more sensible to think of an individual as receiving a part of his income as a wage for his labour, a part as interest on invested capital, and so on, as fits his particular case.

FACTOR MOBILITY

One characteristic of productive factors of considerable importance is their mobility. The simplest aspect of mobility is geographical. It may be observed that, in this sense, some factors like raw materials and small items of equipment can move freely about the country in response to needs, while others are much less able to. In the extreme case of land, mobility is, of course, zero. Labour occupies an intermediate position. People can, at least in principle, settle almost anywhere, though there is often strong social resistance to uprooting.

A second aspect of factor mobility is not so much geographical as economic and concerns transfers from industry to industry or sometimes from one use to another. It is often important to know how easily a factor such as labour can shift from, say, motor vehicle to bicycle production or land from growing wheat to grazing cattle. Factor mobility influences business decision-making, particularly when there is some change in consumer demand conditions calling for adjustment. Only the facts of the specific case are then really relevant. However, two generalisations may be in order. First, factors tend to be more mobile the longer the time period under consideration and, secondly, there is frequently a cost involved in moving. To take labour as an example, if industries in one part of the country decline, it is unlikely that people will immediately leave the area. However, as time passes more and more may do so. Moreover, there are costs incurred in such a move. Houses are needed in areas of expansion while others are left empty. One must also reckon that there may be psychological costs, such as disturbances to family life. Finally, we should mention that barriers to movement are sometimes deliberately created by society. For instance, restrictions may be imposed on the inflow of foreign workers in order to protect certain national interests.

FACTOR COMBINATION

Our understanding of the nature of the different factors of production allows us to examine afresh the way in which they are used. Let us look at the matter again from the viewpoint of an individual business, which is considering how to combine resources in order to produce a given output. This is the question that we already started to answer in terms of what we called choice of techniques. We have emphasised that there is usually more than one way of combining inputs for most kinds of output. Take, for example, the alternative ways in which labour and capital may be employed in a single factory making toffees. Several methods of production may be used, some of which economise more on labour, others on capital. For example, toffee wrapping and packing may be done in several different ways – entirely by hand, by machines which need the attention of operatives for manual loading or by a completely automatic machine.

The choice between different combinations of factor inputs depends on their relative efficiencies, the size of desired output and the price of each factor service. The best combination is known as the 'optimum' and it is important to realise that this may well be different in the short term and in the long term. A new distinction needs to be made here between factors of production according to whether a business is free to alter the amount of them that it uses or not. The supply of some factors, such as raw materials, is variable, in that a business can change the quantity that it uses virtually at will. At the other extreme are fixed factors, like a building the firm occupies. Such factors are fixed only in that they cannot be varied in the short run, though in the long run the firm can move to a larger or smaller building according to its needs; when the lease runs out, for example. It follows therefore, that the optimum factor combination for a business is likely to be different in the short and in the long run. This is, in a sense, an aspect of factor mobility which, as we saw in the last section, tends to increase with the passage of time.

SPECIALISATION AND THE SCALE OF PRODUCTION

Closely allied to the question of techniques is that of the scale on which production is carried on. By and large, the productivity of a factor of production tends to be related to the number of tasks it performs. The fewer they are the more the factor is able to specialise and become proficient in them. Almost any modern factory illustrates the point in countless ways, though it was emphasised by Adam Smith in his book *The Wealth of Nations* as long ago as 1776 as following from the principle of the *division of labour*.

Take a car assembly line, for example. Each individual worker on the line has a limited range of jobs. One puts in the rear lights, another the instrument panel, a third the floor covering, and so on. It must be obvious that the daily output of assembled cars can be maintained with many fewer workers than if each man tried to assemble a complete car himself.

It is hardly necessary to ask why. It is easier for a man to acquire a single skill than to acquire several, and skill and dexterity increase with repetition. Time is saved moving from task to task. Equipment is used economically. Instead of every man having a complete set of tools – hammer, screwdriver, pliers, and so on – he needs only the specific tool required for his particular job. Boring the work may be, but it is technically more efficient. Additionally, we may observe that specialisation stimulates mechanisation since it raises the level of output of a particular process.

The principle of specialisation is not limited in application to manual labour, but can apply to all factors, lowering costs per unit of output as production increases. Highly specialised pieces of capital equipment are used in manufacturing industry because of their efficiency. Managers in large companies are often given specific functions, for example, to oversee sales, exports, finance or personnel for the same reason. It is true also that, on average, costs of advertising and of borrowing money to cover production expenses tend to be lower for large than for small firms.

The presence of production, managerial, sales and financial economies of scale causes some industries to be organised in large units. Examples may be found in chemicals, steel, vehicles and other industries. They are not, however, universal. Other sectors, such as clothing, textiles and retail shops, are commonly organised on quite a small scale because of the absence of substantial economies which accompany large size. It must be added that large-scale production techniques will be used only if the volume of sales is large enough to justify them. One would not expect the same mass techniques to be used for the manufacture of Rolls Royce as for Ford cars. Nor do you find blast furnaces in garages although there are occasional jobs for which they would be useful.

THE DYNAMICS OF BUSINESS

A final question to be asked about businesses is how they react to changes, either in the supply of a factor of production or in sales. The answers are fairly straightforward for a profit-maximising firm. If a fall in availability of one factor is reflected in a rise in its price, then the obvious thing to do is to try to rearrange the process of production in such a way as to economise on the scarce factor, using instead more of other factors which are relatively plentiful. The only important point to make is that it sometimes takes a great deal longer than others to adapt to this kind of situation. It is relatively easy to switch, say, a pet food factory from using sheep offal to pig offal when the relative prices of these materials change. It is more difficult to change from oil to gas fuel for machines that are already in existence. How substitutable factors are in the production process determines the speed of adjustment.

The second kind of change that calls for decisions by businesses is that in the demand for the goods they sell. A firm's reaction here depends again on substitutability, though of a somewhat different kind, in this case how easily production can be switched from one good to another. Unexpectedly, perhaps, the choice facing producers in this kind of situation may be quite different from the way in which a consumer would look at a similar change in the price of different products. The latter would almost always look for a substitute product which performed approximately the same function as the one which was previously cheaper. So if the price of chairs made from steel tubes rose, for example, he would tend to turn to wooden chairs. This is not necessarily so for the manufacturer. His reaction to, say, a fall in the demand for steel chairs would be much more likely to send him into the production of car roof racks or other things made from steel tubing.

EXPLAINING BUSINESS BEHAVIOUR – A SUMMARY

We are now in a position to bring together the arguments of the previous sections so as to outline the major determinants of business behaviour. They can then be put alongside the explanations of consumer behaviour set out in Chapter 1.

Businesses, we have seen, have three questions to answer: what and how much to produce and how to produce it. Basically, the way in which they answer these questions depends on the demand for the goods they produce and on their costs of production. The former settles the prices at which goods may be sold. The latter influences the techniques of production they choose. Costs depend on the price and the productivity of each of the productive factors, which are, in turn, liable to be affected by the scale of operations.

We have seen that the form of organisation and the goals of business are relevant to the explanation of their behaviour. So too is the competitiveness of the market in which firms operate. We need add now only that, in practice, business behaviour is influenced by a number of non-economic determinants which have not so far been mentioned. These are too many to list but it is important to realise that government activity is not infrequently designed to exert pressure on businesses to act in particular ways. The measures used by the state include taxes, subsidies and legal probihitions, such as the outlawing of production processes which pollute the environment and the general prohibition of collusive practices by groups of firms aimed at artificially fixing the market prices of their goods. We shall return to these matters when we come to consider economic policy in Chapter 10.

THE INTERDEPENDENCE OF BUSINESSES

So far in this chapter we have looked at production very largely from the viewpoint of an individual business. This approach is valid for the analysis of many problems, but it must be emphasised that firms and even industries are not independent of each other. Decisions in one industry may have widespread implications and permeate large sections of the economy.

A major cause of interdependence is that the outputs of some industries are the inputs of others. There are some businesses, like those making steel ingots or capital equipment, which do not sell at all to final consumers, and others, like vehicles, which sell part of their output to other businesses for use in their production processes and part to the general public.

The degree of interdependence arising from interindustry transactions may be illustrated by means of what is known as an input-output table (also known as a transactions matrix).

AN INPUT-OUTPUT TABLE

Let us suppose that we have a very simple economy in which there is only one primary factor of production. We can imagine it to be labour, supplied by households. Next, let us assume that there are only two industries, which we shall call agriculture and clothing. Both industries supply goods to households for final consumption but, in addition, each sells some output to the other industry for use as an input. This

Table 2.1 *Input-output table for a hypothetical economy* (£worth)

		Purchasing sectors, i.e. users of input			
		Businesses		*Households*	
		Agriculture	*Clothing*	*(Consumption)*	*(Gross outputs)*
Supplying sectors, i.e. sources of output	Businesses:				
	Agriculture	–	15	10	(25)
	Clothing	5	–	85	(90)
	Households (Labour)	20	75		
	(Gross inputs)	(25)	(90)		

is realistic enough if clothing output consists partly of boots, which are items of equipment for farm workers. If we now add a few numbers to indicate the precise amounts of inputs and outputs involved during a given period of time, we can represent the working of the economy in Table 2.1.[1]

Each of the three sectors of the economy is shown twice in the table, once in its role as producer and once as consumer. The producing, or supplying, sectors appear as rows; the purchasing, or using, sectors as columns. Reading across the top row, we find that the agricultural sector supplied £15 of product (wool) to the clothing industry, and it sold the remainder of its output, £10, direct to households. Its total gross output was therefore £25. The clothing industry, on the other hand, sold £5 worth of boots to agriculture, and £85 of clothing to households, making a total gross output of £90.

If we now read down the table we can obtain some of the same information, but from the user's point of view; for example, the agricultural industry used £5 worth of input from the clothing industry. Total agricultural inputs (production costs) therefore add up to £25 – £20worth of labour and £5 worth of clothing. The clothing industry, on the other hand, used £15 worth of input from agriculture and £75 worth of labour, making a total input cost of £90.

The purpose of drawing up input-output tables of this kind for an economy is to enable an attempt to be made to work out the total effects of any given change of output by one or more industries on all others. Suppose the clothing industry were to expand. It would need additional agricultural production. But expansion of agriculture would, in its turn, call for more clothing. And more clothing would call for even more agriculture, and so on. Now, if we know exactly what are the requirements that one industry has for the products of other industries, for a given expansion, we can use the input-output table to calculate the final size of each industry for the given expansion of one of them, after all inter-industry repercussions have been allowed for. In our example, we are, in fact, assuming that every increase in clothing production by £1 requires one-sixth of £1 worth of agricultural output (£15 out of £90). Similarly, each increase in agricultural production by £1 requires one-fifth of £1 worth of clothing output (£5 out of £25). These fractions are called the input coefficients.

INTER-INDUSTRY RELATIONS IN THE UK

Input-output tables need to distinguish more than two sectors to be of much practical value to production planners. The government in the UK produces sets of such tables on a regular basis, distinguishing more than sixty industry groups. Table 2.2 shows the input coefficients for the UK in 1973 which have been calculated from them. For the sake of simplicity only a portion is reproduced here, but it demonstrates quite dramatically the degree of interdependence that exists in the British economy as well as showing something of the specialisation which takes place.

To find from the table the input requirements for output expansion by any industry, simply read down the appropriate column. In the motor vehicle industry (column 9), for example, £1,000 of final requirements requires £1 of net output from agriculture, £9 from coal mining, £50 from iron and steel, and so on. The table includes both direct and indirect effects. The figures in the table are therefore estimated *net* after all inter-industry transactions are taken into account. So, when output rises in the vehicle industry, its requirements from other industries include not only its direct purchases of iron and steel but also its indirect purchases, such as those of steel needed by the coal industry to meet the expansion in vehicles.

It would be dangerous to leave this subject without making clear that input-output tables must be interpreted with caution and can only give a fairly rough idea of inter-industry relations in practice. This is partly because they are not broken down into a sufficient number of sectors for some purposes. The amount of data needed for the construction of a really detailed table is enormous (the square of the number of sectors). Tables are usually also drawn up on the assumption that input coefficients do not change with the scale of output. We have seen that this is not always the case, but the reason for the assumption is that the tables are complicated enough to construct anyway. Finally, input-output tables are inevitably based on past history and cannot be relied on always to be applicable to the future in a world where so many things, including production techniques, change. The study of input-output tables does, nevertheless, give something of a feeling for the nature of the job of the economist, trying to explain how the economy works.

Table 2.2 *Total requirements per £1,000 of final industrial output in terms of net output, 1973*

	1 Agriculture	2 Coal Mining	3 Mineral Oil Refining	4 Chemicals, etc.	5 Iron and Steel	6 Non-ferrous Metals	7 Mechanical Engineering	8 Electrical Engineering	9 Motor Vehicles, etc.	10 Other Metal Goods	11 Bricks, etc.	12 Timber and Furniture	13 Paper and Printing	14 Other Manufacturing
1 Agriculture	555	0	1	5	0	0	0	1	1	0	1	1	1	1
2 Coal Mining	4	677	1	9	43	5	9	5	9	11	19	3	7	8
3 Mineral Oil Refining	3	1	99	5	3	1	1	1	2	2	4	1	1	2
4 Chemicals, etc.	30	8	14	383	8	6	7	11	10	9	13	9	17	54
5 Iron and Steel	3	36	2	4	391	6	50	20	50	69	7	5	3	6
6 Non-Ferrous Metals	1	3	1	4	6	248	10	15	10	19	2	2	2	3
7 Mechanical Engineering	4	43	6	9	17	8	452	20	15	12	10	4	7	7
8 Electrical Engineering	2	16	3	3	5	12	13	441	16	6	4	2	3	3
9 Motor Vehicles, etc.	3	3	1	2	4	3	4	2	417	2	2	1	1	1
10 Other Metal Goods	6	26	5	12	18	15	33	32	36	414	15	12	5	18
11 Bricks, etc.	6	9	1	5	11	1	6	10	7	4	462	6	1	4
12 Timber and Furniture	2	11	0	2	2	2	3	5	4	3	3	360	2	4
13 Paper and Printing	11	6	3	20	7	7	11	12	9	11	15	9	496	21
14 Other Manufacturing	5	7	2	11	5	4	6	11	24	7	5	7	4	425

Source: *Economic Trends* (HMSO June 1978); additional data kindly supplied by the Central Statistical Office.

INTERNATIONAL SPECIALISATION

We turn, finally, to consider the business of production from an international viewpoint. This provides us with an opportunity to examine an important extension of the principle of specialisation discussed earlier in the chapter.

THE PRINCIPLE OF COMPARATIVE ADVANTAGE

One of the most remarkable contributions of the early economists was to develop what is known as the principle of comparative advantage. The theory is usually attributed to the English economist David Ricardo, who was writing as long ago as the time of the Napoleonic Wars. Ricardo set out to explain why it is advantageous for nations to specialise and trade with each other whenever they are ***relatively*** better at producing certain goods than others. It is important to appreciate the key significance of the word relatively, because the theory does not depend on trade being beneficial when countries have absolute advantages over each other in different products. Comparative (that is, relative) advantage is all that is necessary for a gain to result from specialisation and trade.

The argument can best be explained by means of a simple example of a world in which there are only two countries and only two commodities. Following tradition, we call the countries England and Portugal and the goods cloth and wine. We shall use the abbreviations E and P for England and Portugal and *c* and *w* for cloth and wine.

Let us suppose that P is more efficient than E in producing both *c* and *w*, but that it is *relatively* more efficient in *w*. In the language commonly employed, P has a *comparative advantage* in the production of *w*. Hypothetical figures of productivity in the two countries are set out in Table 2.3. They are given, for the sake of simplicity, in terms of output per unit of labour. Columns (i) and (ii) show the numbers of units of each good that one man can produce in E and P. Reading the table, we see that a man in E can produce either 20*c or* 10*w*, while in P he can produce 30*c or* 40*w*. It is important to note that labour productivity is higher in P than in E in both goods, but that P is four times as efficient in *w* and only one and a half times as efficient in *c* production.

This is what is meant by saying that P has a comparative advantage over E in *w*. E, in contrast, is less efficient than P in both *c* and *w*, but it still has a *comparative* advantage in *c* production. Labour in E is a quarter as efficient as in P in *w*, but two-thirds as efficient in *c*. (It would perhaps be more accurate to describe E as having less of a comparative disadvantage in *c*, but we stick to the conventional terminology.)

Table 2.3 *Output of cloth and wine in England and Portugal*

	Output per man		*In E 5 men on c, 5 men on w; In P 5 men on c, 5 men on w*		*In E 7 men on c, 3 men on w; In P 4 men on c, 6 men on w*	
	Cloth (i)	*Wine (ii)*	*Cloth (iii)*	*Wine (iv)*	*Cloth (v)*	*Wine (vi)*
England	20*c* or	10*w*	100 +	50*w*	140*c* +	30*w*
Portugal	30*c* or	40*w*	150*c* +	200*w*	120*c* +	240*w*
World			250*c* +	250*w*	260*c* +	270*w*

The proof of the proposition that both countries can gain by specialisation and trade can now be demonstrated. Suppose, first, that each country has 100 men in its labour force and uses them, in isolation, 50/50 in the production of *w* and *c*. Columns (iii) and (iv) in table 2.3 show output in each country. Five men in E produce 5 × 20*c* = 100 *c*. The other five men produce 50*w*. Total output in E is, therefore, 100*c* + 50*w*. Output in P can be calculated in a similar way to be 150*c* + 200*w*. Total world product is then 250*c* + 250*w*.

Let us now examine what happens if both E and P specialise to some extent. Let us assume that E uses seven men on *c* and three on *w* production, while P deploys its men in the ratio six on *w* and four on *c*. Output in the two countries is shown in the final two columns of the table. The seven men in E produce 7 × 20*c* = 140*c*. The other three men produce 30*w*. Output in P is 120*c* + 240*w*.

Compare now the total world output in columns (iii) and (iv) with that in (v) and (vi). It has grown from 250*c* + 250*w* to 260*c* + 270*w*. It is not magic but simply the result of specialisation by each country in the production of the good for which it is *relatively* well suited (or in E's case relatively less unsuited). Moreover, it shows the potential gain from trade, even though one country is more efficient than the other, in an absolute sense, in the production of both goods.

Table 2.4 *The gains from specialisation and trade: changes in production and consumption, imports and exports*

	Change in Production		*Trade Exports (−) Imports (+)*		*Change in Consumption*	
	Cloth (i)	*Wine (ii)*	*Cloth (iii)*	*Wine (iv)*	*Cloth (v)*	*Wine (vi)*
England	+ 40*c*	− 20*w*	− 30*c*	+ 20*w*	+ 10*c*	0*w*
Portugal	− 30*c*	+ 40*w*	+ 30*c*	− 20*w*	0*c*	+20*w*

So far, the gain is available for the world as a whole, but trade is necessary for both countries to enjoy it. Let us see how they can both gain from mutual exchange. The figures in Table 2.4 show one possible outcome. They rest on the assumption that exchange on the world market takes place under conditions where $1w$ is worth $1\frac{1}{2}c$.

The table is based on outputs of quantities of *c* and *w* in columns (iii) and (iv) of Table 2.3 compared with columns (v) and (vi). In the first two columns of Table 2.4 we show the *changes* in production in E and P. The next two columns are calculated on the assumption that E exports $30c$ and imports $20w$. P's exports and imports are, of course, $20w$ and $30c$, respectively. The final two columns of Table 2.4 show consumption in both countries, that is the *net* effect of production and trade.

It may be helpful to run through the first row in the table. We start by looking at production before and after trade given in Table 2.3. Thus, E produces $100c + 50w$ before and $140c + 30w$ after trade. Therefore, the change in production in E is $140c - 100c = +40c$ and $30w - 50w = -20w$. These are the figures in columns (i) and (ii) in Table 2.4. E exports $30c$ and imports $20w$. Hence the change in consumption in E is the change in production net of the change in trade: $40c - 30c = 10c$ plus $-20w + 20w = 0w$. E's gain from specialisation and trade is $10c$. The figures for P can be derived in similar fashion to show a net gain of $20w$.

Table 2.4 gives only one possible division of the gain. It is clearly not the end of the story, but readers must be referred to more advanced texts to learn more about it. The principle underlying the result should, however, be clear. As long as a country has a comparative advantage over other counties there is a possibility of gain by concentrating on the production of the goods at which it is best suited.[2] We might add that the bases of comparative advantage lie in a country's endowment of factors of production and accumulations of capital and skills. The gain is a pure result of relative cost differences. For example, P gains because it has been able to buy $30c$ for only $20w$. In isolation, it would have been necessary for P to have taken one man off *w* production at a cost of $40w$ to make $30c$ for itself. The student is advised to restate the reason for the gain to E along the lines of the previous sentence.

The principle of comparative advantage is of widespread application outside the realm of international trade. It explains the advantages of regional specialisation within national boundaries. It also indicates the potential benefits of occupational specialisation and suggests a good reason why highly efficient persons might be well advised not to do everything for themselves. Smith may be a better carpenter than Jones. But he may be a relatively much better mechanic. It should pay them both to specialise; Smith working as a mechanic and Jones as a carpenter, the occupations in which each has a comparative advantage. They can both benefit by doing some work for each other.

NOTES: CHAPTER 2

1 Table 2.1 is prepared on assumptions as follows.

		Sells to			*Uses inputs of*		
Produces		*Clothing*	*Agriculture*	*House-holds*	*Labour*	*Clothing*	*Agric. products*
Agriculture	25	15	–	10	20	5	–
Clothing	90	–	5	85	75	–	15

2 No gain accrues if there is no comparative advantage. For example if P was twice as productive as E in *w* and *c*, there would be no advantage in specialisation. Likewise there would be no gain from trade if transport costs were so high as to eliminate it.

Part Two

PRICES AND MARKETS

Chapter 3

The Allocation of Resources

The first two chapters in this book have looked at economic behaviour from the viewpoints of consumer and producer in turn. We have yet to consider the ways in which the decisions of households and businesses affect each other. But before we get to grips with this subject there is one fundamental matter to deal with. Indeed, it is so central to the nature of economics that many introductory textbooks start with it.

SCARCITY

So far, we have identified a number of characteristics of goods and services which affect economic decision-taking, but we have not yet dealt with one fundamental property that a good must possess before an economist will pay attention to it. This is the quality of *scarcity.*

An economist might be interested, for example, in how much petrol is sucked into a car's engine, but not in how much air is drawn in with it. He might want to know how much people enjoy a swim in the local pool, but not how much they enjoy a dip in the sea. Why? The oxygen in the air is quite as important to the working of a motor car engine as is petrol. And the most obvious differences between swimming pools and the sea are things like salt content, chlorine and waves, which do not sound like critical economic matters.

The explanation is simple enough. Petrol and swimming pools have a prime characteristic in common which distinguishes them from air and sea water, and which is in no way related to their physical properties. It is this. Petrol and swimming pools are not available in sufficient quantities to enable people to have all that they want of them. In other words, they are not abundant, like air and sea water, but are, in contrast, 'scarce', and it is necessary to make a *choice* of how much of each of them is to be produced.

Economists are interested only in the production and consumption of goods and services which are scarce or, to be precise, of goods and services which are produced by factors of production which are themselves scarce. The reason why it is the scarcity of factors, rather than of goods, that is basically important is that there would be little difficulty in producing enough of any one good for everybody to have as much of it as he wanted. Although video-recorders are scarce enough, there would really be no great difficulty in providing every family in Britain with half a dozen of them. And although lager is scarce and water is not, the economy could produce enough lager to supply all the drinking needs of the nation if this was what was really wanted.

OPPORTUNITY COST

There is, naturally, a catch to all this. If we gave everyone in the country six video-recorders or enough lager to bath in, we would have to do without other things that we value. To make video-recorders, labour, machinery, steel, and other raw materials are necessary; but these factors of production are also required for the manufacture of many other goods and services that societies want. That is to say, the factors themselves are scarce. We do not have enough labour or capital to make as much of everything which we want, at the same time. If we use our factors to make a video-recorder, we sacrifice the chance to use them for another purpose. There is a *real* cost involved in employing any scarce factors of production for a particular use. Economists call this opportunity cost, to stress the fundamental lost opportunity which occurs when a production decision involving a scarce factor is made. This concept is central to economics.

Economic goods, then, are defined as those which are produced by at least one scarce factor of production, but the scarcity of the factor is not absolute. It is relative to the value which people place upon it. In the case of water, for example, there is so much more of it falling as rain in Britain than people want that it is an international joke. But in India and California, water is by no means abundant and, even in Britain, water is not freely available in ample quantities to every home. Scarce factors of production are needed to make provision of adequate supplies for domestic purposes. Moreover, a material like rubber, which is at present scarce, need not always remain so in the economic sense of being scarce relative to demand. If, for example, rubber was shown to emit certain rays which caused fatal heart disease the demand might drop to zero and it would no longer be considered by economists to be scarce.

HOUSEHOLD CHOICE

Opportunity cost, or real cost as it is sometimes called, has applications at the individual or household level. Every good or service with a price greater than zero has a real cost which is simply the other goods or services that could be purchased with the same money. It is useful to depict the choice facing the consumer diagrammatically.

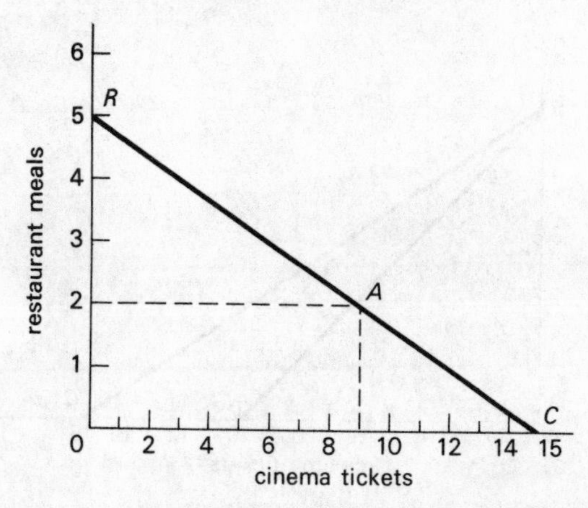

Figure 3.1 *The opportunity cost of restaurant meals.*

Suppose a consumer has, say, £30 a month to spend on meals in restaurants and visits to the cinema. If we know that the average cost of a restaurant meal is £6 and that the price of a cinema ticket is £2, we can represent the alternative ways in which the individual can spend his £30 on the two services as a budget line. In Figure 3.1 this is the line *RC*. The vertical axis of the diagram measures numbers of restaurant meals and the horizontal axis, numbers of cinema tickets. All the points on the budget line represent combinations of the two services available to the consumer for £30. Indeed the line *RC* is sometimes referred to as a consumption possibility curve, a tag which perhaps rather more aptly portrays its meaning.

The budget line intersects the vertical axis at *R* which has the value 5, because this is the maximum number of restaurant meals the consumer could buy if he did not go to the cinema at all. *RC* cuts the horizontal axis at *C*, showing that the consumer could alternatively buy fifteen cinema tickets at £2 each if he never went out for a meal during the month. Along the line between *R* and *C* are other available combinations, such as *A*, which represents two restaurant meals and nine cinema tickets – also costing £30.

The opportunity cost of restaurant meals in real terms is the number of cinema tickets the consumer goes without every time he eats at a restaurant. It can be judged from the slope of the budget line and it is here, in fact, three cinema tickets. This follows from the fact that the price of a restaurant meal is three times that of a cinema ticket. A steeper budget line, say, RC' in Figure 3.2, means that tickets cost £3 each (while the price of a meal remained at £6). The consumer could still buy five meals out, but only ten cinema tickets, on the assumption that he spent the whole £30 on these two goods. The opportunity cost

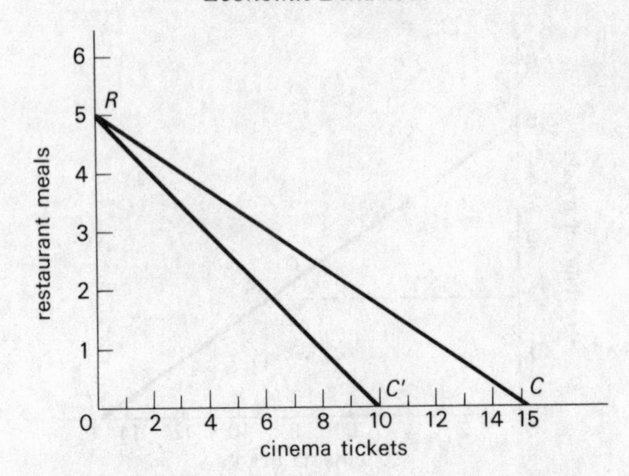

Figure 3.2 *A rise in the price of cinema tickets.*

of a restaurant meal, indicated by the slope of the budget line RC', is two cinema tickets. This follows from the fact that meals now cost twice as much as tickets. Note, however, that the opportunity cost is given in *real terms*, that is, one meal costs two cinema tickets.

For formal completeness, we should add that a change in the amount of money the consumer has available to spend on the two goods is shown by a movement of the whole budget line. The shift will be to a new line parallel to the original so long as no change occurs in the relative prices of the goods or services. For example, a rise in income which allows the consumer to allocate £36 instead of £30 on restaurant meals and cinemas, while their prices remain unchanged at £6 and £2, would shift *RC* to $R''C''$ in Figure 3.3, that is, 'north-east' away from the origin. A fall in the budget allocation would shift the budget line in the opposite direction, still parallel to *RC* but nearer the origin of the graph. (Can you draw it?)

THE PRODUCTION FRONTIER

The discussion of the previous section was designed to show that the idea of opportunity cost was relevant to consuming households. It was to some extent a diversion from the more general theme of scarcity and economic goods. We now return to look at this fundamental concept from the wider angle of national production.

One approach to this question is through the realisation that there is a gap between the wants which people have and the resources which are available for their satisfaction. We can develop this idea and obtain some important conclusions by considering a simplified economy,

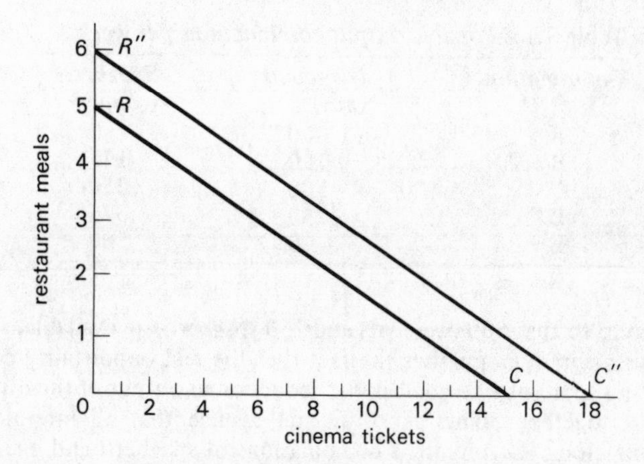

Figure 3.3 *A rise in consumer's income (relative prices unchanged).*

where decisions are to be taken on what to produce over the coming period of time, say, a year. In our economy, we include several factors of production but only two goods which are produced by them. The nature of the goods is irrelevant. To think of an economy subsisting on only two products is so clearly unreasonable that there is no point in pretending that they are realistic. Let us call them, therefore, spaghetti and overcoats.

Imagine, then, that all resources are used to produce either spaghetti or overcoats, or a combination of the two. Consider, further, that we know how much of these goods could be produced per year if resources were employed as efficiently as possible. Say that 1,000 overcoats could be produced if there was no need for spaghetti; 500 (tonnes) of spaghetti if no one wanted overcoats; or that any of the following combinations of the two goods could be produce: 750 overcoats and 125 spaghetti, 500 overcoats and 250 spaghetti or 250 overcoats and 375 spaghetti.

All these production (or output) possibilities can be set out in the form of a table (Table 3.1), which may be described as a production possibility schedule.

Output possibilities can be represented graphically in a manner which is not dissimilar from that used in Figure 3.1 to show consumption possibilities open to a household. If we measure overcoats on the vertical axis and spaghetti on the horizontal axis we can plot each point on the graph (Figure 3.4).

In Figure 3.4, point *A* shows output when all resources are devoted to overcoats (1,000). Point *E* shows that 500 spaghetti can be produced when no resources are used for overcoat production. Point *C* shows the maximum possible output if resources are divided equally between the

Table 3.1 *Possible output combinations per week*

Combination	*Overcoats (nos)*	*Spaghetti (tonnes)*
A	1,000	0
B	750	125
C	500	250
D	250	375
E	0	500

two goods, so that 500 overcoats and 250 spaghetti are available, and so on. This diagram emphasises the fact that the real opportunity cost of producing more of one good is the reduction in output of the other. If we join together points *A* to *E* and assume that all intermediate positions along *AE* represent combinations of spaghetti and overcoats which can be produced (for example, 50 spaghetti and 900 overcoats; 200 spaghetti and 600 overcoats, and so on we have, in fact, a line which represents all the production possibilities which are open to society. This line is called a production frontier, or sometimes a production possibility curve or a transformation curve. It has two features to which we must draw attention.

(1) The production frontier represents only the maximum combinations of the two goods which could be produced if resources are all fully employed and organised as efficiently as possible. Output combinations such as *T* are unattainable and although any combination

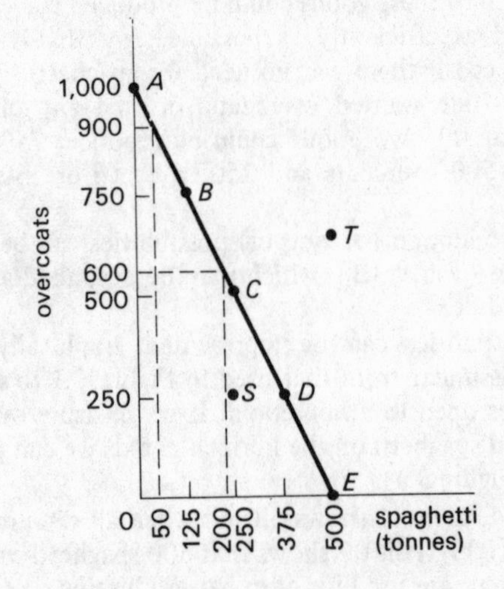

Figure 3.4 *A production frontier exhibiting constant opportunity costs.*

of goods within the space between the line *AE* and the origin 0 is possible, all would involve some waste of resources. At *S*, for example, 250 overcoats and 250 spaghetti would be produced. This must either be an inefficient use of resources or indicate that some are simply lying idle, since we know that if only 250 overcoats were produced, there would be enough resources to produce, not 250 tons of spaghetti, but 375. Alternatively, if only 250 spaghetti were produced, there would be enough resources left for 500 overcoats. In other words *C* or *D* are better combinations of output than *S*.

(2) The opportunity cost of either good can be judged from the slope of the production frontier. The principle involved here is the same as for the budget line in Figure 3.1. It is important enough to explain again.

Consider first the figures in Table 3.1. They tell us the numerical value of opportunity cost. We can describe this cost in either of two ways. If we think of using resources for spaghetti production rather than for overcoats the opportunity cost of 500 spaghetti *in terms of overcoats given up* is 1,000 overcoats. Or, on average, the cost of 1 tonne of spaghetti is 2 overcoats. Alternatively, if we look at the cost of overcoat production in terms of spaghetti given up, 1,000 overcoats cost 500 spaghetti; or, on average 1 overcoat means the loss of ½ tonne of spaghetti.

Now that we know the numerical value of the opportunity cost, let us return to the diagram and find its graphical expression. Imagine all resources are used in overcoat production, that is, the economy is at point *A* in Figure 3.4. Suppose, now, it is decided to start producing 50 spaghetti at the point on the production frontier below *A* corresponding to an output of 900 overcoats and 50 spaghetti. The cost of doing so is the reduction in overcoat production implied in the move, which we know to be 100 overcoats. Or, on average, the cost of each tonne of spaghetti is 2 overcoats. Moreover, as we proceed down the production frontier, using all our resources with maximum efficiency, we shall always have the same opportunity cost facing us – 1 tonne more spaghetti always costs 2 overcoats.

The reason why the slope of the line describes the opportunity cost should now be clear. It may be further clarified in Figure 3.5 where a second production frontier *AF* has been added. On the new curve, we assume that the economy is able to produce the same number of overcoats as before, but only half as many tonnes of spaghetti. If now we again contemplate moving resources from 100 overcoats to spaghetti production, we shall get not 50 tonnes of spaghetti, but only 25. That is to say, the opportunity cost of 25 spaghetti is now 100 overcoats. If we still want 50 spaghetti, we shall have to give up 200 overcoats that is 1 spaghetti costs 4 overcoats on average, and the line *AF* is twice as steep as *AE*.

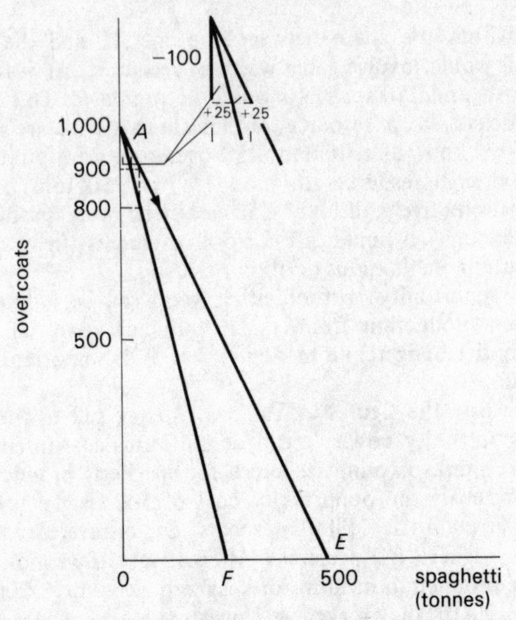

Figure 3.5 *Production frontiers AE and AF. The latter exhibits higher opportunity costs of spaghetti in terms of overcoats.*

COST CONDITIONS

It is necessary to consider that three rather important and different cost conditions are typically encountered.

(1) Constant costs

In the examples used so far, the cost of spaghetti in terms of overcoats is not affected by the amount of either good being produced. In other words, we have been assuming what are called constant costs. This was illustrated geometrically in Figures 3.4 and 3.5 by the fact that the production frontiers are straight lines. The cost of producing one more of either good in terms of the other does not change as we move along *AE*, or along *AF*. There is a proportional (or linear) relationship between them.

(2) Increasing costs

Constant costs are not found in all economic situations. They imply that the resources employed in the production of one good can be combined in the production of another good with equal ease and efficiency, *regardless of how much of either* is being produced. Such a situation occurs if all resources are, as we shall see, neutral as between differing uses. But this is not very likely. One reason is that although the two goods can be made by exactly the same resources (labour and land, for example), each factor of production is probably not equally efficient at producing spaghetti and overcoats. Men work in both lines of output, but their skills are not the same in each. So when resources have to be transferred from, say, spaghetti to overcoat production, it is natural to expect that the men first released will be those who are least skilled at spaghetti production. Then, as more and more resources are moved over, it becomes increasingly necessary to transfer the efficient spaghetti workers to overcoat production. The cost of producing an additional overcoat tends to rise, involving the loss of more and more spaghetti. The farther the economy moves 'north-west' along $E'A'$ in Figure 3.6, the more the cost of overcoats, in terms of spaghetti, increases.

This may be seen quite easily from the graph, where OA' has been divided into equal units ($G'J' = J'K' = K'M' = W'T' = Z'A'$, and so on). Start at E', with all resources in spaghetti production, and move towards A' in 'jumps' representing equal inceases in overcoat production. The cost of doing so, in terms of forgone spaghetti, rises all the time, from $E'G'$ to $H'J'$ to $L'K'$, and so on, until eventually it reaches $S'T'$ and $W'Z'$, as the last units of resources leave the industry and the spaghetti mills close down.

There is a second reason for expecting cost to increase as resources move from one output to another, which has nothing to do with

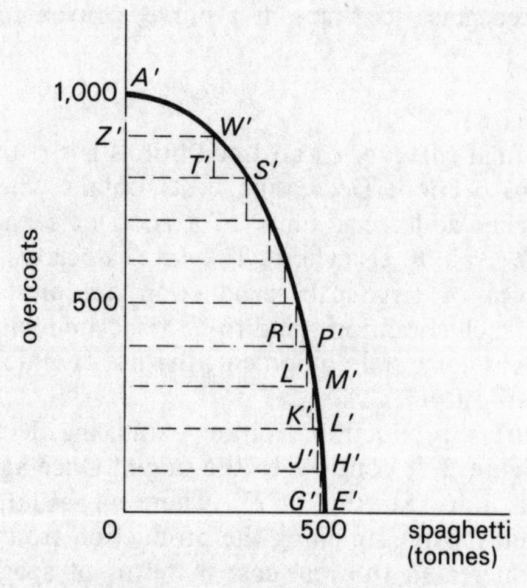

Figure 3.6 *Production frontier curve exhibiting increasing opportunity costs.*

acquired or innate differential skills of the labour force or of any other factor of production. It is concerned with the *proportions* in which factors of production are combined with each other. To demonstrate this, let us assume that some combinations of factors are better than others; that spaghetti, for instance, can be produced most efficiently with a relatively large amount of land, while overcoat production is cheaper with relatively large numbers of workers.

Consider again what happens as we move from E' up towards A' increasing overcoat production. At first, all resources are producing spaghetti and the first factors released are likely to be largely labour, since these are relatively abundant in spaghetti production. All to the good, of course, for the overcoat producers. A lot of labour is what they need, not a lot of land. Worse, however, is to follow as more overcoat production is wanted and we move farther up $E'A'$. Precisely because a relatively large amount of labour was released to start with, there is less available now. Instead, as the transfer of resources continues to the end, relatively larger and larger amounts of land inevitably become available. Lowering output of spaghetti means, therefore, that fewer and fewer overcoats can be made with the newly acquired factors. Certainly, total overcoat production rises, but the opportunity cost of one extra overcoat, in terms of spaghetti given up, also rises.

We shall return to this question again in Chapter 5, where the idea of diminishing returns to a factor of production will be more fully explained. We may be satisfied now with the realisation that a production frontier, which represents rising real opportunity costs of each good in terms of the other as production increases, is not uncommon. We recognise its shape as a curve, convex to the origin, as in Figure 3.6.

(3) Decreasing costs

The third and final category of cost conditions is the opposite of that of the previous section. Decreasing costs obtain whenever the real cost of producing additional units of a good or service call for less resources to be given up elsewhere. They are associated with industries where economies of large-scale production are present. We saw in Chapter 2 that such conditions tend to be associated with the existence of highly specialised capital equipment, the use of which is justified by a large volume of output.

The shape of a production frontier exhibiting decreasing costs is like that in Figure 3.7, concave to the origin. Once again OA'' is divided into equal units. Starting at E'', where all resources are devoted to spaghetti, and moving up along the production frontier, as overcoat production is increased the real cost in terms of spaghetti sacrificed falls. $G''E''$ is greater than $J''H''$, which is greater than $K''L''$, which is greater than $N''M''$, and so on.

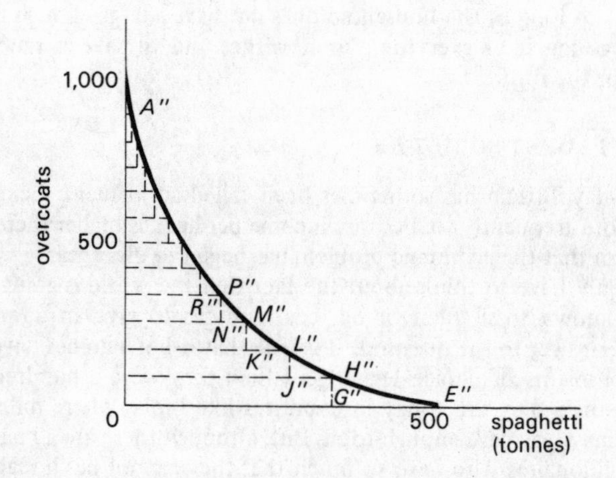

Figure 3.7 *Production frontier exhibiting decreasing opportunity costs.*

'THE ECONOMIC PROBLEM'

The technical matters dealt with in the last few pages were designed to clarify the meaning of the term scarcity in its economic sense. They must not be allowed to blind us to the fundamental issue. It is worth restating the general principle, which is that so long as there is a shortage of goods and services relative to the demand for them, there must inevitably be problems of choice. Households must choose how to spend their limited incomes, and businesses must choose what factors of production they should buy. Economics is essentially concerned with problems of choice. Indeed, the subject has even been dubbed the 'science of choice'. When people talk of the existence of 'the economic problem', they are referring to the way in which an economy, or a person, chooses to allocate scarce resources among the competing uses to which they may be put.

Economic problems exist both for the individual and for society as a whole. In each case the notion of scarcity must be regarded in the relative sense to which attention was drawn earlier. Table 1.1 in Chapter 1 (page 6), for example, demonstrates that the gap between resources and needs is not the same for households in different income classes. For those with incomes of less than £46 a week in 1977, there could hardly have been enough of many goods and services to satisfy quite low requirements. But even households with £123 or more coming in per week faced the problem of choice. If an extra £1 was available next week, what would they do with it? More clothing would 'cost' less entertainment, or fewer other goods. Any decision involves a real cost so long as the household does not have a large enough income to buy as much of everything as it wishes and to save as much as it wants for the future.

THE AFFLUENT SOCIETY

Present-day Britain has sometimes been called an affluent society; the USA more frequently so, because income per head is higher there. Does this mean that the economic problem has begun to disappear?

We only have to think about the fact that the world is going to run out of known fossil fuels of oil, coal and gas to give an unqualified negative answer to the question. It is true that rising incomes have made many problems of choice less urgent than they were a hundred years ago, or than they are today in countries like India, where millions of people may not have enough food. But, although there are a handful of multi-millionaires who have so much that they cannot be thought of as facing any personal economic problems, for any nation as a whole and for the vast majority of people in it the economic problem still exists, though in a perhaps less pressing modern form. Although teenage factory workers with relatively high incomes may sometimes seem to have nearly everything they want, they would usually like more. The range of choice they set themselves, like everyone else, is determined by their means. A man only starts to think of buying a yacht, for example, if his income is great enough to make it a real possibility.

PROBLEMS OF CHOICE

Problems of choice can take many forms. We may illustrate their general nature with three examples.

(1) LEISURE AS A SCARCE COMMODITY

Everyone, even a millionaire, is faced with the economic problem of how best to spend the twenty-four hours of the day. Ignoring, for the sake of simplicity, man's need for sleep, the choice can be portrayed as fundamentally one between work and leisure. In so far as work results in output, the cost of more goods and services is the leisure that has to be given up in order to produce them. Figure 3.8 illustrates the alternatives available: *OB* (i.e. twenty-four hours) of leisure and no goods; *OA* goods and no leisure; and all the combinations of leisure and goods implied by the line *AB*. This is a kind of budget line and is drawn as a straight one, implying that one hour's work always brings a reward of the same number of goods; If, more realistically, there were diminishing returns to work, *AB* would be convex to the origin, like $A'E'$ in Figure 3.6 (page 41).

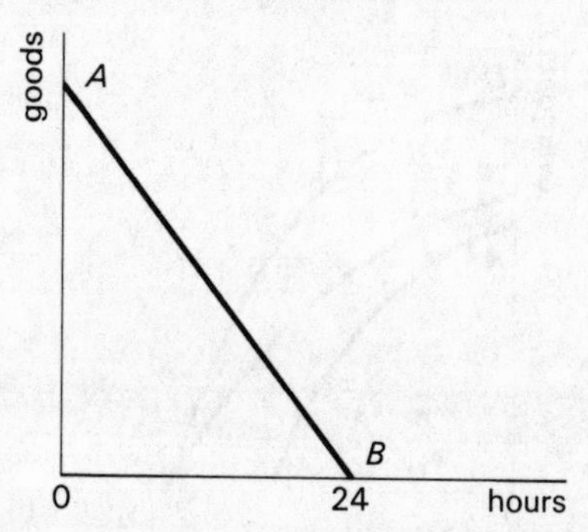

Figure 3.8 *The opportunity cost of goods in terms of leisure sacrificed.*

SOCIAL VERSUS PRIVATE WANTS

The existence of scarcity in an affluent society is also demonstrated by what are known as public goods. These are things like roads, prisons and welfare services, which (for reasons to be considered later) are often provided by the state. They are said to satisfy social as distinguished from private wants, which an individual satisfies for himself by buying food, clothing, and so on, in the market place.

Opinions differ as to what goods and services should be supplied by the government and what the individual should be left to buy for himself. An American, John K. Galbraith,[1] was one of the first economists to argue that the US economy was underproviding for social wants, such as schools, at the expense of private wants, such as automobiles. Galbraith's arguments have been criticised, but there is no room for doubt about the fact that social and private wants compete. The more resources are used to make cars and video-recorders, the less are available for state education, national health services and defence. Figure 3.9 illustrates the choice between a typical private good (video-recorders) and a public good (prisons).

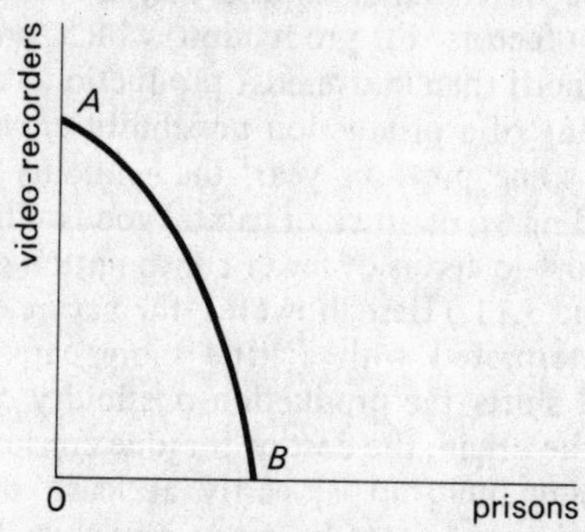

Figure 3.9 *The opportunity cost of private goods in terms of public goods.*

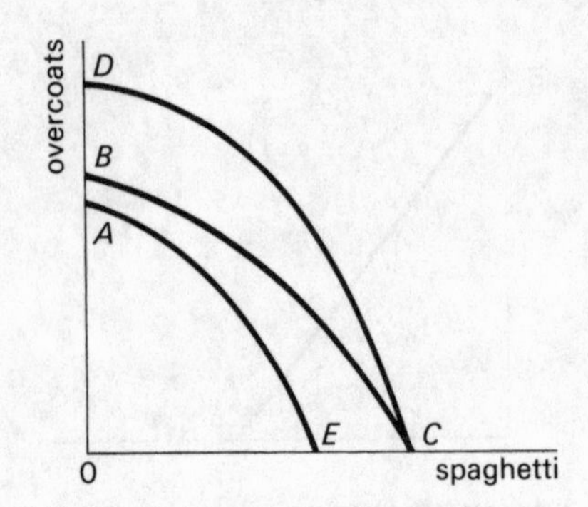

Figure 3.10 *An increase in productivity shifts the production possibility curve to the right.*

ECONOMIC GROWTH

A production possibility curve for an economy is drawn to represent the nature of a particular set of choices during a given period of time, such as a year. It reflects the underlying state of technology at that time, as well as the available resources. Any change in either matter would result in a shift of the production possibility curve.

In Figure 3.10 the original situation of Figure 3.6 (page 41) is repeated in curve *AE*. Curves *BC* and *DC*, on the other hand, represent situations in a later year, when it becomes possible to produce more of both goods than before, because of improved technology, population growth, the acquisition of new natural resources, or some other change. The difference between *BC* and *DC* is that, in the latter, increased productivity is proportionately the same in both spaghetti and overcoats; *BC*, on the other hand, implies that the change increased the supply of those factors of production which are relatively more important in spaghetti than in overcoat production.

Outward shifting of a production possibility curve might be due to the fact that, in some previous year, the economy decided to devote resources to building up its stock of capital goods. This, we know, must have had a real cost in terms of fewer consumption goods in the earlier period. (See Figure 3.11.) Here, however, the nature of the opportunity cost must be interpreted with a little more care. In so far as the additional capital shifts the production possibility curve to the north-west away from the origin, the cost of forgone consumption at the time the capital is being built up is, partly at least, offset by the extra consumer goods that can later be made available. Indeed, one of the most important problems of choice facing an economy concerns the

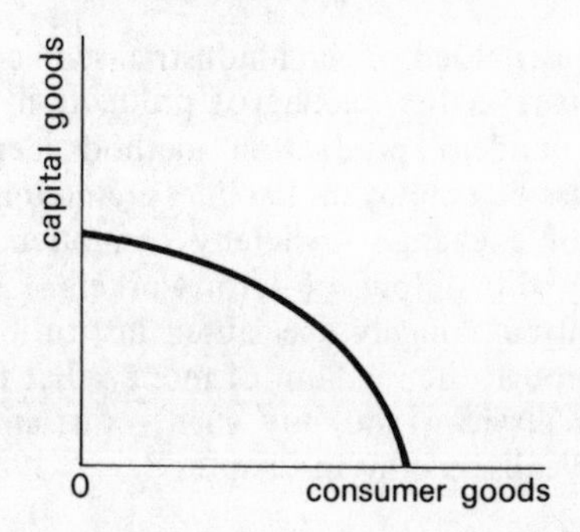

Figure 3.11 *The opportunity cost of capital goods is the consumer goods that must temporarily be sacrificed.*

rate at which it is prepared to forgo present consumption in order to have more to consume in the future. Holding down consumption to increase investment is likely to raise the rate of growth that an economy can enjoy.

SOLVING PROBLEMS OF CHOICE

The first part of this chapter has been confined to describing the problems that scarcity of resources, relative to wants, raises in an economy. The last lap in our introductory overview is concerned with the ways in which the kind of society we live in solves these problems. We know by now that the problems are what to produce, how much to produce and how to produce it.

Consider the first two questions. They ask how society should use its scarce resources. How many overcoats, video-recorders, schools, prisons? How much spaghetti, clothing, Christmas pudding and marmalade? The list is enormous, for it should include everything that society is capable of producing with its limited resources.

It must be admitted at once that there is no single answer to the question of how a society should decide to allocate its scarce factors of production. However, it is usual to distinguish three broad kinds of solution. Societies which rely substantially on one or other of them are known as traditional, command or market economies.

(1) TRADITIONAL ECONOMIES

In a self-sufficient society the decision of what to produce may be made by tradition. A man hunts because his father hunted before him. A girl cooks because that is what her mother did. Each family unit is virtually self-sufficient, and that is an end to it.

In modern industrialised or semi-industrialised economies, tradition may still play a part in the making of production decisions. But the specialisation of modern production methods demands that more complex techniques be employed. Families are no longer self-sufficient, and some form of exchange – whereby computer programmers, for example, can buy the output of farm workers – is needed. Modern societies have evolved a highly specialised institution to perform this function. It is through the medium of money that factors can receive rewards for their services, and buy such goods and services as they happen to want. We discuss this in Chapter 8.

(2) COMMAND ECONOMIES

In complex modern economies tradition plays a relatively minor role in resource allocation. Two different solutions to the economic problem are found. The distinction between them is basically whether decisions are centralised or decentralised. Command economies are those where resource allocation is concentrated in, for example, a central planning agency (which may employ input-output techniques as described earlier in Chapter 2, pages 23–26). Countries such as the Soviet Union and others in Eastern Europe tend to make many economic decisions in this way. So did Britain in wartime. There are important political considerations involved here. However, as far are we, *as economists*, are concerned it does not matter whether the agency is democratically elected, a benevolent dictatorship, or even a tyrannical despot. As long as the decision on what to produce is taken centrally, the economy is known as command, and we can ignore the political pros and cons.

(3) MARKET ECONOMIES

Britain is not a command economy at the present time although some decisions are taken by the government when expenditure on public goods, such as defence and a large part of education and health, is involved. But the bulk of decisions about what to produce in Britain are not taken by the government at all. As we know from Chapter 2, decisions about the production of goods and services are decentralised to a large extent and taken by the business sector of the economy, though they are also influenced by the decisions of individuals as consumers of goods and services.

For the private sector of the economy, where video-recorders and overcoats are produced, there is no commanding authority. Instead, a form of social institution has evolved which allows producers and consumers to get in touch with one another. This institution is simply a market, and the communication that buyers and sellers have with each other is a monetary one, through the medium of what is known as the price mechanism.

THE PRICE MECHANISM

A market in economics is no more than a place or organisation whereby producers, or sellers, of a good get in touch with those who may want to buy what they are offering for sale. Goods are not, however, given away but are bought and sold, and it is possible to regard the movements in their prices as acting as signalling devices which indicate whether too much or too little of each good or service is being produced.

The price mechanism works through the operation of what are known as the forces of supply and demand. We shall devote the whole of the next chapter to some technical aspects of supply-demand analysis. It is possible at this stage, however, to explain the general principles which lie behind the way in which the price mechanism allocates resources.

Consider, for example, the market for the single commodity, say, tomatoes, during a given period of time, say, a week. On one side of the market there are the potential tomato consumers; on the other side are the sellers of tomatoes.

Suppose that the sellers offer their stock for sale at a price which, if they sell it all, will cover their costs plus a modest profit. At this price, however, it does not follow that the quantity that consumers wish to buy will necessarily be exactly the right amount to clear the market. If it is not, then the price must be either too high or too low. If it is too high there will be an excess of supply over demand. And, if all producers are to dispose of their tomatoes before they perish, some of them will have to lower the price. And once price has fallen in one part of the market, it is difficult for any single producer to charge a higher one. Competition among sellers tends to bring the price down for all.

A different situation occurs if price is too low, in the sense that households wish to buy more at this price than sellers are prepared to sell. In other words, there is an excess of demand over supply. The effect in this case is the exact opposite of that described in the previous paragraph. Now it is the buyers who are in competion with each other. There are not enough tomatoes for everyone who wants to buy them. Some sellers will catch on and find that they can sell their stocks even if they raise the price. As before, once price has risen in a part of the market, other sellers may soon follow suit. Competition among consumers for a limited quantity tends to raise market price.

There is, therefore, a tendency for price to move up and down in the market to bring about an equality between the quantity of tomatoes that sellers want to sell and that which consumers wish to purchase. In other words, the price mechanism tends to equate supply and demand. When the wishes of sellers and purchasers in the market happen to be the same, then price is said to be at an equilibrium level. Supply and demand are equal.

PRICES AS SIGNALS

The key to understanding the process by which market economies allocate resources is to recognise that price has a 'signalling' function for those on both the supply and demand sides of the market. This may clearly be seen when the market has been in equilibrium and some external change disturbs it. The argument is not basically affected by whether the initial change comes from the demand side, or from the supply side as, for example when costs of production alter after a new machine is introduced. Let us, however, examine the effects of a change which originates on the demand side.

We know from our brief look at household expenditure patterns in Chapter 1 that demand is likely to be influenced by several factors such as income, tastes and family size. Let us suppose that the size of families among consumers increases. How would this affect the price of tomatoes and the quantity bought and sold? Figure 1.2 (on page 9) suggests that the proportion of income spent on food rises with size of family. So let us assume that the rise in average family size implies an increase in the demand for tomatoes, in the sense that households wish to purchase larger quantities at each and every price, including that which until now has been the equilibrium price in the market. In these circumstances, there is an excess of demand over supply and this tends to produce a rise in price, which acts as a signal both to sellers and to buyers. The higher price acts as a rationing device choking off some of the new demand: only those who value tomatoes highly will be prepared to pay more for them, and price will move towards a new, higher, equilibrium.

The rise in price may have a second signalling effect, however. Provided that there has been no change in the production costs of tomatoes, we should expect that sellers would increase the quantity they wish to sell. If they were making a profit before, they would make a larger one with a higher price, and thus other producers – of cucumbers, for example – might be tempted to switch production to tomatoes. So in the end, when the market has finally settled at a new equilibrium, we may find that the increase in demand, working through the signal of changing price, has brought about an increase in supply to meet it.

CONSUMER SOVEREIGNTY

The allocation of resources brought about by a decentralised market system reflects household demands, which are, in turn, affected by consumer tastes. This feature of the price mechanism has led to its being described as achieving consumer sovereignty. Moreover, the simplicity and low operating cost of the market mechanism compared with central planning administrations can be very appealing. More than two hundred years ago the economist Adam Smith described the system as the 'invisible hand' which guides resources into their best uses, as indicated by the preferences of consumers for different products relative to costs of production. The motive force which is said to bring about this state of affairs is that of self-interest. The wishes of consumers and producers become harmonised through the price mechanism precisely because each side of the market seeks to look after its own interests.

This is, perhaps, most obvious on the demand side. If the price of a good changes, people will tend to buy different quantities of it, because its opportunity cost relative to other goods has altered. By allocating expenditure differently from before, consumers are most likely to get the maximum satisfaction out of their total income.

Less obvious may be the fact that the independent attempt by each producer to maximise his profits can also be in the interest of consumers. If demand increases and price rises in consequence, the incentive of higher profits may be what brings forth a matching increase in supply. Little wonder that some nineteeth-century philosophers studying these matters were enthusiastic supporters of a freely working price mechanism for equating the wishes of self-seeking producers and consumers. They could see that prices act as signals on a track between buyers and sellers – rationing limited supplies among those prepared to pay most for them, and stimulating changes in supply in the light of changing conditions. The so-called *laissez-faire* philosophy of non-interference by the government in the working of the economy flourished on this kind of argument.

MARKET FAILURE

Unfortunately the market system does not work quite as well as its supporters would wish. Explicitly, it can fail to achieve an allocation of resources which best meets society's goals on a number of counts. We shall have to wait until we have nearly finished this book for a full discussion of the causes and implications of market failure.

However, we can already indicate briefly the major reasons for failure. They are perhaps best appreciated at this stage if it is understood that the market mechanism acts efficiently only when certain conditions relating to the market and to the economy obtain. Six such conditions may be distinguished.

(1) Markets must be efficient in the sense that buyers and sellers must be well informed about prices, costs and other relevant market facts. Supply and demand must also respond reasonably quickly to price changes.
(2) There must be effective competition on both sides of the market so that price changes whenever changes in the conditions of supply or demand occur, as when tastes change or new production techniques are discovered.
(3) Buyers and sellers must aim at maximisation of satisfaction and of profits. Consumers must know what they want and be prepared to back their desires with hard cash. They must not be forced through advertising or other means by producers to buy goods which will not give them the satisfaction they except. Producers, likewise, must know what goods are the most profitable to produce.
(4) The distribution of income and wealth between persons must be regarded as in some sense satisfactory, or 'optimal'. The importance of this assumption can be understood if the pricing system is seen as reflecting consumer wants, expressed in the prices that people are prepared to pay for different goods and services. The price mechanism is rather like an electoral system with money for votes. Consumers 'vote' for products by spending money on goods that please them. Popular goods will be those on which consumers want to spend relatively large sums of money. However, people's demand for goods depends, as we know, on their incomes. The rich tend to buy Aston Martins, lobsters and luxury penthouses. Lower-income groups tend to demand Fords, cockles and small semi-detached houses. Inevitably, the distribution of income affects the pattern of national output. A society where the distribution is very uneven will 'vote' for different things than an egalitarian one. How are we to choose between them? The answer is that we cannot do so on economic grounds alone. All we can say is that the forces of supply and demand, operating within a given distribution, produce a certain composition of output. We can only accept the resulting pattern of goods and services as the best if we are prepared to accept the distribution of income as the best also.
(5) The only goods and services must be those which benefit individuals as individuals. This condition excludes public goods, like roads and defence, which benefit the community in a wider sense. It also excludes consumption or production of a kind which involves spillover effects on outsiders, for example, pollution.

(6) The social, legal and institutional framework within which the pricing system operates must be regarded as generally satisfactory. The market operates in a social setting, not in a vacuum. Laws and customs relating to such matters as private property, the family and the freedom, rights and responsibilities of the individual may all affect the manner in which markets work. Society may not be content to see, for instance, traffic in drugs, sex or other activities deemed undesirable. It may be inhibited by custom or outlawed by legislation.

A VERDICT ON THE MARKET MECHANISM

It is clear that all the ideal conditions listed in the previous section do not exist in the British economy. Does that mean that we should necessarily reject the price mechanism for the allocation of resources? The answer is surely no. But it must be recognised that the market system is less than perfect. Some things might be, and are, done to make it function more efficiently. We can only judge whether it is an appropriate machinery if it is compared with other systems, such as central planning, which, too, has advantages and disadvantages. The final verdict requires that the pros and cons of all systems are weighed in the balance. This cannot be done without bringing political considerations into the arena – a matter beyond the scope of this book. We shall, however, return to discuss the efficiency of the market system in Chapter 10.

FACTOR MARKETS

The discussion of the mechanism by which price allocates resources has so far concentrated on the markets for goods and services – that is, with the question of what goods to produce and how much of each of them. We have largely ignored the question to which attention was directed in the chapter on production, of how a given output should be produced, or how businesses should combine productive factors in the process.

We know that the choice of factor combinations depends partly upon their prices, which are themselves affected by conditions in the factor markets. Supply and demand considerations in fact apply in the markets for goods and services. There is a supply and a demand for labour of different types, and these influence levels of wages.

There is a final point to make. In so far as factor markets influence factor rewards – wages, rent, interest and profits – they effect our incomes as persons. They will also influence the distribution of income and wealth. We argued earlier that we cannot judge whether the market system works well or not in general without deciding also whether the distribution of income is in some sense good or acceptable. Income distribution affects the allocation of resources and it directly controls the amounts of goods and services that individuals in the community can buy. It follows, therefore, that we must include factor markets in the assessment of the efficiency of the price mechanism with which we ended the last section.

OTHER MARKETS

We may end this chapter by mentioning the existence of markets other than for goods and services and for factors of production. There are, for instance, markets where the lending and borrowing of money and financial assets takes place, and others where dealers in foreign currencies engage in trading. The same basic principles of supply and demand apply to all these markets, though each possesses certain special characteristics.

All markets provide the framework within which the price mechanism operates to answer the questions with which we have been concerned – what? how much? and how? – as well as others such as who shall enjoy the benefits of the goods which are produced? when shall they be consumed, now or later? and where should they be produced (Cardiff or London)? To understand how these questions are answered we need to know more about the nature of supply and demand, and to this end we turn to the next chapter.

NOTE: CHAPTER 3

1 J.K. Galbraith, *The Affluent Society* (Hamish Hamilton, 1958; Penguin, 1962).

Chapter 4

Supply and Demand in the Market for Goods

In the last chapter we referred to the way in which prices, acting as signals, direct production towards goods and services that people want to buy, and ration the available quantities among persons prepared to pay for them. Our present task is to examine more closely the working of supply, demand and price in the market place. In this chapter we will concentrate on the markets for goods or commodities. In the next, we will look at the working of the price mechanism in markets where factors of production are bought and sold.

We already know that the market price of a commodity depends upon demand and supply. Our next step is to examine more closely each of these. We shall proceed by considering demand and supply from the viewpoint of the individual consumer and supplier of goods. Then, by simply adding together demand by individuals, we can obtain what may be called total, or market, demand for a good. Similarly we can derive a notion of market supply, and finally put the two together to consider the formation of market price.

DEMAND

The demand that is of interest to economists is that which is related to the quantities of a commodity that individuals would be prepared to purchase. This is not the same thing as the quantities that they 'need', or would like to have. Needs and wants obviously lie behind purchases; but resources are limited, and our concern is only with actual market behaviour as revealed in *effective demand* backed by willingness to spend money.

We saw in the opening chapter that the amount of a commodity which people want to purchase is dependent upon many factors. Economists, however, find it convenient for expository purposes to concentrate upon one determinant at a time. The one in which prime interest resides is the price at which a commodity can be obtained.

INDIVIDUAL DEMAND

Let us take an example of a specific good, ice creams, and let us assume that a person's demand for this good, per period of time, depends upon such forces as the price of ice creams, the price of chocolates and other competing goods, the individual's income, his wealth, his tastes, the weather, and any other miscellaneous factors which may influence his desire to buy one. In the short run, we may reasonably suppose that all influences on demand, other than the price of an ice cream itself, do not change. We may then ignore the effect of all the other factors and concentrate on the demand for ice creams related only to their price.

This method of argument is commonly employed in economics when behaviour is known to depend on several factors. In such circumstances the analysis may be very complicated, and economists simplify the problem by a process of abstraction – analysing the influence of each determinant in turn, on the assumption that other determining factors do not change. The assumption is known by the name *ceteris paribus,* from the Latin 'other things remaining equal'. We shall use it several times in this book.

To make the point clearer, we can imagine a list of the quantities of ice creams that would be bought at various prices. Such a list is called a *demand schedule*. Table 4.1 shows demand schedules for two individuals whom we call Alan and Bill. The example is, of course, hypothetical, but it serves to illustrate the fundamental idea that demand has no exact meaning by itself, but only in relation to a particular price.

Table 4.1 *Demand schedules for ice creams* (*hypothetical*) (quantities demanded per week)

Price (pence)	*Alan*	*Bill*	*Bill and Alan*
40	1	0	1
35	2	0	2
30	3	2	5
25	4	4	8
20	5	6	11
15	6	8	14
10	7	10	17
5	8	12	20

Demand schedules like those in Table 4.1 can also be presented graphically. If we measure price on the vertical axis and quantity demanded on the horizontal, we can draw a diagram for Alan and another for Bill as in Figures 4.1 (i) and (ii). D_A is Alan's demand curve. It is constructed by plotting all the tabulated price-quantity combinations on the graph and joining them up. The curve shows, therefore,

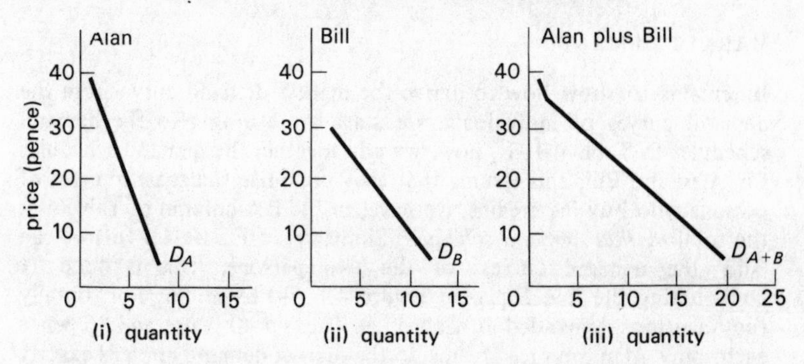

Figure 4.1 *Demand curves for individuals and the market demand for ice creams per week.*

the numbers of ice creams he would buy per week at every price between 5 pence and 40 pence. The same applies to Bill's demand curve in Figure 4.1 (ii).

We must now draw attention to an important characteristic of Alan's and Bill's demand curves. They are both downward sloping. This simply means that each of them demands more ice creams the lower the price. Why should this be so? The answer is related to the satisfaction they get from consuming ice creams. There is a widely accepted assumption in economics that applies generally to most commodities that the *extra* satisfaction (or utility as it is sometimes called) which one gets from consuming *additional* quantities of ice creams tends to fall the more one has of them.

The price one is prepared to pay for a good, it can be argued, depends on the satisfaction one gets from it. Moreover, the price one would pay for an extra unit of the good reflects the extra satisfaction obtained from consuming it. If this extra satisfaction, or *marginal utility*, falls with increasing quantities, then demand will be higher at low prices than at high. To put it another way, the price one would be prepared to pay for an additional unit falls as the quantity rises.

In our example, Alan is prepared to pay 40 pence for a single ice cream a week, but he will only be prepared to buy a second one if the price falls to 35 pence, a third if it falls to 30 pence, and so on. It would take a price of 5 pence to induce him to buy as many as eight.

This characteristic of consumer behaviour is known as the principle of diminishing marginal utility. Marginal utility is the difference in total utility derived from consuming an additional unit of a commodity. The principle can be stated differently. As consumption increases total utility increases, *but at a decreasing rate*. Whichever way the principle is put, it can explain the fact that Alan's and Bill's demand curves are downward sloping.

MARKET DEMAND

It remains to show how to derive the market demand curve from the demand curves of individuals. We start by returning to the demand schedules in Table 4.1. If, now, we add together the demand schedules for Alan and Bill, and assume that they comprise the total number of persons who buy ice creams, we have, in the last column of Table 4.1, the total *market demand schedule*. Similarly, in Figure 4.1 (iii) we can 'add' the demand curves for the two persons. This is done by constructing the line D_{A+B} in Figure 4.1 (iii) by adding horizontally the quantities demanded at each price. Thus, at 40 pence and 35 pence each, only Alan buys ice creams, so the market demand curve is exactly the same as Alan's. At a price of 30 pence, however, Alan buys three ice creams, but Bill also buys two, so the market demand is for five ice creams at that price, and so on. It should be noted, too, that the market demand curve, like those of Alan and Bill is downward sloping. This is not surprising because it is constructed from two demand curves, those of Alan and Bill, which are themselves downward sloping. There is, however, an additional reason. It is simply that falls in price not only induce increasing demand by existing consumers, they also attract new consumers into the market – people who do not consider purchases at higher prices. Referring back to Table 4.1, we can see that Alan is the only consumer as long as the price is 35 or 40 pence. At a price of 30 pence, however, Bill enters the market. The additional consumption of three ice creams is partly due to Alan buying one more, but also to the fact that Bill starts off by buying two ice creams.

The explanation given in the previous paragraph suggests that market demand curves are even more likely to slope downwards than the demand curves of individual consumers. This characteristic of demand curves is believed to have widespread, if not universal, application to demand curves in general.

There is a final feature of market demand curves that must be mentioned. It is that they may be affected by certain factors other than those determining the demand curves for individual consumers. These are all by way of being usually long-run considerations. The most commonly included are the size of the population of a country and the distribution of income within it. The latter is not only a question of size distribution between rich and poor, but also distribution of any kind which might affect total demand. For example, a redistribution of income from older to younger people could easily raise the demand for LP albums and lower the demand for wheeled shopping baskets. In the short run, matters like the size of the population and the distribution of income are included in the *ceteris paribus* assumptions described earlier, that is, they do not change during the period being analysed.

Income and substitution effects of price changes

We may gain further insight into the reasons why demand curves tend to slope downwards by considering that there are really two distinct aspects of a price fall that lead to a change in the quantity purchased. These are known as the *substitution effect* and the *income effect*. The nature of the substitution effect is obvious. When the price of any good falls while the prices of all other goods remain unchanged, there is a natural tendency for people to buy it instead of other goods – that is, to substitute it for similar or competing commodities. But there is an additional reason why demand may change when price falls. Among our *ceteris paribus* assumptions, it may be recalled, is that of a constant level of the consumer's income. But when an individual has a fixed money income and the price of one of the goods he buys falls, this effectively raises his real income, that is, its purchasing power increases. A rise in income means that a person has more to spend on all goods. It is likely that he will use some of this extra to buy more of the commodity whose price has fallen.

Earlier (in Chapter 1, page 7) we distinguished between 'normal' and 'inferior' goods. Those the consumption of which rises (or falls) as income rises (or falls) are called normal. Those which are bought in smaller quantities as income rises are known as inferior. Provided that the good whose price falls is not an inferior good, the income effect of the price change, as well as the substitution effect, will tend to increase the quantity demanded.

Although most demand curves, as argued above, slope downwards, the steepness of the slope varies from one commodity to another. To put the matter differently, when the price of a good changes, the extent to which this leads to a change in demand is not the same for all goods.

The reasons for this are related, to a considerable extent, to what we have called the substitution effect. The more and better substitutes that a good has, the more one may expect demand to increase for a fall in price (or to decrease for a rise in price). In part, this may merely reflect how closely a commodity is defined. 'Kodak 35 mm cameras' have more substitutes than '35 mm cameras', which in turn have more substitutes than 'cameras'. But it is also true that there are more good substitutes for, say, tomato sauce, than for, say, salt.

The income effect is relevant to the extent to which demand for a good responds to price changes. If the good is an inferior one, the income effect will dampen the substitution effect. For a normal good, in contrast, the rise in real income tends to reinforce the increase in demand following a price fall. For any commodity, however, one can add that the more important the item in the consumer's budget, the stronger the income effect is likely to be. A good such as ice creams in our earlier example obviously absorbs so small a part of a consumer's budget that a change in price of a few pence can hardly have a significant effect on his real income. In contrast, a fall or rise in the price of houses, for instance, may very well be expected to make a consumer significantly better or worse off by changing the effective purchasing power of a fixed money income.

A matter relevant to the relationship between price and quantity demanded is the number of uses to which a good may be put. In general, the greater the number of uses, the larger the change in demand to be expected, for the greater is the scope for extending demand after a price fall (and vice versa). Tea, for example, has fewer uses than eggs, so that a fall in the price of tea may be likely to cause a relatively smaller rise in demand than a fall in the price of eggs.

Finally, it should be mentioned that the responsiveness of demand to price changes tends to be larger the longer the time period under consideration. This is true for both rises and falls in price, and reflects the fact that some people often take quite a while even to hear about price changes. Very few people are also so flexible that they adjust their habits instantly the price of a good rises or falls.

ELASTICITY OF DEMAND

Economists have a special way of measuring the responsiveness of demand to changes in price – they call it *elasticity*. Formally, the elasticity of demand is a fraction (or ratio) – the proportionate change in quantity demanded divided by the proportionate change in price. For a commodity which has many substitutes, and whose demand responds easily to price changes, the fraction is larger than 1, and demand is said to be *elastic*. If a 1 per cent price fall causes a 2 per cent rise in quantity, for example, a good would be in elastic demand.[1]

In contrast, a good which has few substitutes, and for which the demand responds weakly to a price change, would have an elasticity of demand of less than 1, and demand would be said to be *inelastic*. A 5 per cent price fall leading only to a 1 per cent increase in quantity would be an example of this kind of good.

Between the two cases mentioned we may discern a third, benchmark, category, comprising goods for which the demand responds to a given percentage price change by changing in quantity by exactly the same percentage. If demand falls by 1 per cent, the elasticity of demand is said to be equal to *unity*. It is not hard to see that, for such goods, total expenditure on the commodity is identical at all prices. But we may observe that for goods for which the demand is elastic, total expenditure increases as price falls (since demand expands relatively more than price falls). Conversely, for goods for which the demand is inelastic, total expenditure increases as price rises (since demand does not fall off relatively as much as price rises).

Before leaving the explanation of the term elasticity of demand, it should be mentioned that the concept of elasticity, measuring the responsiveness of one factor to a change in another, is not confined to demand, but is widely used in economics. For example, the income elasticity of demand measures the responsiveness of demand to changes in income, and there are many others.

CHANGES IN DEMAND

We argued earlier that it was often reasonable to make *ceteris paribus* assumptions about factors such as income, tastes, and so on, which affect demand. These assumptions were necessary in order that a demand curve might be derived at all. But it does not follow that we must always retain the assumptions in our analysis of market behaviour. Suppose in fact, that a change in a *ceteris paribus* assumption occurs. We sometimes refer to such a change as one in the *conditions* of demand. All we need to do is to draw a new demand curve. An example may help to make the matter clear. Imagine something happening, such as the discovery that ice cream stops baldness, which makes people decide they want to buy more ice cream. We could interpret this change as a shift to the right of the demand curve *DD* to *D'D'* in Figure 4.2, implying that *at every price* the quantity demanded is greater than it was before. A fall in income, in contrast, might shift the demand curve back again to *DD*, as might an appropriate change in any one of the determinants of demand other than price.

It must be emphasised that changes in the price of a good itself do *not* shift the demand curve. We read the effects of price changes by moving *along* the curve. It is important to avoid the common error of confusing these price changes with changes in the *ceteris paribus* assumptions. These last shift the whole curve if they vary. The extent and manner in which they alter the position of the demand curve depends upon the nature of the good in question. A fall in the price of

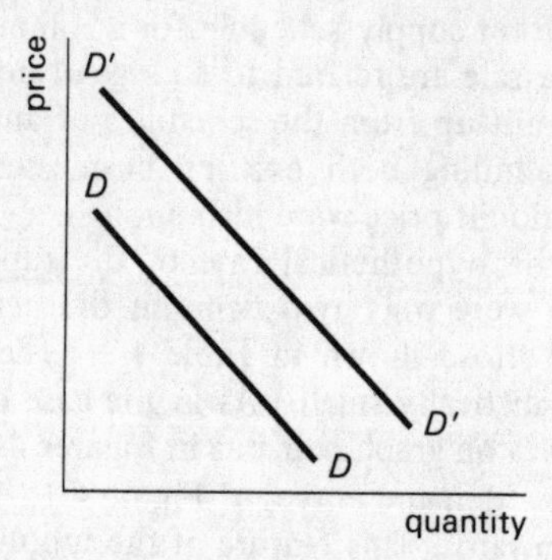

Figure 4.2 *An increase in demand.*

a substitute for a good tends to shift the demand curve downwards – less being bought at every price when there is a cheaper substitute available. But there are also goods which are complementary to each other, which tend to be demanded together, and which cause opposite kinds of shifts in demand curves. Tennis racquets and tennis balls are, for example, complements. A fall in the price of racquets tends to shift the demand curve for tennis balls upwards, more balls being demanded as soon as people buy more (cheaper) racquets.

SUPPLY

We must now shift our attention from demand to examine more closely the determinants of the supply of a commodity. Supply, like demand, depends on many factors. The principal ones are the costs of production, the kind of market in which business operates, and the objectives or goals at which the owners of a business enterprise are aiming.

As we explained in Chapter 2, it is usual in economics to assume, as a first approximation, that firms are in business primarily to maximise profits. Although this is clearly not true in every case, we can safely adopt the assumption here in order to derive certain elementary conclusions about market behaviour. It may need qualification later, when alternative goals, such as maximum sales or growth of the business, are substituted for it. We assume, too, that the market is a competitive one comprising a large number of small firms. We shall return later in this chapter to consider the implications of this assumption.

SUPPLY BY AN INDIVIDUAL FIRM

Our concern at the moment is to relate quantities supplied to price. We wish to derive a market supply schedule for a commodity in which the amounts offered for sale are related to a range of prices. Such a supply schedule must be built up from the schedules of amounts supplied by individual firms, including both existing businesses and firms which might enter production if price were high enough.

Consider again the hypothetical case of the supply of ice creams. Suppose that there were only two firms in the market. Their supply schedules might be those shown in Table 4.2. (The numbers are kept deliberately if unrealistically small.) As in the case of demand, we can plot the supply curves on graph paper as in Figures 4.3 (i) and 4.3 (ii).

In contrast to the demand curves of Figure 4.1, the supply curves of both firms slope upwards. This feature of the supply curve is related to the cost structure of firms. If a firm is to be induced to offer additional

Table 4.2 *Supply schedules for ice creams (hypothetical)* (quantities supplied per week)

Price (pence)	*Firm A*	*Firm B*	*Firm A plus Firm B*
5	1	0	1
10	3	2	5
15	5	3	8
20	7	4	11
25	9	5	14
30	11	6	17
35	13	7	20
40	15	8	23

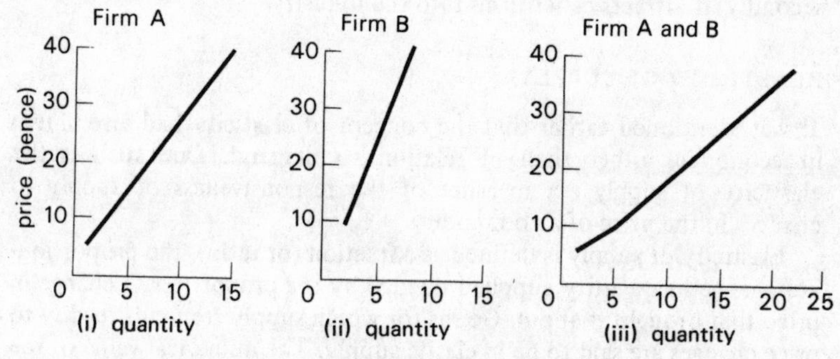

Figure 4.3 *Supply curves for individual firms and the market supply of ice creams per week.*

units of a commodity for sale, it is obvious that the price at which it is able to sell them must cover their costs of production.[2] An upward sloping supply curve implies that the higher the price the larger the quantities that would be offered for sale. The justification for such an upward slope, then, may be that costs rise, at the margin, as output increases. For this reason a rise in price may be seen as necessary in order to cover the addition to total costs occasioned by the higher output.

The changes in total costs attributable to changed output are known as *marginal costs*. We shall assume here that marginal costs rise as output increases, so that we may examine the determination of market price in such a situation. We must realise, however, that if costs do not increase then the supply curve need not be upward sloping. Some of the implications of dropping this assumption may be quite readily appreciated, but the reader is warned that certain others must await more advanced work in economics.[3]

MARKET SUPPLY

The derivation of the market supply curve from the supply curves of firms A and B is straightforward and basically similar to the method of deriving the market demand curve of Figure 4.1 (iii). At a price of 5 pence, firm A offers one for sale, firm B none at all, so market supply is one. At a price of 10 pence firm A offers three, firm B two, market supply is five, and so on.

Finally it should be noticed that the market supply curve like those of firms A and B slopes upwards and in the opposite direction, therefore, to the market demand curve. The reasoning here is basically similar to the case of demand. There are again two explanations. First, a rise in price calls forth a larger quantity from existing suppliers and, secondly, it attracts other firms into the industry.

ELASTICITY OF SUPPLY

It was mentioned earlier that the concept of elasticity had several uses in economics other than in relation to demand. One such is the elasticity of supply – a measure of the responsiveness of supply to changes in the price of a commodity.

Elasticity of supply is defined as a fraction (or ratio), the proportionate change in quantity supplied divided by the proportionate change in price that brought it about. Goods for which supply responds readily to price changes are said to be in elastic supply. The numerical value of the fraction is greater than one, implying that a price rise (or fall) induces a more than proportionate rise (or fall) in the quantity offered for sale. Conversely, goods the supply of which responds only weakly to price changes are said to be in inelastic supply and the numerical value of the fraction is less than one. There is also a benchmark case of unitary elasticity of supply, where the fraction has a value of exactly one and the proportionate changes in quantity supplied and in price are the same.

When we come to identify the factors responsible for deciding whether elasticity of supply is likely to be great or small for a particular good, the question of the availability of substitutes is of great importance, as it was in the case of demand. Substitutes in supply, however, have a rather different significance. In order for supply to be readily responsive to changes in price there must be ready alternate occupations for factors of production. In other words, there must be goods to or from which production can readily be switched.

Compare, for instance, the supply of plastic toy cars with that of potatoes. In the former case, one might reasonably expect that it was relatively easy for a firm to switch labour and other resources from producing plastic cars to any of an obviously wide range of other plastic toys. The responsiveness of supply to changes in the price of toy cars would, then, tend to be relatively greater than that to a change in the price of potatoes. Once potatoes are planted, there is no scope at all in the short run for a farmer to switch to another crop. This example also brings out the point that elasticity of supply, similarly again to that of demand, tends to be greater the longer the time allowed for adjustments to take place.

CHANGES IN SUPPLY

Supply curves, like demand curves, are drawn up on *ceteris paribus* assumptions; in this case to allow the relationship between price and quantity supplied to be isolated. Foremost among the factors which are assumed to remain unchanged over a period are costs of production behind which lie such matters as the state of technology and the prices of the factors of production used by firms. This assumption does not mean that costs do not vary with output, but that the relationship between costs and output does not change over time. If any change of this kind occurs it is often referred to as a change in the *conditions* of supply. We can deal with it in a similar way to that in which we dealt with shifts in demand. We can move the entire supply curve.

Suppose, for example, a new invention makes possible a lowering of costs of ice cream production. We can interpret this as a downward movement of the entire supply curve as from *SS* to *S'S'* in Figure 4.4, implying that a larger quantity would now be supplied at *every price.*

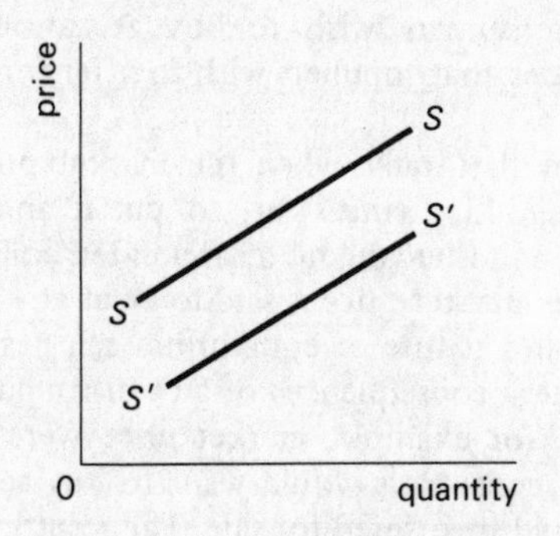

Figure 4.4 *An increase in supply.*

MARKET EQUILIBRIUM

We have now derived independent relationships between demand and price, and between supply and price. Let us put together the market demand and supply schedules and curves which we invented for ice

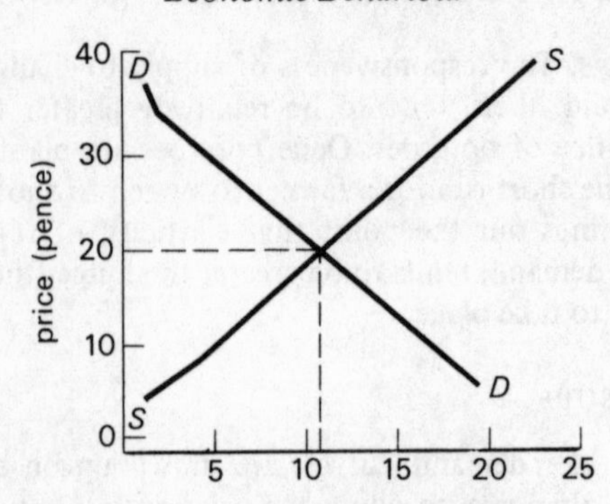

Figure 4.5 *Equilibrium market price, where supply equals demand.*

Table 4.3 *Quantities of ice creams demanded and supplied per week*

Price (pence)	*Market demand*	*Market supply*
40	1	23
35	2	20
30	5	17
25	8	14
20	11	11
15	14	8
10	17	5
5	20	1

creams in Table 4.3 and Figure 4.5. Remember that *DD* portrays the quantities that consumers wish to buy at various prices, while *SS* shows the quantities that suppliers wish to offer for sale at the same set of prices.

It can be seen that only when the market price is 20 pence are supply and demand the same – or, to put it another way, that the market is cleared and there are no disappointed consumers or suppliers. In such a situation, market price is said to be at an *equilibrium* level.

The meaning and nature of equilibrium can best be understood by examining the likely consequences of any other price obtaining in the market. Suppose, for example, market price were below equilibrium, say, at 10 pence, consumers would want to buy seventeen ice creams, but only five would be offered for sale. The resulting excess of demand over supply would tend to force the price up towards equilibrium, as consumers competed with each other for the limited supply. Conversely, at a price in the market above the equilibrium, there would be the opposite situation, an excess of supply over demand. At 35 pence for an ice cream for instance, market demand is only two, whereas twenty would be offered for sale. Market forces on the supply side would now tend to push price downwards, as sellers competed with each other to dispose of their stocks. The market is in equilibrium only where the supply and demand curves intersect, at a price of 20 pence, and with eleven ice creams being bought and sold. Only then is there neither excess demand nor excess supply. The market is cleared and there are no market forces acting on the price to change it.

A word must be added about the nature of market equilibrium, which is sometimes thought to carry with it overtones of desirability. We must emphasise that its meaning is quite technical. The statement that a market is in equilibrium means no more than what it says – that is, that price is such that the quantity suppliers want to sell is equal to the quantity consumers want to buy. There is nothing necessarily good about it.

It is true that we argued earlier in this book that a market system using the price mechanism might achieve an allocation of resources which could be judged as efficient from the viewpoint of consumers. But this statement is highly conditional. It carries the conclusion that such an allocation will in fact be ideal only if certain conditions relating to the market and the economy obtain. These preconditions were listed towards the end of the last chapter, where it was made clear that the market would fail if one or more was not present. We shall return to deal more fully with them later.

APPLICATIONS OF SUPPLY AND DEMAND ANALYSIS

The framework for the analysis of market price just described has an almost unlimited number of uses in economics. A few illustrations may be given.

A CHANGE IN TASTES

Suppose that a market is in equilibrium and there is a change of tastes. Say, for instance, that people start to like ice cream less than they did before.

Readers should be on their guard here against one of the most common mistakes made by students commencing the study of economics, when they confuse *movements along* with *shifts of* a supply or demand curve. Remember always that a demand curve, or a supply curve, is drawn on *ceteris paribus* assumptions to show the relationship between price and quantity demanded or supplied. If there is a change in one of these assumptions, this means that there is a change in the *conditions* of demand or supply, and the entire curve shifts as the relationship between price and quantity alters at every price. In our example here, the change in tastes is just such a change in the conditions of demand, and its effect is to shift the whole demand curve downwards to the left. Since there is, however, no change in the conditions of supply, the lower quantity supplied in the new equilibrium situation results only from the fall in price. The supply curve itself does *not* shift.

We can represent the change in the conditions of demand, as in Figure 4.6 (i), as a downward shift of the demand curve for ice creams from DD to $D'D'$. The effect is that the market tends towards a new equilibrium (E') at the intersection of SS and $D'D'$, where both price and quantity have been reduced, from OP to OP' and from OQ to OQ' respectively.

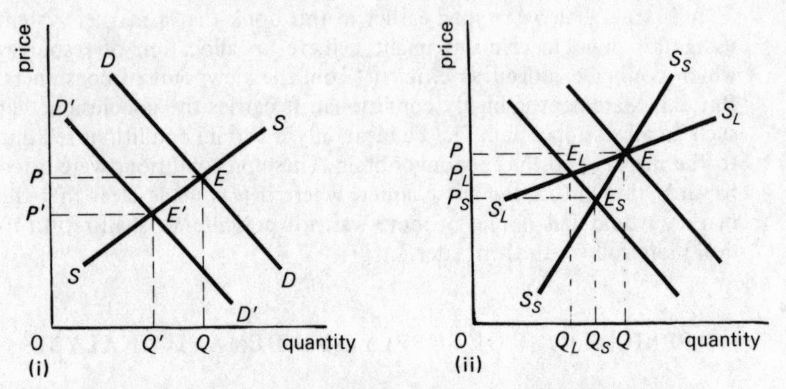

Figure 4.6 *Fall in demand in the short run and long run.*

Short-run and long-run effects

We can take the analysis one stage further if we remember that supply tends to be more responsive to changes in price the longer the period of time we allow for adjustment. In Figure 4.6 (ii) there are two supply curves going through the original equilibrium point (E). $S_S S_S$ is the short period supply curve. $S_L S_L$ is the curve for the longer period. The difference between them is simply that the long-run supply curve shows a higher degree of responsiveness of quantity to a change from the equilibrium price, that is, demand is at that price more elastic, than the short-run curve. It may be seen too that in the long run a fall in demand tends to have a less depressive effect on price, but a larger effect on sales, than in the short run. Initially, the quantity supplied falls only from OQ to OQ_S, causing price to fall from OP to OP_S. But as supply falls further in the long run to OQ_L, market price partly recovers to OP_L.

The influence of time on the demand side can be similarly illustrated. The reader might try to draw for himself a pair of diagrams showing how a decrease in supply, following a rise in costs, can raise price more in the short run than in the long run.

From the analysis in this section, we can derive a general conclusion. The more elastic supply and/or demand, the more a change in either of them is likely to lead to changes in quantities bought and sold, and the less to changes in price. Consider, for example, the two goods in Figure 4.7. In part (i) of the diagram, both the demand for and the supply of pencil sharpeners are assumed to be very responsive to changes from the equilibrium price. The rise in demand depicted has a relatively smaller effect on price than on the quantity demanded and supplied.

In Figure 4.7 (ii), in contrast, the supply of and demand for cocoa are both assumed to be relatively unresponsive to price changes. In this case, the rise in demand is seen to be reflected in a larger change in market price and a smaller change in quantity.

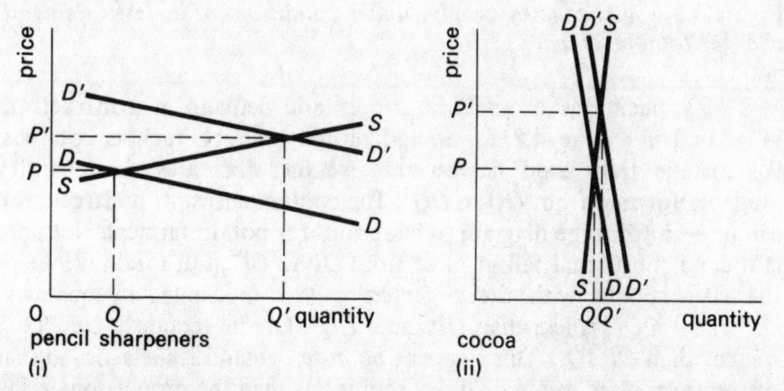

Figure 4.7 *Rise in demand. Elastic and inelastic supply and demand.*

AGRICULTURAL MARKETS

It is no accident that the commodity taken to illustrate the last paragraph and Figure 4.7 (ii) is an agricultural product, cocoa. Both supply and demand tend to be inelastic with respect to price for many agricultural products. Supply is typically inelastic, particularly in the short run. Once a crop is planted, the size of the harvest is likely to be mainly determined by such factors as the weather and the incidence of disease. Even in the longer run the supply of some agricultural products may still be relatively fixed, for example, in the case of orchard crops, where years can elapse between planting and fruit gathering. Price inelasticity tends to be low on the demand side as well. This is true not only for foodstuffs, but also for raw materials, like rubber and cotton. Quantities demanded typically rise and fall more with changes in consumers' incomes than with changes in price.

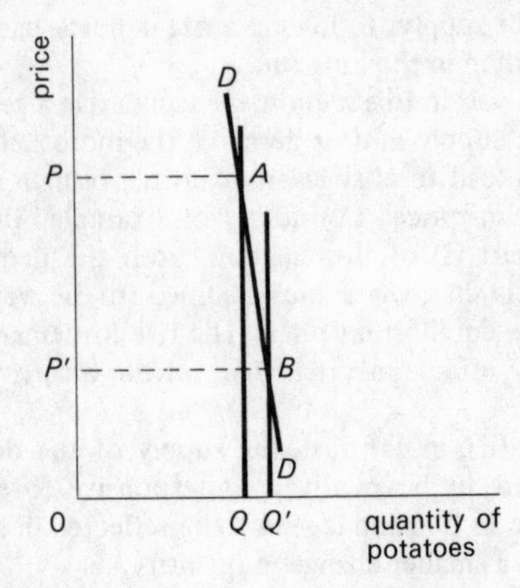

Figure 4.8 *A change in supply, under conditions of inelastic demand, changes total revenue.*

The implications of inelastic supply and demand in a market are illustrated in Figure 4.8 for an agricultural product, such as potatoes. We assume that good harvest-time weather increases the quantity available for sale from *OQ* to *OQ'*. The consequences of the larger crop can be seen from the diagram to be serious for potato farmers. Not only is there a substantial fall in price from *OP* to *OP'*, but total revenue of the farmers falls with the larger crop. Price multiplied by quantity, *OP'* times *OQ'*, is less than *OP* times *OQ*. (Or the rectangle *OP'BQ'* is smaller than *OPAQ*.) This happens *because* demand is inelastic, so that the proportionate rise in quantity sold is less than the proportionate fall in price.

The kind of situation illustrated in the diagram typifies market behaviour for many agricultural products. It is not surprising that, in addition to agriculture being subject to relatively large price fluctuations as crop size varies, farmers' incomes tend also to rise and fall from year to year. Farmers are inclined to be relatively well off when harvests are small, and badly off when they are large. For this reason it is common to find that governments in most countries tend to intervene in agricultural markets with various kinds of schemes to lessen the impact on farmers of short-run market forces, and to stabilise to some extent farm incomes and prices.

TAXATION

A last example of the application of supply and demand analysis is the case of a specific tax on a commodity. Suppose the government decides

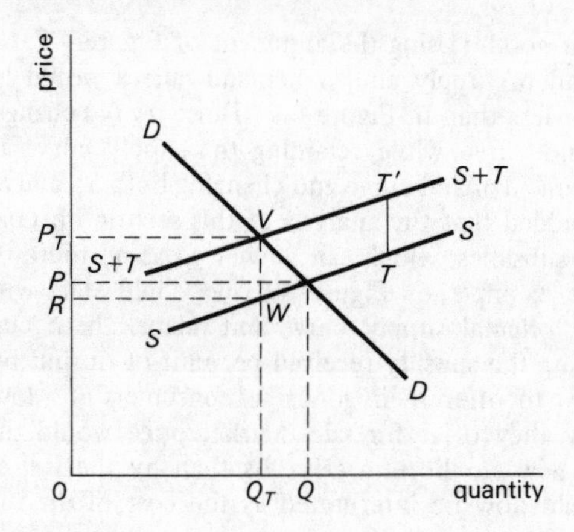

Figure 4.9 *A specific tax; effects on price, quantity and government revenue.*

to impose a tax of a penny on a box of matches. What are the consequences for (*a*) market price and (*b*) sales? And (*c*) how much revenue will the government obtain?

The answers to these questions are suggested by looking at Figure 4.9. *SS* and *DD* are the original supply and demand curves. Market equilibrium is *OQ* sales at price *OP*. A tax equal to *TT′* (representing 1p per box of matches) is now imposed. Assume that sellers are given the responsibility of paying this tax to the government. They will no longer be willing to supply the same quantities at the same range of prices as they did before. We can imagine them adding the tax to each price at which they would be willing to supply a given quantity. We can depict this by drawing a new supply curve ($S + T$) parallel to *SS*, such that the vertical distance between them is equal to the tax itself (*TT′*).

Note that we *cannot* assume that market price also rises by the full amount of the tax. In our diagram it certainly does not do so. When the new equilibrium is reached, market price will be OP_T and sales OQ_T. Consumers' total expenditure is $OP_T VQ_T$, which is what suppliers receive. Out of this total, sellers must pay VW ($= TT'$) per unit to the government, so that total tax revenue to the state amounts to $P_T VWR$. Market price, however, has risen only by PP_T, which is less than the full amount of the tax ($P_T R$). We could explain this phenomenon by suggesting that as market price rose when the tax was imposed, demand started to fall off, and in order to limit the extent of the fall in sales, suppliers effectively absorbed part of the tax themselves.

We cannot investigate the full implications of the analysis in this volume, but enough has been said to show that the effect of a tax on market price may be related to the elasticity of demand and supply of a particular good. (Using the argument of Figure 4.7, can you work out what kind of supply and/or demand curves would lead to price rising more or less than in Figure 4.9? Hint: try (1) changing the slope of the demand curve while retaining the supply curve and then (2) keeping the same demand curve and changing both SS and $S+T$.)

It can be added that the analysis of this section on taxes is equally applicable to subsidies, which can be viewed as no more than negative taxes. In the example of Figure 4.9, we could start with the curve $S+T$ as the original supply curve and relabel the S curve as $S-S$ with TT' being the subsidy received per unit of output by producers, enabling them to offer their goods to consumers at a lower price for each quantity they offer for sale. Market price would then fall from OP_T to the new equilibrium OP (less than by the full subsidy) and $P_T VWR$ would now be interpreted as the cost of the subsidy to the government.

ECONOMIC WELFARE

We have now dealt with a number of situations where the action of the price mechanism leads to an equilibrium situation where supply and demand are equal and the market is exactly cleared. When we first encountered the notion of equilibrium we were at some pains to point out that its meaning was technical and did not carry with it the implication that it was necessarily desirable.

We must return to consider this matter further. Our choice of words was careful and deliberate. Although there is nothing *necessarily* desirable about resource allocation brought about by the market, there is a case to be made that *in certain circumstances* such an allocation might be regarded as in a sense ideal or, to use economists' jargon, 'optimal'.

Some of the advantages of a market system were briefly described in Chapter 3. We are, however, now in a position to understand better the argument why the price mechanism can in certain conditions be regarded as an efficient means of allocating resources. Let us reconsider the case for *laissez-faire*, as we have earlier described it, that economic welfare is maximised in a market system.

THE CASE FOR LAISSEZ-FAIRE

Laissez-faire implies no interference with the market because the price mechanism will allocate resources optimally if left alone. The case for such a policy is not particularly easy to understand and it is most important to follow carefully each step in the argument. It can be put like this. In equilibrium, market price measures two things – the marginal cost of producing a good *and* the marginal utility (or satisfaction) obtained by consuming it. Price measures marginal cost because sellers offer an extra good for sale only if it yields a revenue which covers the cost of producing it. Price measures marginal utility because (if we assume that consumers try to maximise their satisfaction in disposing of their incomes) buyers purchase an extra good only if it yields enough utility to make the expenditure on it worthwhile. Producers go on offering more of a good for sale if price is greater than marginal cost; consumers continue buying more of a good if price is less than marginal utility. Hence, when price is at an equilibrium level, and is the same for all producers and consumers, we can draw the inference that marginal utility is equal to marginal cost.

We may usefully recall, now, our discussion of the true nature of costs in economics. The opportunity cost of producing a good is the sacrifice made in not producing another good. So the equality of marginal cost and marginal utility at equilibrium means that the benefit derived by consumers from purchasing an extra unit of a good is equal to its cost as measured by the opportunity foregone of having more of another good in its place.

If marginal cost is not equal to marginal utility, satisfaction can clearly be increased by switching resources between products. If there is a commodity where marginal utility is greater than marginal cost, it is worth producing more of it because the sacrifice of other goods given up is less than the marginal increase in satisfaction from having more of it. The opposite is true if marginal utility is less than marginal cost. Hence, if marginal cost is brought into equality with marginal utility through the operation of market price, satisfaction of the community cannot be increased by producing more or less of the good. Moreover, if marginal cost is equal to marginal utility in the market for every single good and service, it follows that the distribution of resources is, in a sense, optimal.

It must be emphasised that the case for *laissez-faire* is an abstract one. Its acceptability, in whole or in part, depends on the extent to which it is relevant to the world in which we live. In the last chapter (pages 52–3) we listed six conditions which, if applicable, would mean that a market system would be likely to allocate resources efficiently. They will all be discussed at greater length when we deal with economic policy in Chapter 10. However, we are now in a position to explain why two of them are important for the case for *laissez-faire*.

INCOME DISTRIBUTION AND MARKET ALLOCATIONS

One reason for questioning whether the allocation of resources that results from the free interplay of the forces of supply and demand is efficient arises from issues of justice and equity in the distribution of income in a country. This is, at least partly, a political matter. However, our immediate task is the economic one of showing the implications of income distribution for resource allocation. Let us suppose that we ignore the social issues of equity and accept the distribution of income as given.

The price mechanism will then work in the manner described in the last section to allocate resources so that marginal utility is equal to marginal cost in each and every market throughout the economy. Let us further assume that the initial distribution of income was very unequal. We might then conclude that the market will succeed in securing the production of a fair amount of champagne, yachts, Rolls-Royce cars and luxury hotels.

Suppose we now imagine that it is considered socially desirable to redistribute income more equally by taking from the rich and giving to the poor. It is clear that there will be a shift in demand away from goods of the kinds mentioned above bought by high-income groups. Market forces of supply and demand will still operate to shift resources until marginal cost is equal everywhere to marginal utility. But the collection of goods and services now produced is likely to be quite different. What can we say now? Both allocations result from the free working of the price mechanism, so it is difficult to say that one or other is the 'best'. We can only choose between them if we have some reason for preferring the more or the less equal income distribution, within the framework of which the market system did its work.

The reasoning of the previous paragraph requires us to reassess the implications for economic welfare of equilibrium price and output achieved in a market system. If we are prepared to accept the distribution of income as being in a sense desirable, then we can have no doubts, on this count, about accepting the allocation of resources brought about by the free working of the price mechanism as being optimal. But if we recognise that we, *as economists*, have no special authority to make this kind of value judgement, we must also be careful to avoid concluding also that the market works well. We can only make the much more limited conclusion about the nature of equilibrium – namely, that it is the state of affairs towards which economic forces of supply and demand will tend in the market place. The equilibrium quantity of ice creams, or of anything else, is that quantity which, if produced, leaves no unsatisfied buyers or sellers. But we must remember that supply and demand are really no more than 'catch-alls', behind which lie all the social forces which may influence them. The question of what is the best distribution of income is not at all easy to answer. Economic as well as social considerations are involved and, in so far as inequality might provide incentives for maximising output, they must be taken into account as well as ideas of social justice. We shall return to discuss the implications of these matters for economic policy in Chapter 10.

COMPETITION AND MARKET ALLOCATIONS

A second reason for questioning the efficiency of a market system relates not so much to the social framework as to the nature of the market itself. In order to appreciate the significance of competition for resource allocation in market economies, we shall have to engage in one more piece of analysis.

Most of this chapter has been based on an assumption that markets are competitive. However, there are degrees of competition. Economists classify markets according to whether competition is said to be 'perfect' or 'imperfect'.

(1) Perfect competition

At one extreme there is a highly competitive state of affairs, wherein a large number of small producers each sells a commodity which is no different from that of any other producer and there is complete freedom of entry for firms into the industry. In such circumstances no single seller can *by himself* influence price in the market by withholding supplies; he is too small. He is a price-taker and the market is termed *perfectly competitive.* And, although it may be rare enough in the real world, it provides a useful reference base against which other market situations may be compared.

(2) Imperfect competition

At the other extreme from perfect competition is the case of the single seller or monopolist dominating a market. Monopoly is one of a number of market forms classed under the heading of imperfect competition (though the terms perfect and imperfect relate only to the intensity of competition, not to their desirability or undesirability). Other forms include oligopoly (from the Greek meaning few sellers).

Sources of monopoly power. Firms in imperfect competition are generally in stronger positions than those where competitive forces are intense. Their strength is derived in divers ways. Such firms may control the supply of a raw material. They may hold a patent giving them the sole legal right to some manufacturing process. Their strength may stem from being the only shop selling a certain range of goods in a particular locality. They may market a product which is differentiated from others and for which consumers feel a special loyalty. They may enjoy the benefits of large-scale production economies, so that their costs are too low for other firms to compete with them.

Firms enjoying a degree of monopoly power are not, of course, free to ignore the market entirely. Their actions are constrained to a varying extent by consumer demand and by actions of other firms. The point is only that the competitive forces to which they are subject tend to be weaker. However, firms which do possess some control over the market have one thing in common, wheresoever they draw their strength. They enjoy the opportunity to earn higher profits than would otherwise be the case.

Under conditions of perfect competition, as we have seen, the presence of profit-maximising businesses leads to an inflow of firms into industries making above-average profits. But in imperfectly competitive situations, the sources of market power, whereby firms derive their strength, act as barriers to the entry of other firms. As long as the barriers persist, for example until patents run out, other firms acquire know-how, and so on, those businesses already in the industry are protected from the full blast of competition.

Single-firm monopoly behaviour. The analysis of a firm's behaviour under conditions of imperfect competition are complex and cannot be described fully here. However, one important characteristic must be discussed.

Compare the position of a single-firm monopolist with that of a firm in perfect competition. Assume, too, that both are trying to maximise their profits. The perfectly competitive firm is too small to exert any perceptible influence on the market by changing the quantities he offers for sale. He can sell as much or as little as he likes without affecting market price. In contrast, the monopolist is a price-maker, by definition; he is so large that when he alters his output market price *is* affected. He can only succeed in selling additional quantities if he does lower price. Moreover, since only one price can normally exist in a market for the same commodity, when the monopolist lowers price to sell another unit, he must lower it on *all* the units that he sells.

The implications of this feature on the output policy of a firm can be understood by reconsidering what is meant by our earlier statement that a seller offers goods for sale up to the point where the price he gets for them covers his marginal costs. This is true for the firm under perfect competition, because the price he receives is only another way of saying the increase in revenue he obtains from selling an additional unit. Economists call the change in receipts following an increase in the quantity sold *marginal revenue*. It is defined as the total revenue from the sale of n units, minus the total revenue from the sale of $(n-1)$ units.

For a small firm in perfect competition, marginal revenue is equal to price. But for a monopolist, the sale of an extra unit of a good is only

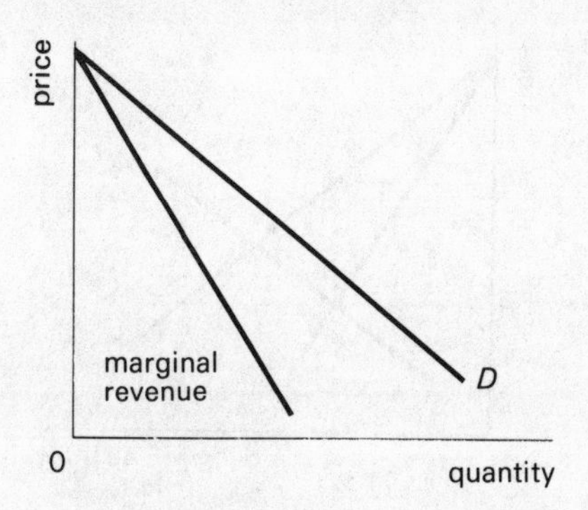

Figure 4.10 *Marginal revenue under imperfect competition.*

attainable by reducing price, not only for the additional unit, but for all the goods sold. In other words, marginal revenue is always less than price, and we can draw a marginal revenue curve which lies below the demand curve, as in Figure 4.10.

An example may help to make the matter clear. Suppose a large firm can sell 60 units at a price of £1.00 each, but in order to sell 61 units the price must be lowered to 99 pence. The increase in total revenue which the monopolist receives from the 61st sale is not 99 pence but 39 pence. He adds 99 pence by selling one more unit at 99 pence but loses 1 penny on each of the 60 previous sales. In other words, his marginal revenue of 39 pence is the total revenue from 61 units (61 × 99 pence) *minus* the total revenue from 60 units (60 × 100 pence).

Whereas we said earlier that a firm produces up to the point where marginal cost is equal to price, we now know this really meant: up to the point where the extra cost was just covered by the extra receipts – i.e. where marginal cost equals marginal revenue. Although price and marginal revenue are the same for a firm in perfect competition, the monopolist, as we have seen, finds that marginal revenue is less than price. Hence, he maximises profits by producing *less* than the competitive output. In Figure 4.11 the equilibrium position is where the monopolist produces an output of *OA* that is, where the marginal cost curve cuts the marginal revenue curve. Competitive output, where marginal cost equals marginal utility, would be *OB*.

Monopoly and market efficiency. After this brief excursion into the analysis of monopoly equilibrium, we must return to the question with which we started. How does the existence of imperfect competition affect the conclusion that the price mechanism allocates resources in an optimal manner? The particular feature of the monopolist's behaviour in Figure 4.11 that is relevant is that the profit-maximising output *OA*

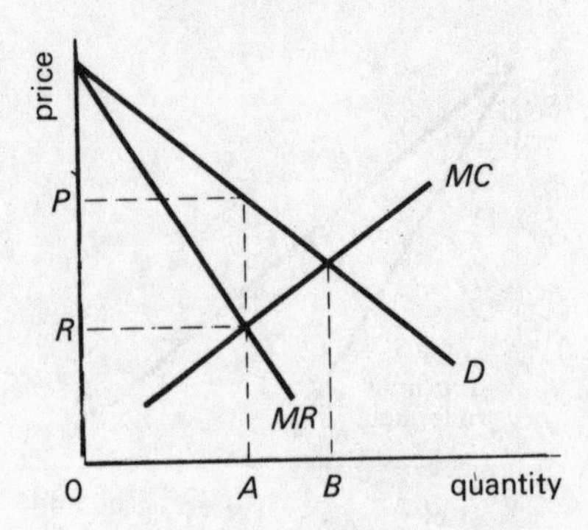

Figure 4.11 *Monopoly*

sells in the market at the price *OP*, which is greater than the marginal cost *OR*. If we recall that price is a measure of marginal utility of a good to consumers, we must draw the implication that monopoly equilibrium tends to result in marginal utility being greater than marginal cost, and that an increase in output would add more to consumer satisfaction than to costs. Since costs in economics are opportunity costs, this means that, *prima facie*, resources used in the output of a good produced in such circumstances involve, at the margin, a sacrifice of other goods of less value than the satisfaction that they provide to consumers.

We may conclude that the presence of monopolistic elements in a market tends to lead to less production than would occur under competition; and that (by the standards which we applied for judging the efficiency of the price mechanism for allocating resources) output is, *ceteris paribus*, less than optimal. Since we know that the world is characterised by markets in which competition is to varying degrees less than perfect, we have good reason to view with caution the argument for non-interference in the working of the market system. We must be equally careful, however, not to jump to the conclusion that the price mechanism should necessarily be jettisoned, though it clearly cannot be relied on to work in a completely free fashion to secure an optimal allocation of resources.

Even the case against monopoly outlined above, which rests on underproduction, is not complete. For one thing, there are reasons for believing that the economies of large-scale production, mentioned earlier as sources of monopoly power, really do mean that costs may be lower for single firms than for several. In terms of Figure 4.11, this means that the curve labelled *MC* would be downward sloping. Breaking up such 'natural monopolies', as they are called, in order to promote competition would only involve higher costs of production on average.

So it becomes a matter of judgement to decide whether or not, on balance, the presence of monopoly involves less than optimal output.

To complicate matters further, it should be added that monopolies may be inefficient in another sense. Their costs of production may be higher than they need be. They are not under the same pressure to minimise costs as if they were in more competitive situations. Such higher production costs are said to be the result of 'X-inefficiency'.

We may conclude that the question of judging the efficiency of market systems is a complex one. We shall reconsider it in Chapter 10 when we deal with economic policy. Meanwhile we turn to a consideration of the way in which supply and demand work in markets for factors of production.

NOTES: CHAPTER 4

1 The most common formula for the calculation of elasticity of demand (known by the symbol η_d) is:

$$\eta_d = \frac{\text{change in quantity}}{\text{quantity}} \div \frac{\text{change in price}}{\text{price}}.$$

So if a fall in price from £100 to £99 brings about a rise in quantity demanded from 200 to 204:

$$\eta_d = \frac{4}{200} \times \frac{100}{1} = 2.$$

Readers are advised to consult more advanced texts about alternative ways of interpreting the formula.

2 Costs here are defined to include an element of profit, which economists call 'normal profit', defined as the minimum necessary to persuade a firm to produce in its existing market. Normal profits are related to the opportunity cost of capital – the amount that could be earned by switching resources to an alternative industry.

3 There are even difficulties in drawing a supply curve at all.

Chapter 5

The Prices of Factors of Production

The purpose of this chapter is to show how economics can help answer such questions as why people have different incomes. Variations are really quite considerable. In Britain in 1977, average income was more than £2,500. However, the top fifth of the population received about double this sum and people in the top 1 per cent had on average £17,000 – nearly seven times as much.[1] How can we account for differences like this?

THE DISTRIBUTION OF PERSONAL INCOMES

The answer to this question is a complex one. In the first place there are several sources from which we derive our incomes as individuals. We may get wages or salaries as employees; we may get some income in the form of interest on capital, such as in a building society account; some of us may earn rent from the ownership of land or houses; others may derive profit from the ownership of a business. Finally, some incomes are received as transfer payments, for example, retirement pensions, unemployment and other social security benefits. It was pointed out in Chapter 2 (page 16), when we were discussing the rewards received by the different factors of production, that most individuals receive some part of their income in more than one form.

The first part of an answer to the question why some people have higher incomes than others, therefore, is simply that some have more sources of income and own, for instance, a lot more capital than others.

The first explanation for differences in income is important but it is not the only one. This is clear if we recognise that there is a spread of income also for each factor of production. Take labour, for example. In 1978, on average, men in mining earned about 10 per cent more than the average of all manual workers, while those in textiles earned roughly 10 per cent less. These figures are, of course, only averages, and conceal wide differences within industries. Skilled workers earn more than unskilled, and men more than women. There are other differences too, due, for example, to geographical location, for example, wages tend to be higher in London and the South-East than, say, in Scotland.

SUPPLY AND DEMAND FOR FACTORS OF PRODUCTION

Wages are no more than the price of labour. Having seen how the forces of supply and demand determine the price of goods and services, the reader will hardly be surprised to learn that we propose now to examine how these forces operate in the markets for factors of production. The content of this chapter is in fact not much more than an extension of the last. Its main purpose is to apply the general principles of price formation to factor markets though, because we shall need to use analysis more fully explained earlier, we shall quite frequently refer the reader back to sections of Chapter 4. There are, moreover, certain features which are to some extent peculiar to the way in which supply and demand apply to the prices of factors of production. We shall illustrate our discussion of price determination in factor markets by looking closely at one factor – labour.

THE LABOUR MARKET

Our approach to the question of wage determination follows that used in the case of goods and services. We shall derive, in turn, demand and supply curves, starting at the level of the individual and the firm, and proceed to analyse price determination in the market.

One complication needs to be faced at the outset. Men and women are individuals and differ from each other in many ways, especially in ability, skill and motivation. These individual differences are most relevant to questions about why incomes vary and we shall have to deal with them. However, we need to establish a relatively simple framework of analysis to start with and we shall ignore them in the early sections of the chapter. We assume, then, for the purposes of simplification that any one unit of labour can be substituted for any other or, to use the technical jargon of economists, that labour is a homogeneous factor of production.

THE DEMAND FOR LABOUR

The most important difference between the nature of the demand for a factor of production, such as labour, and that of the demand for a good or service is that labour is not wanted directly for itself, but for what it is capable of producing. For this reason, we usually speak of the demand for labour's services as being *derived* from the demand for the good or service which it helps to produce. Labour, of course, is generally combined with other factors of production – capital, land and raw materials.

The way in which economists normally approach the demand for labour by a business is by focusing attention on the productivity of the labour employed. In the short run, a firm may have a *fixed* amount of capital equipment which may be used together with a *variable* number of workers. If men are added one at a time to its labour force, the firm can observe the effect on total output. The difference in total production which results from employing an additional man is known as the marginal product of labour. When the marginal product is valued at the price at which it sells in the goods market, we obtain a measure of the marginal product in terms of money. It is this marginal product which lies behind the demand for labour as a factor of production.

Consider the following example. Imagine that a firm, working with its fixed land and capital, obtains total outputs of turnips from men as shown in the first column of Table 5.1. The figures are, as usual, hypothetical. Table 5.1 shows that one man working on 1 hectare of

Table 5.1 *Turnip output per week on 1 hectare of land*

Men employed	*Total production (tonnes)*	*Marginal product (tonnes)*
1	2	2
2	5	3
3	9	4
4	12	3
5	14	2
6	15	1
7	15½	½

land produces 2 tonnes of turnips. When a second man is added, total output rises by 3 tonnes to 5. Marginal product is, therefore, the difference between output with one and two men – that is $5 - 2 = 3$ tonnes, in physical terms. To find the marginal product in money terms, we need to know its market value. If we assume that turnips sell for, say, £80 per tonne, marginal product in the last column of the table becomes £160, £240, £320, £240, £160, £80 and £40 worth of output.

Let us plot the figures in the final column on a graph as in Figure 5.1. We get the curve labelled 'marginal product'. The important feature of this curve is that after a certain point it starts to fall. This tendency for marginal product to decline whenever units of a variable factor, such as labour, are added to work with a fixed factor, such as land, arises

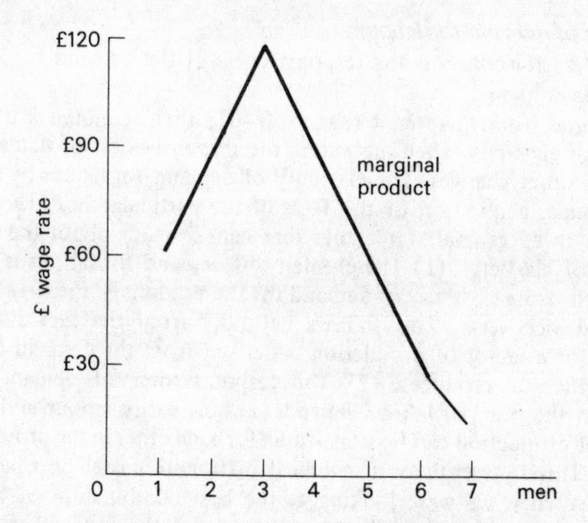

Figure 5.1 *Diminishing returns to a variable factor of production.*

because of the different proportions in which factors are combined. It is given the status of a 'law' in economics – 'the law of diminishing returns'. The 'law', it must be stressed, obtains only in the sense that it is thought to be of widespread application. It follows logically from the principle of the division of labour, explained earlier (see Chapter 2, page 21) and it certainly describes the state of affairs existing in much of industry and is regarded as being a sufficiently typical state of affairs on which to base analysis.

It must next be explained why a firm's curve of marginal product turns out to be the same thing as its demand curve for labour in the short run. The reason is simple enough. Firms are assumed to be in business to make a profit. Provided the employment of an extra man adds more to revenue than to costs, it pays to employ him. Suppose the wage rate is £80 per week. It is obviously profitable to employ one man, since he adds £160 to total revenue of the firm. A second man adds £240, a third £360, and so on. It is worth engaging six men, in fact, but a seventh man costs the firm £80, but only adds £40 worth of turnips to total revenue. So we can read the curve of marginal product in Figure 5.1 as being, in effect, the demand curve for labour of the firm.

The total *market* demand curve for labour is obtained by adding together the demand curves of individual firms in a similar way to that used in the goods market to derive the total demand curve for a commodity. (See Figure 4.1, page 57.) There are two aspects of the market demand curve which must, however, be dealt with before we turn to look at supply.

Elasticity of demand for labour

The first matter concerns the responsiveness of the demand for labour to changes in its price.

We know from Chapter 4 (pages 60–61) that economists use the concept of elasticity when measuring the responsiveness of demand to price and other changes. The elasticity of demand for labour by a firm is, of course, a question of the facts of the particular case. However, there are three general statements that can be made about the determinants of elasticity. (1) The elasticity of demand for labour is likely to be high if the elasticity of demand for the product of the firm is also high, and vice versa. This follows naturally from the fact that the demand for a factor of production is derived from the demand for the goods which it produces. (2) The responsiveness of demand to a change in the price of labour depends on how easily labour and other factors of production can be substituted for each other in the production process. This is essentially a technical matter, discussed in Chapter 2 (page 20) when we were looking at the best combination of factors for a business to employ. We noted then that the best combination would depend on the prices of the factors. So all we are saying now is that a fall in the price of one factor, labour, will increase the demand for it by the firm, the more so the easier it is to substitute labour for other factors. (3) Finally, the effect of a change in the price of labour will tend to be greater or smaller depending on whether labour costs are a large or a small proportion of the firm's total costs of production. This is intuitively fairly obvious. One would expect a producer to react more sharply to a change in the price of a factor which bulks large rather than small in its total costs.

The short run and the long run

The second feature of the demand for a factor of production that needs attention relates to the period of time under consideration. This matter is immediately applicable to the content of the previous paragraph on elasticity. In the first place, it may be observed that it is as generally true for labour as it was for goods and services that responsiveness to price changes tends to be greater in the long run than in the short run, because substitutability between labour and other factors of production becomes easier as time passes. In the long run, factors which were previously fixed become variable; for example, machinery wears out and is ready to be replaced.

Take a very simple example. A building firm may use a primitive technique for mixing cement and sand. Because labour is, let us suppose, cheap, the mixing is done with shovels and buckets of water. If the price of labour rises, there will be an incentive to economise on labour, but it is relatively expensive to change techniques immediately, especially if the firm has just bought a lot of new shovels and buckets. However, if the higher price of labour persists long enough, the idea of setting up a more capital-intensive technique, by changing the buckets and shovels for a concrete mixer, becomes a real possibility.

The example given is, of course, an oversimplified one. But that should not be taken to imply that the matter under discussion is either simple or unimportant. As a matter of fact, the way in which production is organised in countries like Britain is heavily influenced by changes in the relative costs of different factors of production. In so far as technological advance and other forces have brought about a long-run rise in the cost of labour relative to capital, the search for mechanisation can be substantially attributed to it. That is why we have seen machines replacing craftsmen in an enormous range of industrial and other processes, for example.

A final point to be made about the demand for labour in the long compared with the short run concerns the shape of the demand curve. It was emphasised earlier that the law of diminishing returns only applied when units of a variable factor were used in conjunction with a fixed factor. In the long run all factors become variable and the law is not relevant. This means that changing output no longer necessarily involves changing the proportions in which factors of production are employed together. It does not, of course, affect the main conclusion that the demand for a factor of production is derived from its productivity in terms of the value of the goods it produces. It simply affects the shape of the demand curve.

Varying the quantity of inputs while keeping the proportions between them fixed is known as changing the scale of production.

THE SUPPLY OF LABOUR

Let us turn now to the supply side of the market and approach it in the familiar way of building up a market supply curve of labour offering its services at a range of wage rates.

Individual labour supply

Consider first the individual faced with the decision of how many hours to work. Our first thought might be that he will want to work longer hours the higher the hourly wage rate in the market. In other words his supply curve would slope upwards, like the supply curves for goods in Chapter 4, Figure 4.3 (page 63). This may in fact very well be the case. If we delve a little more deeply, however, it will be apparent that the supply curve need not necessarily have an upward slope at all.

Look at the decision from the worker's point of view. It was put above as whether to work or not to work. That was a negative approach.

An alternative would be to regard his choice as being whether to work or to take leisure. If leisure is enjoyable, working means sacrificing leisure and the amount of it a man is prepared to give up depends on what he can earn by working.

Let us start again and ask how a worker will react to a rise in the price of labour. We can now see that the question would be exactly the same if it were asked about the effect of a rise in the price of leisure, because the cost of leisure to the worker, in terms of income given up, is now greater. The answer that must be given to the question might not at first look any different. Work brings a higher reward, so the individual will tend to substitute work for leisure and work more hours.

But we cannot leave the matter there. It will be recalled from Chapter 4 (pages 59–60) that a change in price has two effects which can, in principle, be separated. One is a substitution effect. The other is an income effect. The substitution effect of a rise in the wage rate is what we have considered in the previous paragraph. It leads people to work for longer hours and implies, therefore, an increase in the supply of labour. In other words, it suggests that the supply curve is upward sloping.

Turn now, however, to consider the income effect. It will be recalled that this is the effect on real income of a price change on the assumption that all other prices remain the same. What does that mean to a worker? If the price of labour rises, it means simply that he receives a higher real income, or purchasing power over goods and services, from working any given number of hours than before. He gets a higher wage per hour. What will be the effect of such a rise in real income, brought about by a rise in the wage rate? There is no certain answer to the question. The probability, however, is that he will be inclined to prefer more leisure, and therefore work less, because he has more to spend on things that he can enjoy in his leisure-time.

A rise in the price of labour must, of course, take account of both the income and the substitution effects of the price change. What can we say about the net effect in general? Unfortunately, from first principles, very little. We have seen that the two effects tend to work in opposite directions. The substitution effect of a rise in wage rates tends to lead to an increase in labour supply; the income effect, to a fall.

It has, therefore, to be concluded that the net effect of a change in the price of labour could go in either direction. The theory tells us that everything depends on the relative sizes of the income and substitution effects. In practice, the evidence is almost equally indecisive. Studies show that in some cases labour supply appears to rise with a rise in wage rates, while in other cases the reverse is true and it falls. The only helpful statement that might be ventured is that the substitution effect is liable to be of relatively greater importance at low levels of income and the income effect at higher levels. This would mean that rises in the wage rate tend to increase the supply of labour up to a point and then to reduce it. The rationale behind such behaviour could be that people work more as wage rates rise until they reach a certain income level and thereafter start to work less. The turning point might be subsistence level income. For until that is reached there would hardly be much point in taking more leisure. But 'subsistence level' is a rather subjective concept and the conclusion seems to be of more general significance. If the statement is reliable then it implies that the supply curve of labour is like that in Figure 5.2. It slopes upward at low wage rates, indicating the predominance of the substitution effect. When the wage rate reaches *OW*, however, the income effect predominates and the curve starts to 'bend backwards', with rises in the price leading to fewer hours' work being supplied.

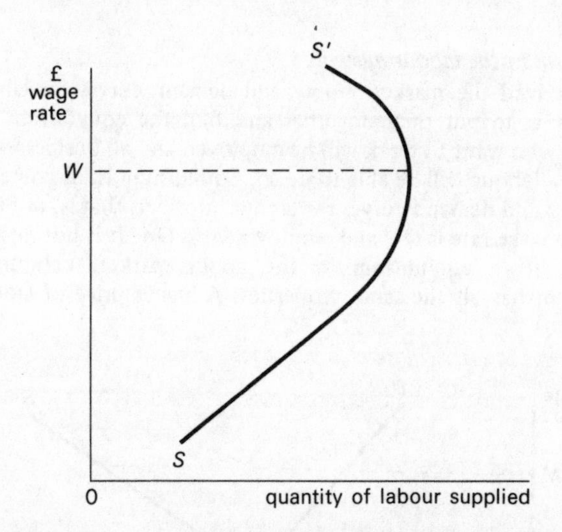

Figure 5.2 *Backward sloping supply curve of labour.*

Market labour supply

The supply curve of labour in the market as a whole is found in the now-familiar way, by adding the supply curves of all individuals in it. Some of these curves may be backward sloping, others upward sloping. But it should not be forgotten that the extent to which individuals are free to alter the number of hours that they work is considerably restricted in many cases.

Moreover, the market supply curve is more likely to have an upward slope than is that of any individual's supply curve. For the market supply curve reflects not only the change in work by each worker, but also the number of persons entering the labour market. Even if one worker supplies less labour as the wage rate rises, others may enter the market seeking work. For example, the total labour supply tends to rise as married women are attracted into the labour force by a higher price of labour. The supply of labour to a particular industry or occupation will also tend to increase as relative wage rates rise and individuals move from lower- to higher-paid occupations.

Finally, it must be said that there is likely to be a difference in the shape of the supply curve in the long run and in the short. Apart from the usual features of higher responsiveness to be expected to wage rate changes the longer the time period under consideration, we also have to recognise that long-term considerations such as the size and age distribution of the population must be taken into account as well as institutional factors, such as the legal minimum or conventional school-leaving age.

Equilibrium in the labour market

Having derived the market supply and demand curves for labour, the final step is to put them together and find the equilibrium price at which all who want to work will be employed and all businesses seeking to employ labour will be able to do so. Equilibrium is, of course, where the supply and demand curves for labour intersect, that is, in Figure 5.3 where the wage rate is OW and employment is OA. It is not different, in principle, from equilibrium in the goods market. Labour market equilibrium has all the same properties. A higher price of labour, say,

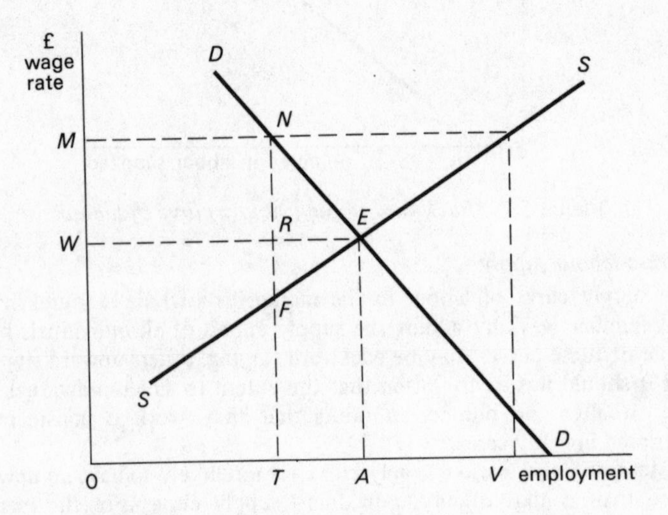

Figure 5.3 *Equilibrium in the labour market.*

OM, will result in an excess of supply over demand (*TV*) and a lower price will have the reverse effect. Market forces in either situation will tend towards equilibrium. Moreover, both supply and demand curves are drawn under the usual *ceteris paribus* assumption, so that equilibrium does not carry with it the implication that it is necessarily desirable.

The framework of analysis of Figure 5.3 can be used, as usual, to examine an effect of a change in demand resulting from a change, say, in the productivity of labour, or in supply following, for example, a change in the school-leaving age. (Make sure you know which way the curves shift for each kind of change.)

Minimum wages

One example of the way in which the market operates can be seen by examining the effect of the introduction by the government of a law laying down minimum wage rates. The analysis is fairly straightforward. Suppose the supply and demand curves are *DD* and *SS* as in Figure 5.3. The equilibrium price is *OW*, and at this price employment is *OA*. Suppose now a minimum wage rate is laid down. If it is less than *OW* then it will have no effect, but let us assume it is *OM*. At this wage, the number of persons offering their services is *OV* and the number demanded is only *OT*. Market forces cannot bring the wage rate down, by law. So, the effect of the excess supply over demand in these circumstances is to be seen in the level of employment. Only *OT* workers will actually find jobs and a measure of the effect of the minimum wage policy is that *AT* fewer workers would be employed than under a freely working market system.

We might try and go a stage further and ask how effective the policy has been. In terms of raising wages the answer must be that it has done its job. Wage rates are higher than before (by *MW*). But there has been a cost; namely, *AT* unemployed. We cannot therefore give an unequivocal answer to the question unless we are prepared to judge whether the higher wages of those still working more or less compensate for the sufferings of the new unemployed. The answer surely depends very much on who the *AT* unemployed losers are, and whether their better-off colleagues are able and prepared to compensate them.

We cannot say anything very useful about their preparedness, since it is not really a matter of economics. However, the question of ability is fairly straightforward. Total wage receipts after the introduction of the minimum wage are *OM* times *OT*, or the area *OMNT*. Before legislation the wage bill was *OW* times *OA*, or the area *OWEA*. Since *OWRT* is common to both areas, the answer depends on the relative sizes of *WMNR* and *TREA*. If the former exceeds the latter, the increase in total wages of the *OT* workers still in employment is sufficient to give them enough to compensate their unemployed colleagues. In the reverse situation there is not enough for them to do so. Whether the former or latter obtains is a question of the elasticity of demand for labour. The less elastic the demand curve, the more likely it is that the fall in employment will be proportionately less than the rise in wages so that the wage bill increases after the minimum wage is imposed. In the diagram, the demand curve has an elasticity of demand of approximately unity, so that the total wage bill is the same in the two cases.

Finally, we should return to answer the question of *who* the unemployed workers are. On the assumption, with which we are still working, of homogeneous labour, the answer is not particularly interesting. It is a matter of negotiation and of relative indifference to employers. Perhaps workers with the shortest service, or the youngest, will go first. But if we now drop the assumption and recognise that labour is not a homogeneous factor of production, the answer is quite significant. One would expect that the least productive workers would find employment hardest to obtain at high wage rates. This conclusion arises simply from our knowledge of the fact that the marginal productivity of labour lies behind the demand for its services by businesses.

A qualification is perhaps necessary to prevent anyone reading into this section the view that minimum wage legislation is undesirable. Such is not necessarily the case. Our analysis has only shown that such a policy, taken by itself, may cause unemployment. If accompanying measures can prevent this happening the conclusion may be quite different. We shall consider this matter again in the next section when looking at the activities of trade unions.

IMPERFECT COMPETITION AND THE LABOUR MARKET

The discussion in the chapter so far has been based on an implicit assumption that the forces of supply and demand in the labour market act in a competitive manner. As explained in Chapter 4 (page 75) such a situation obtains when the number of traders is so large that actions by a single one of them are too insignificant quantitatively to have a perceptible influence on market price. However, labour markets are often typified by characteristics previously described as imperfectly competitive and we shall now have to consider them. There are two ways in which imperfect competition can affect the situation.

(1) The goods market

The first, and easiest to deal with, is when the product of the industry sells in an imperfect market, as when the firm is a monopoly producer. This means that the firm's demand curve for labour must be differently interpreted. The curve itself still derives from the demand curve for the product, but it will not be the same as the demand curve with which the firm would be faced if it could sell as much as it pleased at the ruling market price. As explained in Chapter 4 (pages 76–7), a monopolist has to lower price on all his sales in order to sell additional units of a good. The marginal revenue (the additions to total revenue) to the firm is what is relevant. So the value of each unit of output produced by labour is not the price at which it sells but its marginal revenue. The implication of this is simply that the demand curve for labour of a monopolist will tend to slope down more steeply than that of a firm in perfect competition.

(2) The labour market and trade unions

The second way in which the presence of imperfect competition affects the labour market relates not to the goods market in which products are sold, but to the labour market itself. This is a much more complex matter and we can only touch on some of the more important features in this book.

Imperfect labour markets mean that the number of buyers or sellers is small enough to influence the price of labour. This is in practice very common and one of the major reasons for it is the existence of trade unions. Associations of workers in an industry or occupation are able to act in a manner similar to that of monopoly producers of goods, described in Chapter 4 above. A trade union, acting on behalf of its member workers in an industry, brings pressure on the level of wages by exercising control over the supply of labour seeking employment. In so far as trade unions can regulate supply by controlling entry into an occupation or industry, they can do just this. Their action could then be illustrated by Figure 5.3, used previously to describe the effects of the introduction of a minimum wage. Reinterpreting the diagram, a trade union might, by restricting labour supply to *OT*, for example, secure a wage rate of *OM*, though again at the cost of the same unemployment, *AT*.

Trade unions exist in most industries and their activities on behalf of members are not confined to striving for increasing wage rates. They negotiate on many other matters, extending to holidays, pensions, hours and conditions of work, and so on. Unions' strength stems from their ability to control the supply of labour and also from their power to call, or threaten to call, strikes and go-slows.

In collective bargaining with employers, trade unions have, however, another tactical weapon in their armoury. If they can raise the level of productivity of their members, they can to the same extent raise employers' demand for labour. Consider Figure 5.4, which reproduces the situation depicted in Figure 5.3. If the union wished to establish a wage of *OM* without causing unemployment, it can succeed provided it

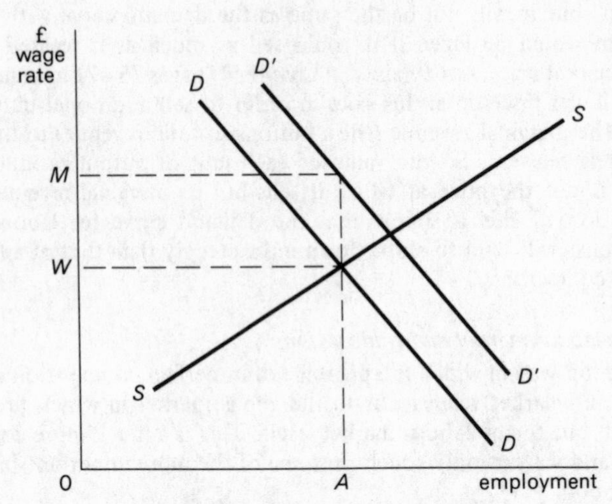

Figure 5.4 *Trade union activities*

achieves an upward shift in the demand curve for labour from *DD* to *D′D′*. It does not matter as far as the analysis is concerned whether the rise in productivity is due to management, to the union, or to a combination of the two. There may be considerable uncertainty in practice also about the precise value of the marginal product of labour, and this may itself prevent unemployment.

A final feature of imperfect competition in the labour market, which must be mentioned for formal completeness, is the existence on the demand side of employers' organisations exercising a degree of monopoly power. In so far as collective bargaining takes the form of negotiation between monopolistic buyers and sellers of labour the resulting agreement may be very hard to forecast. The analysis of such situations is complex and would take us well beyond the bounds of this introductory book.

DIFFERENCES IN WAGES

We have come quite far in this chapter by way of acquiring tools of analysis, but less far in terms of answering the kind of question with which we started. Why *do* wages differ by region, occupation, sex, industry and other characteristics?

Answers to this question are not purely economic. But the framework of supply and demand analysis used so far can aid considerably in throwing light on the reasons for wage differentials.

A good starting point is to retain the assumption that labour is a homogeneous factor of production so that we can ignore, for the time being, any differences in skill and ability between individuals. The most general conclusion that follows from this assumption is that the action of the price mechanism in the market for labour will lead to a tendency for equality of wages in all occupations throughout the country. The argument is simply that if wages were *not* the same everywhere, there would be a natural inclination for workers to switch from low-paid to high-paid jobs. Shifts in labour supplies would act as equilibrating forces.

Of course, it would be a caricature to suggest that the world is like this and that all jobs are equally remunerated. The idea is, however, a useful guide to clear thinking and we can explain differentials by identifying what is wrong with the theoretical scheme which suggests that they are.

Four explanations may be offered.

(1) First, labour is not homogeneous. Men and women differ in innate skill and ability and differentials are reflected in their different marginal productivities. These lead, therefore, to different labour demand curves. Skills are not, moreover, all innate. Some are acquired by education and by training. We referred to this matter in Chapter 2 (page 18) and pointed out that some skills acquired by training might perhaps be regarded as the result of investment in 'human capital'. The longer the training period, the higher one would expect the earnings of a particular type of labour to be. Lawyers, doctors and accountants, for example, spend several years before they are qualified professionally, and the fact that their earnings are higher than those of unqualified labour can be regarded, at least in part, as a return on investment in human capital.

Labour is not homogeneous in one other respect too. Some people prefer hard work, not to mention risk, to an easy life. They may earn more as a result of working harder or longer hours, or even working in risky occupations, as, for example, steeplejacks, test pilots or mercenaries.

(2) A second reason for the existence of differentials is that labour is not completely free to move from place to place, or from job to job, whenever there is a wage incentive to do so.

Job mobility is related to the subject of the previous section in so far as retraining to acquire new skills is concerned. But geographical mobility is not everyone's cup of tea and many people prefer to stay near home and with their old work-mates rather than move to a new locality to earn more. Mobility is also costly. It takes time to search for a better-paid job. It may involve giving up work and living for a time on past savings and not everyone is prepared to do this.

(3) The third explanation of different money wage rates between individuals arises from the existence of what are called the 'non-pecuniary' advantages and disadvantages of particular occupations. These should be notionally added to monetary wages to obtain a realistic picture of the full reward for each job. Assembly-line workers in a noisy factory have a relatively unpleasant task and must, therefore, be paid enough to ensure a sufficient supply. Farm workers, on the other hand, often seem to enjoy their work in the open air. This is probably part of the reason why their wages tend to be below the average of other industries.

(4) The final reason why wages are not everywhere equal is related to variations in the competitive conditions in the market for different kinds of labour. We have already seen how the activities of trade unions, for example, can raise wages. Since trade union strength varies from industry to industry we can attribute some of the differences between wage levels to the differential strength of trade unions by industry.

ECONOMIC RENT

There is one final characteristic of factor markets that must be examined before ending the chapter. It is commonly associated with the return to land as a factor of production, though it is of more general application and we shall look at it first in the context of the price of labour.

The wage that must be paid in order to attract a worker to a job must be at least as high as that which he could get in his next most remunerative occupation. This is called his transfer earnings – another term for what is effectively the opportunity cost to him of working in a given job. An upward sloping supply curve of labour implies that transfer earnings vary between individuals. Look, for example, at Figure 5.5. The supply curve, *SS*, implies that one man would work at a wage of *OT*, another at a wage of *OV*, another at a wage of *OW*, and so forth. In other words, one man has transfer earnings of *OT*, another of *OV*, and another of *OW*, and so on.

Let us suppose that the demand curve for labour cuts the supply curve at point *E*, and the equilibrium wage *OB* is paid to all *OA* workers. The (*OA*th) man who finds it marginally attractive to work in this occupation at the wage *OB* has zero transfer earnings. But all other workers receive a wage in excess of their transfer earnings. The man who would offer his services at a wage of *OT* receives an excess of *TB* over his transfer earnings; the man with transfer earnings of *OV* receives an excess of *VB;* and so on. The difference between the wage received

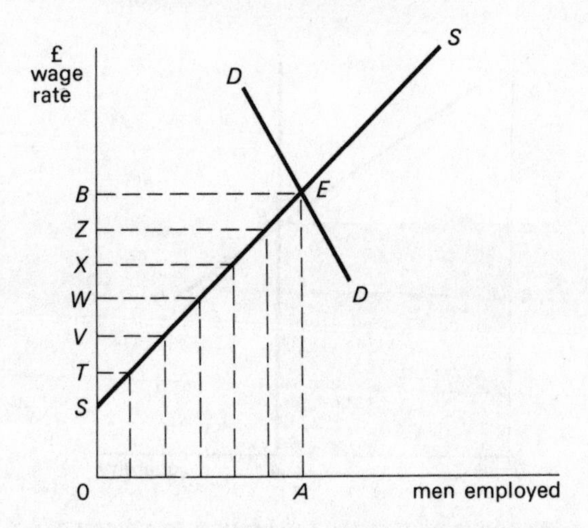

Figure 5.5 *Economic rent* (BES). *The difference between the wage bill* (OBEA) *and total transfer earnings* (OSEA).

and the transfer earnings of an individual is a kind of 'surplus', and is sometimes known by the special name of economic rent. In the diagram, the total economic rent earned by all workers in the industry is *BES* (that is, the wage bill, *OBEA*, minus total transfer earnings, *OSEA*).

The concept of economic rent relates not only to labour but to any factor of production which has an upward sloping supply curve. To take an extreme case, if there were a factor the supply of which was absolutely fixed, the supply curve would be a vertical straight line; implying that the factor had zero transfer earnings and that the same amount would be offered for sale whatever the price. The entire payment to such a factor of production would consist of economic rent, which does not need to be paid in order to secure its being offered for sale. In Figure 5.6 the equilibrium market price is *OB*, where the quantity demanded, *OA*, is equal to the quantity supplied. However, *OA* would also be supplied at any other price, for example, at a price of *OC*, or even of zero. The total return to the factor, *OBEA*, thus consists of economic rent.

The quantity of land in existence is, to all intents and purposes, fixed in supply. This fact gave the nineteenth-century American economist Henry George the idea that the government could impose a tax on land without causing any reduction in the quantity in use. It is important to note that the economic argument for a tax on land does not involve taxing improvements, such as buildings. This might affect the supply of factors of production which are used to make the improvements and tend to cause such factors to shift into other industries

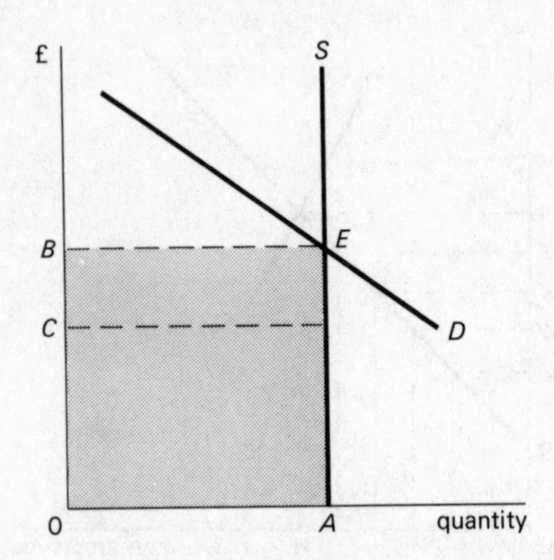

Figure 5.6 *Economic rent, as the total return to a factor of production in fixed supply.*

or occupations which were not subject to the tax. The fairness of taxing land-owners in this manner is, of course, quite a separate issue, but it is important to understand the economic case for imposing a tax on a factor in fixed supply.

Note, however, that the argument holds only in the case of land if the tax is universally imposed on this factor. If only farm land, for example, were taxed, there would tend to be a reduction in supply, because land would be shifted to other uses, for instance, for building purposes. In other words, there is a real opportunity cost of employing land in one use rather than another, which consists of its transfer earnings in the alternative use.

THE DETERMINATION OF FACTOR PRICES

The aim of this chapter has been to show how price is determined in markets for factors of production. The framework for analysis has been that of supply and demand and it is important to remind the reader that these do not operate in isolation but take their shape and position in a social setting. If we wish to examine the effects of, say, a raising of the school-leaving age or of a lowering of the age of retirement, our tools of analysis will show that the supply curve of labour will shift to the left in either case. However, we must not lose sight of the social origins of the movement any more than we should fail to recognise that people's attitudes to work and leisure influence the shape of the supply curve itself.

The arguments of the chapter have been very largely illustrated from the example of the factor of production labour. But we can use the same tools of analysis to study price formation in markets for other factors of production, such as land and raw materials. Demand is still derived from factor productivity; supply still reflects opportunity cost; and barriers to factor mobility of divers kinds can still explain differential payments. Moreover, our results may be different in the long run and the short, as well as in markets which are competitive or monopolistic.

It remains to add that there are two factors of production whose rewards are of a rather special kind. The first is enterprise. As explained in Chapter 2 (page 18), pure profits, or the return to 'enterprise', are something of a residual for a business after all other factors of production have been paid their rewards. It is difficult to treat profits in exactly the same way as other factor prices, but there can be little doubt that supply and demand have their influences even here.

The second remaining factor is capital, whose return, the rate of interest, also possesses rather peculiar characteristics. Supply and demand play important parts in price formation, but the forces lying behind them have certain special features. In particular, market supply and demand curves cannot be adequately constructed in the manner used for other factors. We defer consideration of interest rates until Chapter 8 because, in order to understand properly how they are determined, it is necessary to introduce material of an altogether different nature from that used so far in this book. In order to bring them in we need to look at the economy as a whole and this involves a quite different approach. There is a branch of economics, known as macroeconomics, which emphasises aggregate behaviour of the economy as a whole and it is time to look at it.

NOTE: CHAPTER 5

1 These averages are peculiar ones. The source of data for the calculation of the average is the 'tax unit', which lumps together incomes of husbands and wives on the one hand, and single persons on the other. So the average is something between household and individual income.

Part Three

NATIONAL INCOME, OUTPUT AND THE PRICE LEVEL

Chapter 6

The National Income

So far in this book we have concentrated attention on the behaviour of consumers, producers and factors of production in individual markets. Our object has been to show how resources are allocated by a pricing system.

There is, however, another way of looking at things. This is to ignore the fine details and to step back and view the economy as a whole. The time has come to adopt this wider approach, which concentrates on the aggregate behaviour of major components of the economic system.

MACROECONOMICS

The branch of economics which deals with aggregates, such as the total national income, is known as macroeconomics, as opposed to microeconomics, which examines questions of resource allocation in individual markets and which we have so far been studying. In macroeconomics we shall still be concerned with production and prices, but our interest will now focus on *total* output, expenditure and employment and on the average general level of prices.

The approach in macroeconomics does not differ basically from that of microeconomics. Supply, demand and equilibrium will still be involved. We shall simply employ these concepts in a new perspective – viewing the economy as a whole and the national income in particular. We might do worse than begin by asking what exactly the national income actually is.

THE CIRCULAR FLOW OF INCOME AND EXPENDITURE

We may, for once, start with a definition. The national income, or national product, is a measure of the total value of goods and services produced by a country in a given period of time. Goods are valued at their money prices because this is the most convenient and meaningful way of adding together different quantities of goods and services, like hats, hearing aids and haircuts.

The national income is a measure of output, expenditure and of the income of the factors of production. The identical nature of these magnitudes can be demonstrated with the help of a diagram, which emphasises the circular nature of the flows of income and expenditure.

AN ULTRA-SIMPLE ECONOMY

It is easiest to begin with the simplest possible case. Let us suppose that we are faced with an isolated economy which does not engage in any dealings with foreign countries. Suppose, also, there is no government activity, so that there are only two sectors, a business sector and a household sector. We further assume that businesses do all the producing of consumer goods which they sell to households; while the latter own all the factors of production which they sell to businesses for the purpose of producing the national output of goods and services.

Figure 6.1 shows the circular flow of income, expenditure and output

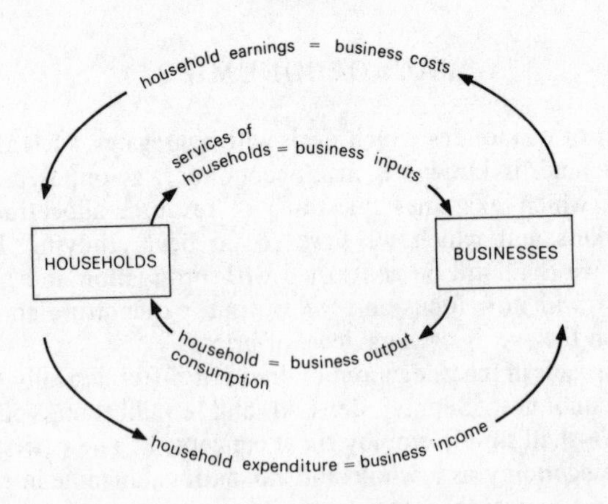

Figure 6.1 *The circular flow of expenditure and income.*

for this two-sector economy. Consider, first, the lower portion of the diagram. Business output is shown as flowing to households in return for household expenditure. These two flows are necessarily equal. The total expenditure by households on goods and services must be the same as the total value of the output that they buy. What is more, businesses only derive their income as a result of households purchasing their output. So total expenditure by households can be viewed a third way, as being the same as total business income. Hence, the lower portion of the diagram shows there are three identical ways of looking at this flow of payments and receipts. Total expenditure is the same as the value of output which is the same as total business income.

The upper portion of Figure 6.1 illustrates the counterpart flows of the services of the factors of production and payments for them. The arrows starting in the household sector represent the money value of the flows of the services of these factors, as members of households work for businesses in return for wages and provide capital in return for interest, and so on. These two flows are equal because total spending by businesses on factor services (that is, their total costs) is the same as total receipts (or earnings) of households for providing these services.

There is one last important equality to notice. Total business income is paid out to households by way of payments for the services of factors of production. Therefore, total business and household incomes are equal. The money value of flows in the upper and lower portions of the diagram are then also equal to each other. We conclude that the value of the national output of this ultra-simple economy is the same as its national expenditure, which is the same again as its total national income.

Profit is treated as a reward accruing to the factor of production enterprise. There is, therefore, no residual 'profit' remaining in the business sector. All business income is passed on to households, who own all factors of production.

Value added

There is one technical but important matter which must be disposed of before proceeding. It is correct to say that calculations of national income, expenditure and output should all give the same result. But we must be especially careful when using the output measure in any cases where production is not sold directly to final consumers. If some output is bought by other industries for further processing (called intermediate output) we should make a mistake if we added together the total output of all industries and called that national output. The figure we should arrive at would be too large because we would have double-counted 'intermediate output'.

In order to avoid this mistake the procedure is adopted of including only the *value added* by each industry. Value added is defined as the value of output less the cost of materials and semi-finished products bought in from other firms. Let us take a simple example. Suppose a farmer sells plums for £100 to a manufacturer who sells jam for £160 to a retailer who sells it to consumers for £200. The values added at each stage of the production process are £100 by the farmer, £60 by the manufacturer (£160 − £100) and £40 by the retailer (£200 − £160). The sum of values added is £100 + £60 + £40 = £200, which is the same as the total expenditure by consumers on jam.

MORE COMPLEX MODELS

The two-sector model of an economy described in the circular flow diagram of Figure 6.1 contains several simplifying features which, nevertheless, do not affect its general purpose of identifying the equality of income, expenditure and output flows. There are, however, two important complications that must be taken care of if our hypothetical economy is to bear sufficient resemblance to the real world for our purposes. The first arises from the fact that we need to deal with an economy which has two sectors in addition to businesses and households. The second complication pertains to the fact that national output includes items of capital equipment as well as of consumer goods.

(a) Circular flows in a four-sector economy

The two sectors which we now add to our simple economy comprise the government and the rest of the world. They appear in a slightly more complicated diagram, Figure 6.2, which is otherwise of the same general form as Figure 6.1.

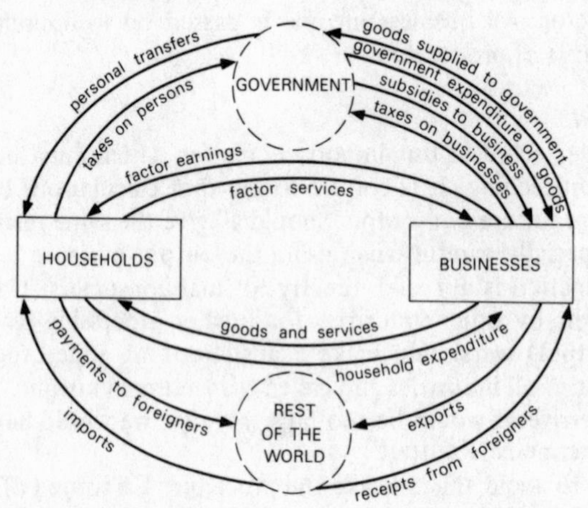

Figure 6.2 *Circular flows in an open economy with a government sector.*

(i) Government. The state enters the picture in two main ways. In the first place, the government supplies certain goods and services, such

as schools, hospitals and armies, itself. In the second place, the state acts as tax-gatherer and disburser of transfer payments to supplement the incomes of private individuals and others. The chief of these flows of income and expenditure are shown in the upper portion of Figure 6.2.

Taxes are levied on households (for example, personal income taxes) and on businesses (for example, corporation tax), and these appear as flows from the two private sectors to the government. Transfer payments, on the other hand, are shown as flows from the government; they are also made both to households (for example, retirement pensions and unemployment benefits) and to businesses (for example, subsidies to industries which the government wishes to support). In Britain, a large part of all expenditure is channelled through central and local governments. Hence it is obviously vital to take account of the influence of the state if we are to be able to relate our argument to the real world.

(ii) The rest of the world. The need to incorporate the rest of the world in our circular flows of income and expenditure is due to the fact that most countries today are not self-sufficient economically, but engage in trade with foreigners. For the United Kingdom, this matter is of immense importance. About a third of all income and expenditure flows are attributable to international transactions of one sort or another.

The major international payments and receipts are for imports and exports. Figure 6.2 portrays them in the lower portion of the diagram, where a sector termed the 'rest of the world' is shown. Note, incidentally, that the diagram shows that both households and businesses are involved in transactions with the rest of the world. This implies that some of the outputs of (British) businesses supply consumers elsewhere and emphasises that overseas countries exercise an influence on the British economy, affecting the size of business income in Britain and, therefore, the level of the national income. At the same time, the fact that the British purchase goods and services from foreign countries shows that their economics are equally open to influence from Britain's. It should be added that payments and receipts are made for a variety of purposes as well as for imports and exports. They are considered in a later section dealing with the balance of payments (see below, pages 118–20).

Capital investment

There is one further kind of complexity that needs attention over and above the introduction of government and international transactions into our scheme. We must introduce a distinction between output of consumer goods and of capital goods.

We first encountered the idea of capital as a factor of production in Chapter 2. Capital includes machinery, factories and equipment which are not wanted for themselves but because they indirectly help businesses to produce consumer goods. Additions to a nation's stock of capital during a period of time is called *investment*. We shall find it useful to distinguish between expenditure on consumption and that on investment. The principle for distinguishing between them is straightforward, but we have to recognise that the word investment is used in certain special ways.

Stocks. In the first place, it is necessary to point out that, by convention, economists include *changes* in the value of stocks of goods and materials as part of investment. Stocks (inventories in American terminology) consist of output in the pipeline, as it were, between production and consumption. They include raw materials and semi-manufactured and unsold consumer goods, classed as 'working capital', to distinguish them from 'fixed capital', such as plant and machinery. The former are almost part of consumption, but are not really so until they are actually bought by consumers.

The size of the nation's stocks is part of the national capital existing at a point in time. Provided there is no change in the volume of stocks between the beginning and the end of the period over which we wish to estimate the national income, there is no reason to take account of them. If, however, there is a change in the quantity of stocks, the situation is different. For instance, if the volume of stocks increases during the period, this amounts to an increase in capital and, therefore, should be treated as investment. Likewise, and for the same reason, a decrease in the volume of stocks is considered negative investment.

Durable consumer goods. A second example of the unusual way in which economists use the term capital investment arises from the inclusion of some output which would naturally be thought of as consisting of consumer goods being classed as capital. We have already met some of these in the previous paragraphs when we saw that working capital comprised stocks of unsold consumer goods. There is another sense, however, in which expenditure on certain consumer goods is regarded as capital investment. One way of explaining why this is so is to regard the word consumption as implying the immediate satisfaction of wants directly by consumers – using up or even destroying goods in the process, for example, the eating of an egg, the tipping of detergent into a washing machine or the burning of petrol when driving a car. However, some consumer goods, such as cars and houses, provide a service over a long period of time. Durable goods of this kind represent, in a sense, capital, because they are not used up immediately but are available for future consumption without further production. We shall sometimes find it useful to include such outputs as part of the nation's investment.

THE STANDARD OF LIVING

We now know that the national income is a monetary measure of the total flow of goods and services available to a country during a period of time such as a year. The reader could be excused for thinking that it was therefore a measure of the standard of living of the people. It is in fact not entirely untrue. We write deliberately in the double negative to give pause for thought. The national income is one indicator of living standards, but the two are not the same thing. The differences between them are particularly important when making comparisons of living standards either between countries, or within one country over a period of time. There are several reasons why such comparisons based on statistics of national income may be misleading.

(1) PRICE CHANGES

The first important reason why a change in the value of national income need not carry with it the implication that living standards have changed also is that the prices at which the national output is valued may have risen or fallen. Economists distinguish between *nominal* and *real* income changes. The former merely reflect movements in prices, while the latter refer to increases or decreases in the real volume of output.

The value of a set of goods and services is no more than their volumes multiplied by their prices. It is possible, therefore, to estimate the extent to which a change in national output, indicated by its nominal or monetary value, is a real one or is simply due to changing prices. In periods of inflation it is essential to make this distinction.

The method used to isolate changes in real national income when its money value is rising or falling requires information on movements in the general level of prices. Figures are collected of the prices of a representative collection of goods and services bought by households in Britain. The percentage change in each item is given a bias (or 'weight') corresponding to its importance in household expenditure. The average price change, so calculated, is representative of the changing cost of living, and is not unduly influenced by very large price changes in minor items. Statistics measuring average price movements are generally in the form of index numbers. They are constructed by taking one year, which is called the base, and referring to the average price level in that base year as 100. The price index number of another year is then expressed as a percentage of that of the base.[1] For example, a figure of 150 indicates that prices have risen by 50 per cent since the base year.

Price index numbers can be applied to statistics of the money value of national income measured in the prices current in each year in order to allow for inflationary (or deflationary) elements. To take an extreme example, if between two years the national income doubles in money terms while the general level of prices also doubles, the real national output will be the same in both years. If prices increase, but by less than nominal income, real income rises but by less than nominal income, and vice versa. It remains to say that there are many practical problems involved in the construction of price index numbers, particularly over long periods when goods in the shops may be changing physically (for example, electric blankets instead of hot water bottles). The use of such price indices, however, provides an effective way of linking, even approximately, national income and living standards.

(2) POPULATION CHANGES

National income is a measure of total output available to a community. If the numbers living in the community rise (or fall), even without any change occurring in the size of the national income, the standard of living is liable to fall (or rise) as a direct result. A better indicator of living standards is, therefore, obtained if national income is divided by the size of the population to give a figure of income per head (or per capita).

(3) CONSUMPTION VERSUS PRODUCTION

National income includes goods and services of all kinds, some of which are capital items and exports, which do not lead to the physical well-being of the population in the period under consideration. The standard of living in any given year is likely to be more closely related to consumption expenditure than to total output including investment. (It may be associated also with imports and with the running down of stocks of goods held by businesses and households.)

Capital items, like machinery and factory buildings, as we know, may raise consumption in future periods, but it is common to talk of living standards being held down in order to build up capital or, in the opposite event, to be 'artificially' kept up by 'living on capital'. Moreover, as existing capital equipment wears out or becomes obsolete as it gets older, an economy usually needs to set aside some portion of its resources simply to maintain the real value of its capital, replacing it as necessary. Without such a depreciation allowance, as it is called, the value of the nation's capital would gradually fall, and living standards would sooner or later follow. Estimating the depreciation (or capital consumption) allowance that should be made for this purpose is a somewhat tricky job, particularly since it involves, in part, predicting the future. Unless you know in advance whether a machine will last five or ten years, for example, you do not know how to estimate the portion of its value you should count as having depreciated during any year of its life.

We cannot go further into this important question here. But it is useful to know that capital consumption is estimated to have absorbed approximately 10 per cent of the resources available in the UK over recent years. We should regard national output as the flow of goods and services which is available for all purposes in the economy, including maintaining the value of the nation's capital stock intact.

It should be added only that foreign transactions ought to be regarded in a similar fashion. A nation can live 'above its means' for a period by importing more than it exports or by selling off its foreign investments.

(4) EXCLUSIONS

National income does not measure everything that helps the people of a country to have a certain standard of living. Four major kinds of exclusions may be distinguished.

(a) Non-marketed goods and services

By and large the statistics of national income are based on the goods and services that are bought and sold in the market. This is not absolutely true, since government-provided output (for instance, on health and education) is valued at cost and included in the official estimates.[2] But there are many non-marketed goods and services which do not figure in the national income totals. Some of the more important exclusions are the services of housewives and do-it-yourself jobs by householders. Consequently, if every married man divorced his wife and employed her as his housekeeper and, at the same time, worked as a paid odd-job man for his neighbour instead of doing DIY jobs for himself, the national income could rise without there being any material change in circumstances. Illegal activities, such as the supply of drugs, are also excluded from national income estimates. And the statistics of the value of the services of 'professional' household repairers and others who work 'for cash only' in order to lower their tax liabilities are less than they should really be.

It is difficult to estimate precisely the effect of making allowance for non-marketed excluded activities on the real national income. It is important to bear them in mind if there is any suspicion of a significant increase or decrease in their scope. There is evidence of a rise in the size of the 'cash economy' in Britain in recent years, for instance, which would imply that national income estimates understate the real rise in the volume of output. Moreover, growth rates of some Third World countries may, for a similar reason, be *over*estimated. Economic development is often accompanied by a switch from subsistence living within the family to growing reliance on specialisation and the exchange of goods and services in the market. Hence if the market sector only is included while this is happening, the growth rate of national income is exaggerated.

A last, rather different, kind of economic activity which is not marketed consists of negative outputs, or economic 'bads' as they are sometimes dubbed. These include the undesirable by-products of a growing economy – like traffic noise and pollution of the environment. They have received increased attention in recent years.

(b) Quality changes

A second exclusion from the measured national income is the quality dimension of goods and services. Statisticians try to make some allowance for quality changes, but it is virtually impossible to do so with great accuracy. How much 'better' is today's car than that of twenty-five years ago? It is certainly quite a different article. Some people even claim that quality has deteriorated because comfort has been sacrificed for performance. But even if we ignore the possibility of quality deterioration, the problem of valuing higher quality persists. How much better off are we really watching our colour televisions than we were when we only had black and white sets (or when an earlier generation was listening to the radio)?

(c) Leisure

The third exclusion from the national income as conventionally measured – leisure – is perhaps the most important. Living standards are certainly influenced by the amount of leisure there is, as well as by the way in which it is spent. Average hours worked have come down fairly steadily in postwar Britain. More significant, perhaps, is the fact that the typical annual holiday for industrial workers has risen from one to three weeks over the same period. (There has also been some upward movement in involuntary leisure in years of relatively high unemployment, though one would certainly not want to argue that this should be counted in the same way.)

It is possible to make some adjustment to the national income for increasing leisure and attempts have been made to do so. The number of extra hours can be counted more easily, however, than they may be valued. It has been suggested, for example, that one might reasonably value an hour's leisure at the wage sacrificed by taking it – that is, using the concept of opportunity cost (see Chapter 3, pages 34–6 above). But some people regard this as wrong because they believe that the intrinsic value of leisure-time is unvarying and not subject to change with the general level of wages.

(d) Non-economic factors

We should, finally, take account of the fact that a nation's living standards are affected by a variety of what should probably be regarded as non-economic factors which are not included in the national income measure. Geographical circumstances are a good example. Other things being equal, it is cheaper to live in a warm climate than in one with long hard winters. You need less well insulated houses, less fuel and warm clothing. Similarly, it costs less to live in a country whose geographical configuration is such that transport is easy and cheap. There are, therefore, more resources available for other things.

One must be a little careful here about the implications of different living costs when comparing national income statistics between countries or regions. Transport costs are high in some large cities not solely because of geographical, but also as a result of man-made, factors – people have wanted to make them that way. In so far as individuals have a choice about whether to live in high- or low-cost areas, it is doubtful whether there is a real justification for taking cost differences of this kind into account.

(5) THE DISTRIBUTION OF INCOME

The last reason for emphasising the fact that the national income is not necessarily a good measure of living standards is related to the question of the distribution of income. The main point to be made here is simply that the income of any one individual need not move together with the average income per head of the population. Not everyone's income need rise proportionately when the average national income goes up. Some people's may even fall.[3]

An associated matter relates to the activities of government, which raises revenue by taxation and other means and supplies goods, services and income transfers to some individuals (for example, those in retirement and the unemployed). The distribution of taxes and benefits falls unevenly on members of the population and some allowance should arguably be made for them.

The most common allowance deducts the taxes made on income from personal pre-tax income and adds transfer payments to obtain what is called 'disposable income', that is, the sum an individual retains and which he can decide to spend (or save) as he pleases. There are, however, other taxes raised by the state (for example, VAT, import duties, and so on) as well as benefits provided by government, other than the transfer payments already mentioned.

These are important items. Taxes on expenditure account for not far short of half of government revenue and have been increasing. They should, together with state-provided benefits, be allowed for in measuring individual living standards. It is not, however, a simple matter. Some public services like health and education can, in principle, be allocated to individual persons. But there are immense conceptual and practical problems involved in doing so. There are even some categories, like expenditure on defence, which benefit the community at large rather than specific individuals, and there is no obvious way to allocate them at all.

Our discussion of the relationship between the standard of living and the national income has been long enough to warrant a concluding comment. The implications of all the arguments put forward in this section is that the two indicators are certainly not the same and that we must view with caution any statement which suggests that living standards necessarily move in line with measured national income. We have shown how adjustments can be made to national income estimates to take account of some particular problems (for example, due to population changes, investment expenditures and government activities), but we have seen also that there are many conceptional and practical difficulties in doing so. The search for a better measure of economic welfare than national income has occupied economists for several years. New indicators have been developed, and will doubtless be improved, but there will never be a single one which is entirely adequate to measure living standards for everyone in the population. The national income will almost certainly continue to be used for many years to come. We should remember to interpret it in the light of the comments that have been made in this section.

THE NATIONAL INCOME OF THE UNITED KINGDOM

We are now ready to leave the domain of simple model economies and to study the national income of the UK. Reference to official statistics tells us that the national income of the UK in 1978, in very rough terms, was about £150,000 million. This means that all the goods and services produced during the period between 1 January and 31 December in that year were worth approximately that amount, or about £3,000 per man, woman and child in the population.

However quickly this book gets into your hands, it is certain that the figures will be out of date. You should therefore make a point of looking up for yourself what the national income was estimated to have been for the latest years you can find.[4] Work out, too, how much it has increased in percentage terms since 1978. It will bring home to you that it is much more interesting to examine trends in the national income as time passes than to pay great attention to its value in any particular year.

Figure 6.3 has been prepared to show the trend in the national income over the fifty years since 1930. There are two lines on the graph. Concentrate first on the unbroken line and ignore the war years. The line is labelled 'money national income' and it shows what has happened to the volume of goods and services valued at the prices current in each year.

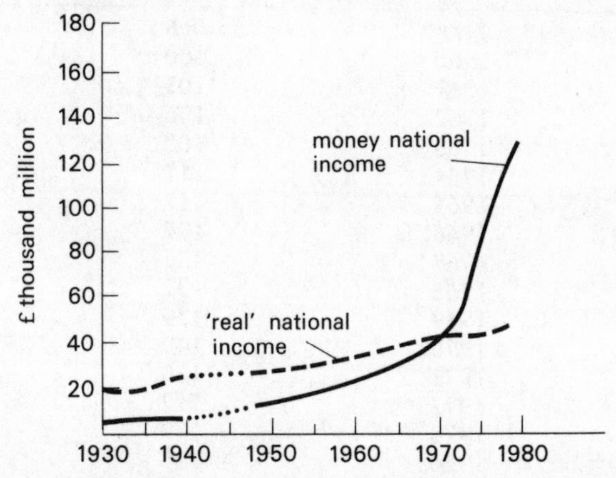

Figure 6.3 *National income at current prices and at constant (1970) prices since 1930.*

Sources: Central Statistical Office, *National Income and Expenditure*, annually; *The British Economy, Key Statistics, 1900–1970* (Times Newspapers for the London and Cambridge Economic Service, 1972).

As can be seen from the graph, the value of money national income rose by a multiple of about thirty in the half-century since 1930. There are two distinct reasons why this could have taken place. The first is the straightforward one that the physical quantities of goods and services rose, and there is no doubt that this is part of the explanation.

INFLATION

The second reason for the large rise in the value of the national income arises from the fact that the prices at which national output has been valued have not remained constant since 1930, but they have risen. As everyone knows, we have been living in an inflationary age of rising prices and a part of the explanation of the increase in national income is simply that it has been growing more rapidly in nominal than in real terms.

We explained earlier that it was possible to estimate the inflationary component of changes in the value of output by the use of price index numbers (see above, pages 107–8). A series of such price index numbers for the UK is given in Table 6.1. It shows that prices rose about 3 per cent between 1960 and 1961 and that they were roughly four times as high in 1978 as they were twenty years earlier.

Table 6.1 *Price index numbers of all goods and services sold in the UK*

Year	*Index*
1960	100
1961	103
1962	106
1963	108
1964	112
1965	117
1966	122
1967	125
1968	132
1969	139
1970	149
1971	160
1972	712
1973	189
1974	228
1975	283
1976	330
1977	369
1978	406

Source: CSO *National Income and Expenditure* (HMSO 1979).

Let us now turn back to figure 6.3. In order to make an assessment of the extent to which the increase in national income since 1930 was attributable to the rise in prices, we make use of a series of price index numbers. Over so long a period we should not regard such an index as having a very precise meaning. The physical goods in the shops were not the same at the end of the period as they were at the beginning, so that we have to approximate for price changes where old goods disappear and new ones take their place (for example, electricity instead of candles). But defects of detail can be overlooked as our need is only for broad magnitudes.

In Figure 6.3 we have used a price index to deflate values calculated at current prices to produce what is known as *real* income – that is, income adjusted for price changes. This means effectively revaluing the output of each year at a set of constant prices. For the purpose of the diagram the prices ruling in 1970 have been used to construct the broken line on the graph which shows the course of real income over the same period as that of the unbroken line, which represents nominal money income at current prices. Real income rose much less than money income, in fact between two- and three-fold since 1930 compared with the thirty-fold increase noted earlier in nominal income. In other words prices must have risen more than ten-fold over the period.

It is important to point out that the general level of prices has not been increasing over the half-century at a steady rate. During the 1930s the price level was fairly steady. This was in fact a period during which the economy was heavily depressed and prices actually fell during the first few years of the decade. After the Second World War, in contrast, prices began to creep upwards at figures of 2 to 4 per cent per annum. In the 1970s the rate of inflation sharply accelerated into double figures for most years, reaching a rate of well over 20 per cent around the year 1975. It ought to be noted that this increase in the rate of inflation, which characterised the 1970s, was experienced in most industrial countries of the world. British inflation may have been greater than that of several other countries, but there is no doubt that inflation had become a world problem.

Inflation, especially if unanticipated and accelerating, has important social and economic consequences, including those on the distribution of income, employment and economic growth. We shall have to look shortly at the causes of inflation and later return to discuss its policy implications in Chapter 9.

ECONOMIC GROWTH

The statistical series of the national income in the UK since 1930, displayed in Figure 6.3, shows the real long-term rate of growth of the economy. This growth rate has averaged about $2\frac{1}{2}$ per cent per annum since the end of the Second World War and compares favourably with previous peacetime periods of the century. In the interwar years the rate was nearer 2 per cent, while between 1900 and 1913, it was only around 1 per cent. The postwar British growth rate compares less favourably with those of several other countries. In the third quarter of this century the USA achieved around 3 per cent, France, Italy and West Germany nearer 5 per cent and Japan over 8 per cent. A country that achieves an annual growth rate of $2\frac{1}{2}$ per cent succeeds in doubling its national income in twenty-eight years. Its income per head, however, will grow more slowly if its population is increasing. The size of the UK's population has been held steady over the last few years, but it rose by around 10 per cent between 1950 and 1970 and this has to be taken into account if (as explained above, see page 108) one wishes to use a measure which more closely approximates living standards.

The subject of economic growth has become of major interest in recent years and the question arises as to what causes economies to grow at all. This is an extremely difficult and controversial area in economics and we shall not be able to say very much about it in this introductory book. However, it must be clear that economic growth is basically dependent on the quality and quantity of the factors of production available and the efficiency with which they are employed. Labour productivity is affected by education and training and the number of workers depends on such matters as the rate of growth of the domestic population, emigration and immigration. The age distribution of the population is also relevant. The larger the proportion of the adult population below retirement age, for example, the greater the supply of workers will be.

The factor of production on which attention is often correctly focused when economic growth is being discussed is capital. We have argued several times in the course of this book that investment expenditure in machinery, plant and equipment tends to raise productivity and can, therefore, be an important determinant of growth. The UK has invested about a fifth of its resources in capital of one sort or another in recent years, while certain other countries have maintained higher proportions of investment to total expenditure. This has been a common explanation for lower growth rates in this country than elsewhere, though it is certainly not the whole story.

It is necessary to emphasise that large investment expenditures need not necessarily lead to high growth rates. For one thing, although production costs may fall initially as capital is accumulated, one might even expect the law of diminishing returns (see above, pages 82–3) to apply to increasing amounts of capital being used with a relatively fixed supply of labour (and land). Quality of capital is clearly as important as quantity and there is no doubt that economic growth is very heavily dependent on technological advance.

Finally, it should be added that productivity, and therefore growth, are subject to the influence of what, for want of a better expression, we might call the 'socio-economic environment'. If a society is imbued with a strong work ethic, economic growth is more likely to be high than if people are interested mainly in leisure. It is beyond our domain to consider whether business and labour motivation and morale is associated with particular social systems, competitive atmosphere, taxation policies, and the like.

We should end this discussion by drawing attention to the current controversial issue of whether economic growth is a very desirable objective anyway. There used to be a conventional wisdom that growth was a necessary precondition for solving certain major social and economic problems, like the existence of poverty. But recent opinion has emphasised the costs that are associated with growth, such as the loss of 'old values' and the pollution and spoilation of the environment. One is tempted to conclude that there is, perhaps, an optimum rate of economic growth which maximises the advantages and minimises the costs. Regretfully, we cannot pursue the matter further here.

CYCLES IN ECONOMIC ACTIVITY

Our discussion of trends in real national income has concentrated on its long-term growth. In the short run, changes in the national income have been variable rather than steady. This variability was barely visible in Figure 6.3 because of its scale. Figure 6.4 has therefore been prepared by plotting the increases or decreases in the real national income of the UK for each year since 1921 as a percentage of the income of the previous year. It can be seen that year-to-year fluctuations have been considerable. In some years the national income grew by as much as 8 per cent, in others hardly at all and, in a few years, it actually declined. But illustrations restricted to individual years hide the important fact that good and bad years do not appear at random, but tend to come in runs, leading to alternate periods of prosperity and depression.

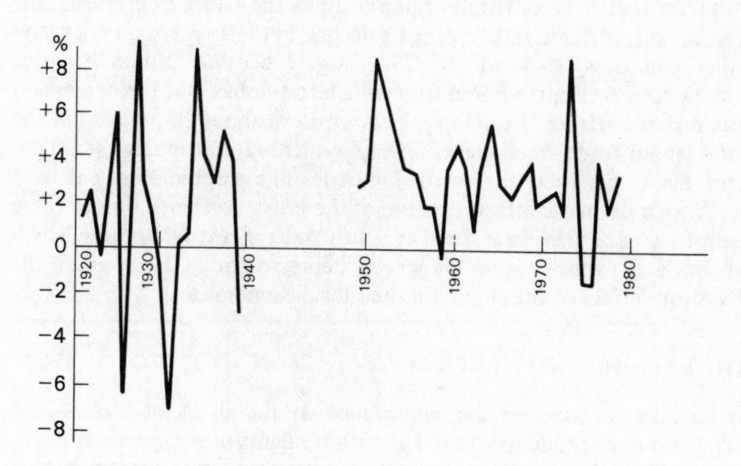

Figure 6.4 *Year-to-year changes in national output since 1921 (per cent).*
Source: as for Figure 6.3.

The cyclical behaviour of economic activity is termed the trade, or business, cycle by economists. It characterised the British economy in the nineteenth century and has continued, though in somewhat modified form, since then. Cycles of different duration have been observed. In the last century a fairly regular nine-year cycle occurred as well as others of shorter duration and there is some evidence for the existence of much longer cycles. Four stages can be distinguished in the classic cycle: (1) boom; (2) crisis (or recession); (3) slump (or depression); (4) recovery.

A typical boom is characterised by business optimism, rising output and employment and, eventually, rising costs and prices. At the upper turning point, or crisis, business optimism turns sour, bankruptcies increase, investment falls off and the economy moves into depression, the opposite phase to the boom. Output and employment fall, or stagnate, until the lower turning point of recovery is reached when business optimism returns, investment picks up and a new boom is launched. These very stylised characteristics have been common to most cycles. So has the tendency for investment expenditure to fluctuate a good deal more widely than that of consumption.

Despite common features, it must be heavily stressed that cycles have varied historically, and in some cases markedly, from each other. Differences extend to the duration and intensity of booms and slumps and to the proximate causes of turning points. It is not, therefore, sensible to regard any one cycle as more typical than any other. We should, however, refer to the particularly severe slump in the 1930s which followed the boom in the 1920s. This slump was prolonged and so severe that it is sometimes referred to as the Great Depression. The UK, in fact, suffered rather less of a decline in the 1930s than did many other countries, such as the USA, largely because Britain had not experienced so sharp a boom from which to tumble. But the depression was real enough to 2½ million jobless workers, about 20 per cent of the total labour force. Even higher unemployment rates, topping the 40 per cent mark, persisted in certain industries like shipbuilding, coal and steel, with dramatic effects because of the heavy concentration of these industries in certain areas, such as South Wales, Scotland and the North of England, which were known as depressed areas because of the disastrous effect of the slump on their local economies.

THE BALANCE OF PAYMENTS

It remains to consider the importance of the flows of income and expenditure of residents of the UK with residents of other countries.

A nation's international transactions are recorded in what is known as its balance of payments, which is simply an account of its dealings

Table 6.2 *Balance of payments, United Kindgom, 1978*

Outflows		*Inflows*	
Current account			
	£m.		£m.
Imports		Exports	
visible	36,607	visible	35,432
invisible	16,467	invisible	18,085
	53,074		53,517
Current account balance	+ 443		
Capital account			
UK private investment overseas	3,575	Overseas investment in the UK	2,771
		other (net)	361
	3,575		3,132
Capital account balance	− 443		

Source: *Monthly Digest of Statistics*, August 1979.

over a period of time with the rest of the world. A very brief form of the balance of payments of the UK is shown in Table 6.2. It should be understood that this is for illustrative purposes only and the reader is advised to seek up-to-date figures, as for the national income (for sources see note 4 to this chapter, page 122).

The balance of payments is conventionally divided into two sections. The current account comprises receipts and payments for imports and exports both visible and invisible (invisible trade includes items such as banking, insurance and foreign travel). Flows of funds for investment are entered in the capital account, as are official transactions of a capital nature by the government and changes in the UK's holdings of reserves of foreign currencies.

The expenditure flows in the balance of payments are of great importance to a country like the UK, not only because of their absolute size relative to the national income, but also because of their volatility which carries with it a threat to internal instability.

Transactions between countries cause the booms and slumps of trade cycles to spread throughout the world. When one country is enjoying a boom period its rising incomes tend to pull in higher imports from other countries, whose exporters find their own incomes rising as a direct result. The reverse happens in slumps. Falling incomes lead to falling imports – that is, falling exports and incomes in the rest of the world.

International monetary flows occur, as we have seen, not only for the purpose of paying for trade in goods and services, but also for other reasons. If the return that can be secured by investors is higher in one country than in another, for example, capital flows can be switched to take advantage of higher interest rates. In practice, capital flows can be extremely unstable at times – not only because of differences in interest rates, but also because of sudden changes in confidence of dealers and speculators on the international exchanges.

Any sharp increase in the net outflows of funds for trade and/or capital purposes from a country can cause severe problems, especially in the case of a country like the UK which trades so much with the rest of the world. This combination of instability and heavy dependence are major reasons why the government intervenes in the foreign exchange market. Indeed, the world as a whole has an interest in reducing the level of instability internationally and nations often get together and act in a concerted way, such as by offering loans to tide a country over short-term crises, and so on. We shall return to the subject of international economic policy in Chapter 9.

STAGFLATION

A feature of the behaviour of the economy of major importance in recent years has been a marked change in the course of the general level of prices. Whereas in the classic cycle prices tended to rise, mainly in the later stages of the boom, there now appears to be a pronounced long-term upward movement in the price level with virtually no falls at all. Even more to the point is the fact that the rate of inflation appears to have been accelerating, even in periods of recession. This has given rise to a new phenomenon, dubbed 'stagflation', when stagnant or even falling output is accompanied by increases, at times sharp, in the price level. A second important change of recent years is that the level of unemployment has moved upwards in the 1970s. In the first twenty years or so after the end of the Second World War unemployment in Britain was historically low – varying between 1½ per cent and 2½ per cent of the labour force. In the early 1970s it rose to 3½ per cent and in the second half of the decade had reached figures of 4 per cent, 5 per cent and 6 per cent.[5]

The social and economic consequences of fluctuations in economic activity are great. Hardship is caused by high unemployment and productive output is lost when the economy is operating below full capacity. Price instability, especially when it takes the form of accelerating inflation, is also widely considered to have serious consequences. We shall return to consider these matters in Chapter 9. Meanwhile it may be said that the concern of economists with the trade cycle goes back a very long time. It is generally recognised that a major breakthrough in understanding the causes of the cycle is due to the work of John Maynard Keynes. His book, *The General Theory of Employment, Interest and Money*, published in 1936, has probably been the most influential book by an economist in the present century. We shall be taking a look at some of his ideas in the next chapter. The recent coexistence of high inflation and high unemployment associated with stagflation has, however, called into question the applicability of at least some of Keynes's views to the present-day world and we shall have to consider more recent developments before returning to deal with the question of what can be done to promote economic growth in an environment of full employment and price stability.

THE NATIONAL ACCOUNTS

We should end our discussion of the national income by learning the standard forms used to present it statistically in the national accounts. Although this is to a certain extent a technical matter, it is important to understand the meaning of the official statistics for the UK in order to be able to interpret and comment on them. This section merely introduces the names given to the various measures by the compilers of the national accounts and relates them to ideas discussed earlier in the chapter.

Three distinct ways of defining income, expenditure and product are employed.

(1) Gross versus net

This distinction is used to allow for the capital consumption that takes place. A depreciation allowance is deducted from gross national product (GNP) to arrive at the net national product (NNP), which assumes that the value of the national capital is the same at the beginning and end of the period.

(2) National versus domestic

As the words imply, this distinction is used to differentiate domestically produced income from national income, which includes transactions with the rest of the world. Net income from abroad is added to gross domestic product (GDP) in order to arrive at gross national product (GNP).

(3) Factor cost versus market prices

If a tax is placed on a commodity, a gap is created between the cost of producing it, represented by the amount paid to all the factors of production, and the price at which it is sold in the market, Two alternative valuations of the national output are therefore available.

One is the national product at factor cost, the other at market prices. The difference between the two is accounted for by taxes on expenditure, such at VAT, net of any subsidies. Thus taxes are added to and subsidies are subtracted from GNP at factor cost to arrive at GNP at market prices. It should be noted that the term GNP is often used without further specification to mean GNP at factor cost.

These relationships may be summarised as follows:

GDP + net income from abroad = GNP

GDP − capital consumption = NDP

GDP at market prices − taxes on expenditure + subsidies

= GDP at factor cost.

NOTES: CHAPTER 6

1 The index number is based on a weighted average to distinguish it from a straightforward average. An example may be helpful. Suppose there are only two items in the family budget, clothing, the price of which doubles, and food, the price of which trebles. The price index for clothing alone is 200 and that for food 300 on the base of 100. If the two goods are equally important in household budgets they have equal weights. The weighted average index is (50 per cent of 200 and 50 per cent of 300 =) 250. If food was four times as important as clothing the weights would be four and one (or eight and two). The index would now be (80 per cent of 300 and 20 per cent of 200 =) 280. The rise in prices appears higher because food, the price of which rose the more, has the larger weight.

2 Official estimates also include, for example, allowances for the value of food produced and consumed on farms and of the rent 'imputed' as income to owner-occupiers of houses.

3 A somewhat more subtle point is that the change in income distribution may relate to real and not to money income because of changes in relative prices. If, for example, as in the illustration in note 1 above, inflation leads to a greater proportionate rise in the price of food than that of clothing, this will tend to bear more heavily on low- than on high-income households, because expenditure on food tends to fall relative to income as income increases. This would effectively amount to a redistribution of income; *ceteris paribus*, of course.

4 Try the *Annual Abstract of Statistics*, *National Income and Expenditure*, or *Economic Trends*, all published by HMSO for the Central Statistical Office.

5 Unemployment is not a simple phenomenon, but results also from causes other than falls in the demand for labour associated with the trade cycle. Some unemployment is seasonal; other is frictional or structural arising from changes in the structure of the economy as progress leads to expansion in certain industries and contraction in others (see below, page 179, for further consideration of the nature of unemployment). An alternative indicator of the severity of cyclical unemployment, which allows for at least some unemployment of other kinds, is the difference between the number of workers seeking jobs and the number of vacancies for them.

Chapter 7

The Determination of The National Income

In Chapter 6 we explored the national income from a largely descriptive point of view. We discovered something about the meaning and measurement of the national income and we obtained an idea of the trends and fluctuations that have charted its course in the UK in recent years. We have not yet asked, however, why the national income reached its particular level. Our objective now is to answer this question – to see how national income is determined.

The task before us is a formidable one and we shall devote this and the next chapter to it. Its difficulty arises chiefly from the fact that we cannot reach simple conclusions about income determination without dealing at the same time with other important macroeconomic variables, especially aggregate employment and the general level of prices.

Progress was easier in microeconomics. We made full use of the assumption of *ceteris paribus.* This was legitimate and useful when we were examining only a part, often a small part, of the economic system. We could safely examine the operation of supply and demand in the market for ice creams, for example, on the assumption that the prices of other goods remained unchanged.

In macroeconomics we can get into difficulties if we make simplifying assumptions of this kind because we need to look at the economic system as a whole and interactions between its components are an integral part of the explanation of how it works. Of course, we shall make simplifying assumptions to begin with, but we shall eventually need to look carefully at the interrelationships between the market for goods and services, the market for labour and the money market.

AGGREGATE DEMAND

Our starting point is a simple one. We shall modify it as we proceed in order, hopefully, to end up by being able to discuss some current problems of economic policy in Chapter 9. The immediate objective, however, is the limited one of reaching an understanding of the way in which output, employment and prices behave in the aggregate. We begin by turning aside for the moment from questions of employment and the general price level in order to focus attention on the aggregate demand for goods and services. This is a major simplification and the reader is warned that some important conclusions in this chapter may need modification when the analysis is made more realistic and, necessarily, more complex. We cannot start with everything at the same time, however, and we shall deliberately leave the question of inflation to the next chapter.

In one sense, aggregate demand is no more than the sum of the individual demands for each and every good and service in the economy. We can not, however, simply add together all the familiar market demand curves in order to arrive at a total, aggregate, demand curve for the economy as a whole, because such curves, as we know from the first part of this book, show quantities demanded at different *prices.* If, as now, we are interested in the determination of national income, we need a new-style aggregate demand curve, which portrays the flow of demand for goods and services at different levels of *income.*

PLANNED AND REALISED EXPENDITURES

In order to understand the forces that determine income at the macro-economic level, we must first distinguish two separate ways of looking at economic events. Our approach to the national income in the previous chapter was a historical one. We accepted that events had taken place. The year was over and past. We looked at what goods had been produced, what incomes had been received and at what expenditures had been made. We observed what had actually happened. This way of looking at events *after* they have occurred leads to observations of what are termed realised (or *ex post*) magnitudes of income and expenditure.

In contrast, there is an alternative viewpoint from which to observe the same economic behaviour. We can interest ourselves in events *before* they occur. This way of looking at things allows us to consider determinants of behaviour. So, when we discuss planned (or *ex ante*) expenditure or output (as it is called), we shall be concerned with what people plan, desire or intend to spend or produce, rather than on what was realised (*ex post*) after the event.

As a matter of fact, we used these concepts implicitly earlier in the book when we were discussing the determination of equilibrium price though we did not use this terminology. What we called demand curves are no more than (*ex ante*) statements of the amounts that consumers plan to buy of a product at a range of prices. Supply curves, similarly, are statements of the *planned* quantities that would be offered for sale over the same price range. The realised quantities, on the other hand, are the amounts actually bought and sold. The latter are only the same as the planned quantities if market price happens to be at equilibrium.

Suppose market price is not at but below equilibrium.[1] We know this means that in such conditions demand will exceed supply. Now, however, we can appreciate that this is true only in the *ex ante* sense – that is, the quantity that consumers plan to buy at the market price is greater than the quantity that sellers plan to sell. It is not true in the *ex post,* realised sense, because the quantity of goods actually sold must inevitably be the same as the quantity actually bought. When we look back at what happened in the market, *ex post,* we see only this equality of realised magnitudes, and not any frustrated plans of buyers and/or sellers. If, as here, the plans or desires of consumers and producers do *not* coincide, we know that the market is not in equilibrium, and that the forces of demand and supply will normally operate to change price.

In contrast, consider the situation in equilibrium. The amount consumers plan to buy matches that which sellers plan to offer for sale. Planned (*ex ante*) demand equals planned supply, and there is no pressure on market price. Our definition of equilibrium turns out to be: where *planned* demand and supply are equal.

Let us now transfer our new-found terminology from the realm of the individual market place, where prices act as an equilibrating force, to macroeconomics. Here, as we shall see, changes in the level of the national income can take on the role of bringing about equality in the plans of the whole community.

AN ULTRA-SIMPLE ECONOMY

Let us approach the question of the determination of national income initially in an ultra-simple economy in which the following assumptions hold:

(1) there are only two sectors, households and businesses;
(2) the only goods are consumer goods;
(3) the price level does not change, so that income is measured in real terms.

This economy is in fact similar to the one with which we became familiar in Chapter 6, which was represented diagrammatically in Figure 6.1, page 102. The most important observation we made there about that economy, which is now of the utmost relevance, was that total income was equal to total output which was equal to total expenditure. We can go further and say that the income was generated by the expenditure on goods and services. It was because people bought goods and services that the factors of production derived their income from the proceeds. Expenditure, in a sense, created income.

This treatment involved an *ex post* way of looking at what actually did happen, and we cannot therefore tell whether planned expenditure matched income or not. Look at it from the *ex ante* point of view. Suppose that people plan to spend, during the current year, exactly all their income. Planned expenditure exactly matches income and is precisely the right amount to purchase total output. When income is at such a level it is described as being in equilibrium. Moreover, as we shall see, there are no economic forces to bring any pressure to change the level of income.

Schematically, we have the kind of situation shown in Figure 7.1 (i). Start at position 1, with a level of income equal to the size of the rectangle below the number, determined by expenditure of the same amount. Assume that the community plans to spend the whole of its income, neither more nor less, as indicated by box 2. Expenditure is exactly enough to buy total output. Income is in equilibrium. It will remain at the same level so long as the community plans to spend all its income, as shown by the fact that the boxes labelled 2, 3 and 4 are all of the same size.

Suppose now, however, instead that the community plans to spend less than its income, as depicted in Figure 7.1 (ii). As before we start with a level of income equal to the size of the box under number 1. Planned expenditure, box 2, is less than income and is insufficient to purchase total output. The amount of income generated, box 2′, is necessarily equal to total expenditure, box 2. Income is not in equilibrium. It has fallen and will continue to do so because, in the diagram, consumers never plan to spend all of their income. Note that even when income is not in equilibrium, looking back (*ex post*) realised income is, nevertheless, equal to realised expenditure. When the year is over, the statisticians will measure income and find that it was not the size of rectangle 1, but was the same as expenditure, because $2 = 2'$.

Figure 7.1 (iii) is reproduced for symmetry. It shows how planned expenditure greater than income tends to cause income to rise. There should be no need to explain it. We should, perhaps, mention that planned expenditure greater than income is perfectly feasible, provided one has past savings to draw upon or can obtain credit from a shopkeeper, a bank, or some other quarter.

THE DETERMINANTS OF EXPENDITURE

The previous section has identified the characteristics of equilibrium and disequilibrium income. What we have done is to suggest that

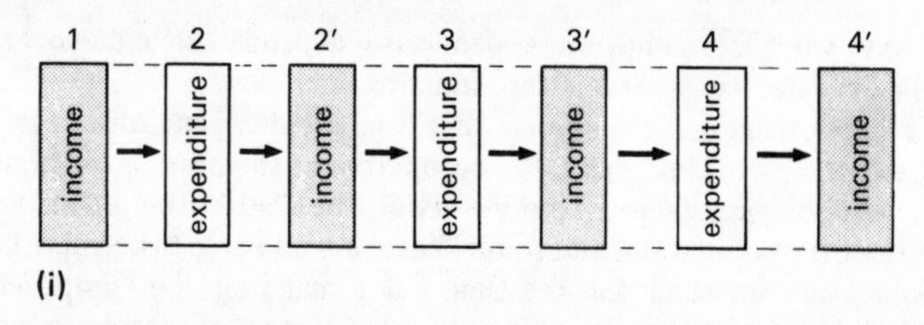

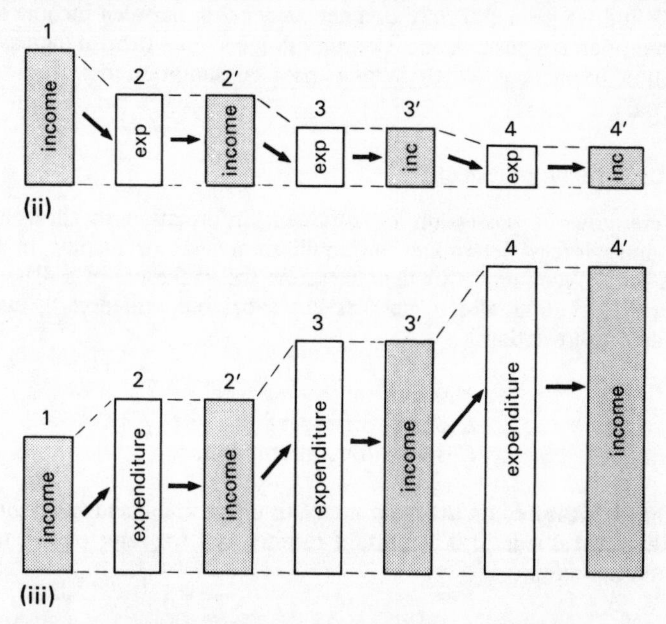

Figure 7.1 *Income and expenditure flows in equilibrium and disequilibrium. (i) Equilibrium, income constant (ii) Disequilibrium, income falling (iii) Disequilibrium, income rising*

national income will be in equilibrium when the community's spending plans exactly match its income or output. We have not explained how or why income should tend to settle at the equilibrium level.

In order to demonstrate the forces working in this direction we need some additional information. We require an expenditure function, which is the name given to the statement which describes the determinants of expenditure plans.

In the oversimplified economy which we are considering the extra information is easily supplied. There is, by assumption, only one type of expenditure, that on consumer goods and services. Hence, we need only say what consumption expenditure depends on and we have supplied the necessary expenditure function.

We know from earlier chapters that household expenditure depends on many things – family size, the occupation of the head of the household, psychological factors forming tastes, the distribution of income, the size of the population, and so on. These are all liable to be important at times, but we shall for the time being make another simplifying assumption that the only relevant determinant of aggregate consumption expenditure is total income. The assumption is fairly soundly based and we need add only that the association between income and consumption is a positive one. Consumption becomes then an increasing function of income. When income rises consumption rises too, and vice versa.

INCOME DETERMINATION

We are now in possession of sufficient information to show how economic forces determine the equilibrium level of income in our ultra-simple economy. Our demonstration will make use of a diagram, Figure 7.2. Let us also sometimes cut short our sentences by using standard abbreviations:

Y stands for income [2]
E stands for expenditure
C stands for consumption.

Income is measured on the horizontal axis of the graph and expenditure on the vertical axis. It is important to note that the same scale is used for the two axes.

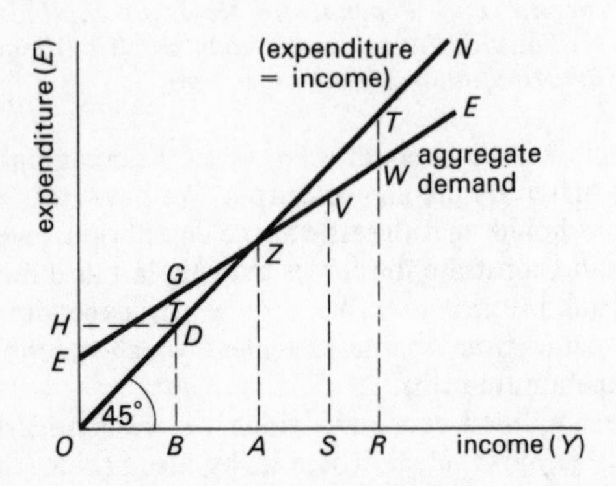

Figure 7.2 *The determination of equilibrium income.*

Let us first construct a curve of planned total expenditure or *aggregate demand.* We have assumed that the only constituent element of expenditure is consumption, which is solely dependent on income. We therefore draw the line *EE* to represent the community's planned consumption spending at every level of income. *EE* slopes upwards because we also assumed that consumption was an increasing function of income.[3] Thus if income has a numerical value represented by the horizontal distance *OB* (that is if $Y = OB$), planned consumption $= BG$. If $Y = OA$, planned $C = AZ$, and so forth. The curve *EE* is known as the aggregate demand curve, because it represents the total demand of the community, that is, its total planned expenditure at different levels of income.

Next let us inspect the line *ON*, which is drawn by bisecting the right-angle made by the two axes at the origin. *ON* is sometimes known as the 45° line.[4] At every point along *ON*, *E* and *Y* have the same value. At *D*, for instance, $OB = OH$, and so on. That is the geometry. The economic significance of the line *ON* is straightforward. Since we know that equilibrium income must occur at a level at which total planned expenditure exactly matches income, it follows that equilibrium must lie at some point along *ON*.

However, we have already drawn an aggregate demand curve (*EE*) which shows total planned spending at different income levels. Actual income, as repeatedly stated, is generated by expenditure and must therefore lie along the line *EE*. The only value of income which can satisfy the condition that expenditure is just, and only just, sufficient to purchase total output is where *EE* cuts the 45° line, *ON*, at *Z*. Hence equilibrium income is *OA*.

Consider the implications of this conclusion. When $Y = OA$, the line *EE* tells us that planned $E = AZ$. But *Z* is on the 45° line; therefore $AZ = OA$. In other words, the community's planned expenditure, the sole constituent of which is here consumption, precisely matches its income at *OA*. Total expenditure out of *OA* income is the same as total output. *OA* must be the equilibrium level of income.

The mechanism by which equilibrium is reached may be further clarified by supposing that income happens not to be at the equilibrium. If income is above equilibrium, say, at *OR*, we know from the aggregate demand curve *EE* that the community will plan to spend only *RW* of its income. This expenditure is less than income (by *WT*). If only *WR* is spent, the income generated will also be equal to *WR* – that is, less than *OR*. *OR* cannot, therefore, be the equilibrium level of income. It is too high to be sustained. *WR* is not, however, an equilibrium of expenditure, so income will not remain at this level. This can be seen in the diagram, where *OS* has been marked off equal to *WR*. At this, lower level of income, consumption expenditure (read off the *EE* curve on to the vertical axis) is *VS*. But since *V* is not on the 45° line, expenditure is still less than income. *OS* income will not, therefore, be reproduced. Income is still above equilibrium. The only level of income at which expenditure is such as to absorb total output, and which therefore reproduces itself, is *OA*.

In order to make sure that the argument is understood, let us suppose that income is less than equilibrium, say, *OB*. Planned expenditure corresponding to income *OB* is *BG*, which is greater than *OB* (by *DG*). If *BG* is spent, income generated will be also equal to *BG. OB* income cannot be sustained. It is too low. The only level of income which generates expenditure which reproduces itself is where spending plans match income, at *OA*. If income is above equilibrium, economic forces will tend to force it down. If it is below equilibrium, the same forces will tend to raise it. Only at equilibrium are there no economic pressures to change the level of income.

A SIMPLE ECONOMY

We have spent long enough with our ultra-simple economy. It is time to relax one of the assumptions which made it so unrealistic, that consumption is the only component of aggregate demand. We shall for the moment continue to deal with a closed economy without a government sector. But we shall introduce a second vitally important category of expenditure: investment.

SAVING AND INVESTMENT

Investment, it will be remembered, comprises expenditure on capital equipment, like machinery and factory building. Expansion of the capital basis of a business takes time and needs to be financed immediately, whereas returns flow in only later when output has risen. It takes place, therefore, when the economic outlook appears favourable and the costs of borrowing are relatively low. We shall have to return later to consider the determinants of investment, but we may accept for the moment that it depends on factors other than the level of income. Investment expenditure is therefore, by assumption, treated as a constant and does not change when income changes.

Our aggregate demand function now comprises two components, consumption and investment expenditures. We continue to assume that all consumption expenditures are made by households and we now add that investment expenditures are made by the business sector, which finances them by borrowing from institutions such as banks.

We have one final matter to deal with. It is one of definition so it should not cause problems. We need a word to describe the portion of income which is not spent on consumption. The term used by economists for this purpose is saving. Note that saving does not necessarily mean quite the same thing as it does in everyday speech. Saving is simply defined as income not spent on consumption. Using the standard symbols of S for saving and I for investment, our assumptions can be expressed as:

$$S = Y - C^5$$

$$I = \text{a constant.}$$

We must now examine the implications of introducing savings and investment for the question of income determination. The first observation to be made is that the basic conclusion drawn from the ultra-simple economy remains true. Equilibrium still obtains so long as the community's expenditure plans exactly match its income. The only difference now is that expenditure plans comprise spending on investment as well as on consumption.

Figure 7.3 (i) gives a schematic representation of expenditure flows in our economy which, though greatly simplified, exactly fulfils this condition for equilibrium. Households plan to spend their income on consumption or to save it. (By definition they cannot do anything else.) Investment expenditure is made by businesses, who finance their operations by borrowing. If you understood Figure 7.1, you can tell that, because the rectangle representing expenditure plans is equal in size to the income rectangle, income is at equilibrium.

The equality of planned savings and investment

There is another important conclusion to be drawn from Figure 7.3 (i). *In equilibrium,* not only does planned expenditure match income, but planned saving is equal to planned investment. This sounds good sense. If households want to abstain from consumption exactly as much as businesses want to use for investment, then total expenditure plans must match income and output.

The necessary condition for income to be in equilibrium can be expressed then as that the amount the community does *not* want to spend on consumption must be equal to the amount it wishes to spend on investment. But not consuming is, by definition, equal to saving. Therefore, the equilibrium condition can be alternatively stated as *planned savings must equal planned investment.*

There is nothing very new about this statement. It does no more than state in different words the condition we already know, namely, that planned expenditure ($C + I$) must be equal to income. We can even reinterpret income in Figure 7.1 and income OA in Figure 7.2, where

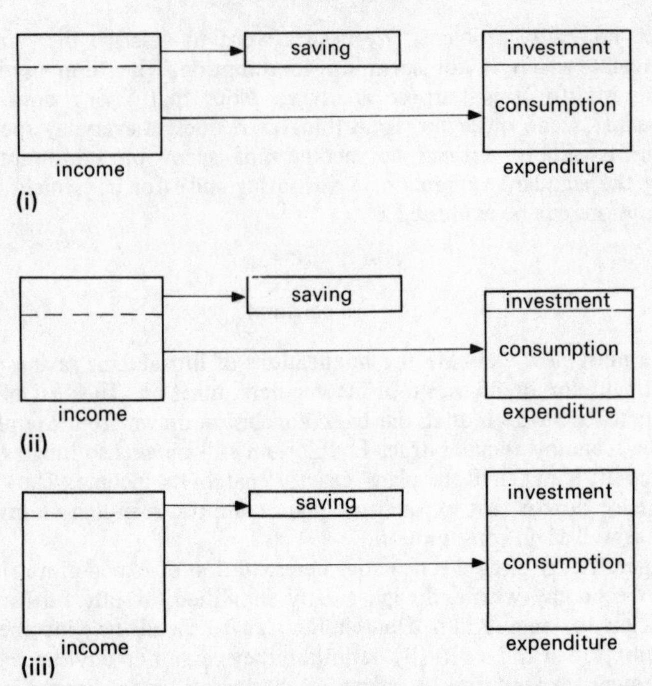

Figure 7.3 *Income and expenditure flows in equilibrium and disequilibrium: planned saving and investment. (i) Equilibrium: planned saving equals investment (ii) Disequilibrium: planned saving greater than investment (iii) Disequilibrium: planned investment greater than saving*

no investment was allowed in the model, as being equilibrium situations because savings plans were implicitly zero.

The manner of expressing equilibrium is, however, novel and may take a while to grasp. It is the key to understanding the relevance of expenditure flows to income determination. Let us try to get accustomed to this way of thinking by examining a situation which starts when income is *not* at an equilibrium level.

Figure 7.3 (ii) depicts a state of affairs when income is above equilibrium. This situation can be expressed in one of two ways, either (1) planned expenditure is less than output or income, or (2) planned savings are greater than planned investment. Both are shown schematically in the diagram by the facts that (1) the size of the two-compartment box labelled expenditure is smaller than that of the box marked income, and (2) the savings box is larger in dimensions than the investment box. The business community wants to spend less on investment than households want to give up consuming (that is, to save).

Hence there is a surplus part of income that no one wants to spend. Income does not, as it were, reproduce itself in full. It is too high to be self-sustaining and tends to fall.

Figure 7.3 (iii) illustrates the reverse situation, where planned investment exceeds planned saving; the investment section of the expenditure box is larger than the savings box. Now business wants to spend more on investment than households want *not* to consume (i.e. to save). Expenditure is larger than output. So income must be below equilibrium and tends to rise.

The explanation of why income tends to an equilibrium level where planned savings are equal to planned investment in terms of box diagrams is only a rough-and-ready method. We have used it in order to give a general idea of the way in which economic forces operate. Let us reconsider the argument with the use of a graph showing the aggregate demand curve with which we are already familiar. Figure 7.4 is in two parts. Look first only at the top half, section (i), which has axes, scale and a 45° line drawn exactly as Figure 7.2. The line *CC* denotes

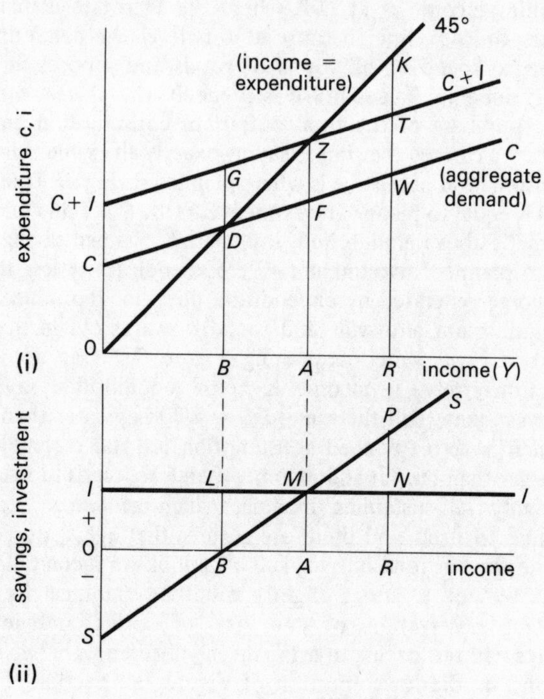

Figure 7.4 *The determination of equilibrium income, savings equals investment.*

consumption expenditure at different levels of income. It replaces *EE* in Figure 7.2, since we previously defined expenditure as being all on consumption. Investment was, by implication, zero. We now assume, however, that investment is positive, though unrelated to income. Diagrammatically, planned investment is shown as the difference between the lines *CC* and $C+I$, which is now the curve of aggregate demand. These two lines are parallel to each other because investment expenditure does not vary with income. It is $GD = ZF = TW$, that is, the vertical distance between *CC* and $C+I$.

Planned savings are not directly measurable from the diagram, but if we remember that the 45° line shows equality of income and expenditure we can measure savings plans by taking the difference between planned consumption and income. For instance, if income is *OR* (= *RK*), planned consumption expenditure is *WR*. Therefore, planned savings must be *KW*. If income is *OA* (= *AZ*), planned saving is *ZF*. If income is *OB* (= *BD*), planned saving is zero; while if income is less than *OB*, planned saving is negative – people plan to spend more than their income.

Equilibrium income is at *OA*, where the aggregate demand curve ($C+I$) cuts the 45° line, because at this level the community as a whole plans to spend on all forms of goods and services an amount equal to its income. Expenditure is precisely the correct amount to finance the purchase of the total output of consumption and investment goods. We can see that this is saying exactly the same thing as that the equilibrium level of income is where planned saving *ZF* (the 45° line minus *AF*) is equal to planned investment *ZF* (the $C+I$ line minus *AF*).

If income is above equilibrium, say, at *OR*, planned saving (*KW*) is greater than planned investment (*WT*). Expenditure is less than total output. Income generated by expenditure does not reproduce itself. It is above equilibrium and will tend to fall towards *OA* in the manner described when we were considering Figure 7.2 (see above, pages 129–30). Conversely, if income is below equilibrium, say, at *OB*, planned investment (still the same, $DG = WT$) is greater than planned saving, which is zero (planned consumption is total income). Expenditure is larger than output and income, therefore, tends to rise towards *OA*. The only self-sustaining income, which generates expenditure exactly equal to itself and therefore ensures that aggregate demand is precisely the same as total output, is the equilibrium income, *OA*.

It is convenient to use a slightly modified graphical form which allows direct observation of the size of saving and investment expenditures without having to estimate the differences between curves. This is done in the lower portion of Figure 7.4. Section (ii) of this diagram portrays precisely the same relationships as the top section (i) in a slightly different way. We measure income on the horizontal axis as before; but instead of showing expenditure on the vertical axis, we show savings and investment directly. The scales of the two portions of the graph are exactly the same. Note only the position of the zero point of the vertical scale in section (ii).

The line for planned investment expenditure is now *II*, which is drawn parallel to the income axis, because planned investment expenditure is always the same ($BL = AM = RN = GD = ZF = TW$). The line *SS* shows planned savings directly, and corresponds therefore to the difference between the *CC* line and the 45° line in Figure 7.4(i). For instance, when all income is spent on consumption, at *OB* income in section (i), savings are zero in section (ii). When income is *OR* and planned consumption is *RW* in section (i), planned saving is *KW*, which is equal to *PR* in section (ii). Equilibrium income in Figure 7.4(ii) is still *OA*, where savings and investment plans coincide, since *SS* here intersects *II*. At incomes greater than *OA*, planned savings exceed planned investment, and income tends to fall. At incomes below *OA*, planned investment exceeds planned savings and income tends to rise.

THE ROLE OF STOCKS

The meaning of the equilibrium level of income should now be clear. So should the general tendency for upward and downward changes in income to occur when planned investment is greater or less than planned saving. There is only one more basic aspect of the theory of income determination to be explained. It involves the mechanism by which economic forces tend to move the level of income towards equilibrium.

So far we have deliberately oversimplified the argument by ignoring a key component of actual investment. This is the change in the value of stocks of goods (including consumer goods) in the economy. By definition, investment expenditure embraces all output, other than that which is consumed. Therefore realised investment includes changes in the value of stocks of consumer goods held by businesses. Such changes may not be planned, in which case they play a critical role in the explanation of income movements.

To understand why this is so, let us return to the main argument and suppose that income happens to be below equilibrium. As we know, this means that planned saving is less than planned investment, or, to put it the other way, that planned expenditure on consumption and investment is greater than total output. The only way that aggregate expenditure on consumption can exceed the current output of consumer goods is by the release of stocks. Hence businesses will find that they are selling goods faster than they are producing them and their stocks fall. This *unplanned* reduction in stocks is, as previously stated, a part of realised investment. Indeed, the difference between the totals of realised investment and of planned investment must measure this change in stocks. If you like to think of it in another way, the unplanned reduction in stocks explains how it can happen that realised investment can exceed planned investment.[6]

The logic of an unplanned fall in stocks must be taken one step farther. Businesses, observing that their stocks have fallen, will understandably take action to restore them to their previous level. This will require an increase in production, requiring extra resources. Businesses will, therefore, tend to employ more labour and other factors of production, paying them additional incomes. Hence total income tends to rise following an unforeseen reduction in stocks. It will only stop rising when planned expenditure exactly equals output, that is, when income is at the equilibrium level and there are, therefore, no unplanned changes in stocks held by businesses.

The argument applies in reverse when income happens to be above equilibrium, that is, where planned saving exceeds investment. If, now, consumers spend only what they planned, while the business community spends on capital goods only what it planned, expenditure does not absorb total output and businesses find an unplanned build-up of their stocks. In these circumstances, businesses will tend to lay off workers and close down parts of factories, so as to allow stocks to fall to the lower, desired level. This action, however, sets in motion a downward movement in income.

CHANGES IN EXPENDITURE

The analysis of the previous sections has focused on the nature of equilibrium national income in the context of given spending plans. We can, however, use the same framework to examine the effects of changes in consumption or investment plans. Such changes can be handled in a manner very similar to that used for the analysis of changes in supply and demand within a market mechanism. A change in either consumption or investment which involves greater or smaller expenditure at every level of income means that the entire curve shifts.

Suppose, for example, that there is an increase in investment plans, due, say, to business men viewing economic prospects more optimistically. This would be shown in Figure 7.4 as an upward movement of the $C+I$ curve in section (i) of the diagram or of the II curve in section (ii). In both cases the new curves remain parallel to the old, provided there is still no association between income level and investment spending. A fall in consumption spending plans, due, say, to an increase in expectation of life after retirement, would shift the CC

curve downwards in section (i) and the *SS* curve upwards in section (ii) of Figure 7.4.

The propensity to save

Let us consider in more detail the possibility mentioned at the end of the last paragraph of a fall in planned consumption expenditure. The other way of looking at such a change is, of course, to regard it as a rise in planned saving. We want to ask the question what the effect will be on total savings and national income of an attempt by the community to save more of its income than previously.

The analysis can be followed with the help of Figure 7.5, which is virtually identical to Figure 7.4(ii). It will be helpful to introduce one convenient term which has not been used before – the propensity to save. The line *SS* has been described so far as the line of planned savings. It is also often referred to as a graphical expression of the *propensity to save.* As we know, *SS* represents the quantity of saving desired by the community at each income. If income is assumed to be at any given level (say, *OA*) we call the relationship between planned saving (*AG*) and income (*OA*) the propensity to save. To be even more precise, we refer to the ratio $\frac{AG}{OA}\frac{S}{Y}$ as the *average propensity to save* (APS). There is a similar definition for the average propensity to consume (APC). In Figure 7.4(i) at income *OA* the average propensity to consume is $\frac{AF}{OA}$.

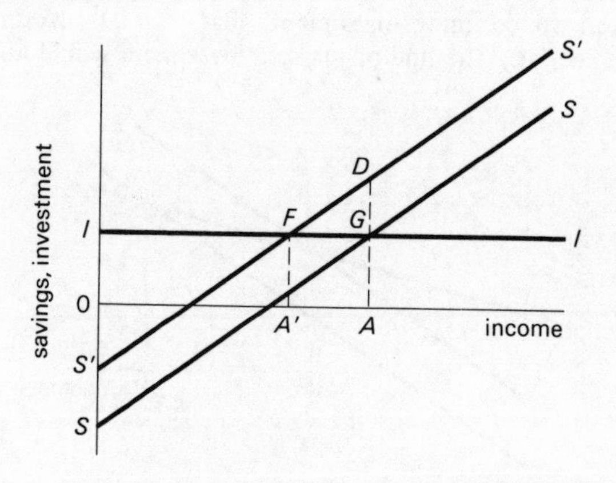

Figure 7.5 *The Paradox of Thrift (investment constant).*

The 'Paradox of Thrift'

In Figure 7.5 planned saving is equal to planned investment at income OA. Assume now we start at equilibrium, and that there is an increase in planned saving. People want to save more at every level of income than they did before. SS shifts to $S'S'$. Planned saving now exceeds planned investment (i.e. $AD > AG$), so income tends to fall, until it reaches OA', where savings and investment plans match each other, both being equal to $A'F$.

The remarkable feature of the result of this analysis, which has caused it to be known by the name of the Paradox of Thrift, is that the new level of savings in the equilibrium is no higher than before there was an increase in the propensity to save ($A'F = AG$).

The key to understanding the paradox that the desire by the community to save more did not increase total savings is to appreciate that it led to a decrease in income. At the lower level of income people want to save less. Income only stops falling when it reaches the point at which planned saving equals planned investment. Since investment is, by assumption, constant even when income falls, it is not really surprising that the situation ends up in equilibrium with savings at the same level as before.

Variable investment. The assumption that investment expenditure is given as a constant, determined by forces outside those we have been considering, is unsatisfactory. We cannot deal yet with all the theories of investment. But a plausible first approximation might be that investment is positively associated with income. It is of some interest to carry this idea over to the phenomenon of the paradox of thrift, which becomes thereby doubly 'paradoxical'. Suppose, for instance, that falling incomes lead to declining investment, that is, that investment is a function of income. The line of planned investment would not then be

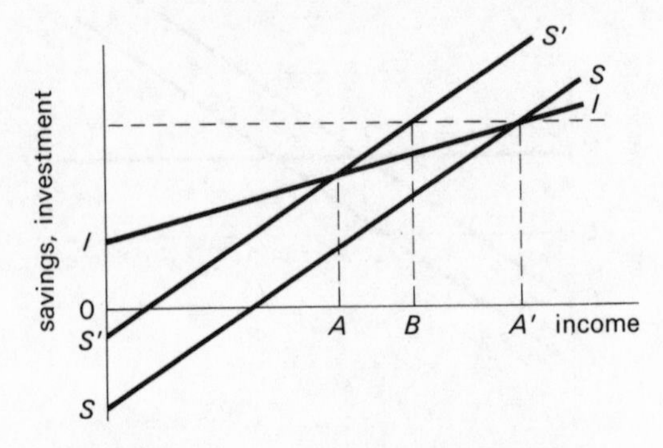

Figure 7.6 *The Paradox of Thrift (investment dependent on income).*

parallel to the horizontal axis. It would have an upward slope, like that of II in Figure 7.6, which portrays a positive association between income and investment. That diagram shows, too, that an increase in the propensity to save, such as from SS to $S'S'$, would lead to a bigger fall in income than would take place if investment did not decline when income fell. When a slump occurs, as it did in the 1930s, incomes tend to fall sharply. We can see one reason why from the second version of the paradox of thrift. Aggregate demand falls off, because of an increase in the propensity to save.* The level of income then declines, giving rise, in turn to a reduction in investment.

The multiplier

Having considered the consequences of a change in savings plans, we must next examine the effects of a change in investment. We should, by now, be sufficiently familiar with the kind of analysis to expect that a decline (or rise) in investment would lead to a fall (or rise) in income. This is likely to be true, but there is another important conclusion to be drawn. A change in investment in circumstances of the type we have been considering leads not only to a change in income in the same direction, but also a greater change in income than the change in investment itself. The relationship between a change in investment, written as ΔI and a consequent change in income, written as ΔY, between two equilibrium positions, is termed the *multiplier*.

The simplest way to explain the working of the multiplier is to introduce a last piece of terminology relating to the propensity to consume. Previously, we defined the average propensity to consume (APC) at any level of income as $\frac{C}{Y}$, and the average propensity to save (APS) as $\frac{S}{Y}$. We now define the *marginal propensities to consume and to save* as the *changes* in consumption and saving relative to the *change* in income, or $\frac{\Delta C}{\Delta Y}$ and $\frac{\Delta S}{\Delta Y}$.

An example may help to make these definitions clear. Suppose that when income rises from 1,000 to 2,000, consumption rises from 900 to 1,500. We can calculate the average and marginal propensities to consume by means of Table 7.1.

Return now to our definition of the multiplier, $\frac{\Delta Y}{\Delta I}$. Suppose investment rises by 100. Incomes of the factors of production rise at once by 100. What happens to the extra 100 of income now created? The answer is that some of it is spent, and creates additional income, and some is saved. How much of each? The MPS and the MPC tell us the answer.

*Or a fall in planned investment. See next section.

Suppose, as in our example in Table 7.1, the MPS = 0·4 and MPC = 0·6. Then an income rise of 100 leads to 40 more saving and to 60 more consumption. An increase in income of 100 will cause income to rise, therefore, by 160 (60 more than the original 100). But the process does not stop there. The extra 60 of income will again either be spent or saved, according to the MPC and the MPS. So the full rise in income, given that we are not worried about how long it takes, is a series:

$$100 + \frac{6}{10}(100) + \frac{6}{10} \times \frac{6}{10}(100) + \ldots \text{etc.}$$

or

$$100 + \frac{6}{10} \cdot 100 + \frac{6}{10^2} \cdot 100 + \ldots \frac{6}{10^n} \cdot 100$$

or

$$100 + 60 + 36 + 21{\cdot}6 + \ldots, \text{etc.}$$

The series is an infinite one which gradually approaches the limit, 250. If an increase in investment causes an increase of income of 250, the multiplier is said to be $2\frac{1}{2}$ $\left(\frac{\Delta Y}{\Delta I} = \frac{250}{100} = 2{\cdot}5\right)$.

It may not have escaped the reader's attention that the multiplier is the marginal propensity to save upside down (its reciprocal).[7] We may be satisfied with the realisation that there is a perfect, though inverse, relationship between the multiplier and the MPS. This is natural enough. Only expenditure creates income. Savings are a kind of leakage. The greater the amount of saving from any given change in income, the less extra income is created. If, for instance, the MPC was $\frac{1}{2}$, and the MPS also therefore $\frac{1}{2}$, the stream of new incomes created would be $100 + 50 + 25 + 12\frac{1}{2}$, etc., approaching 200. The multiplier would be only 2.

Figure 7.7 gives a graphical representation of the multiplier. An increase in investment from *I I* to *I′I′* raises incomes from *OA* to *OA′*. The multiplier therefore is $\frac{\Delta Y}{\Delta I} = \frac{AA'}{LM} = \frac{RM}{LM}$. Moreover, the MPS, $\frac{\Delta S}{\Delta Y}$, appears on the graph as the slope, or gradient, of the line *SS*. The steeper the line the more savings increase as income rises, that is, the greater the MPS and the less the MPC. Hence, if you drew a steeper line going through point *R*, and assumed that investment rose as in Figure 7.7, you would find that the ensuing increase in income was less than in the diagram. The multiplier would be smaller because the MPS was greater.[8]

The multiplier process helps in understanding the way in which a slump can snowball downwards. If falling incomes lead to falling invest-

Table 7.1 *Calculation of the propensity to consume and to save*

Income rises from 1000 to 2000 and consumption rises from 900 to 1500

	PROPENSITIES			
	Average propensity			*Marginal propensity*
(APC) $\frac{(C)}{(Y)}$	$\frac{900}{1,000} = 0.9$	$\frac{1,500}{2,000} = 0.75$	MPC $\frac{(\Delta C)}{(\Delta Y)}$	$\frac{1,500 - 900}{2,000 - 1,000} = 0.6$
(APS) $\frac{(S)}{(Y)}$	$\frac{100}{1,000} = 0.1$	$\frac{500}{1,000} = 0.25$	MPS $\frac{(\Delta S)}{(\Delta Y)}$	$\frac{500 - 100}{2,000 - 1,000} = 0.4$

(Note that the MPS + MPC = 1 = APS + APC, because income can only be saved or consumed.)

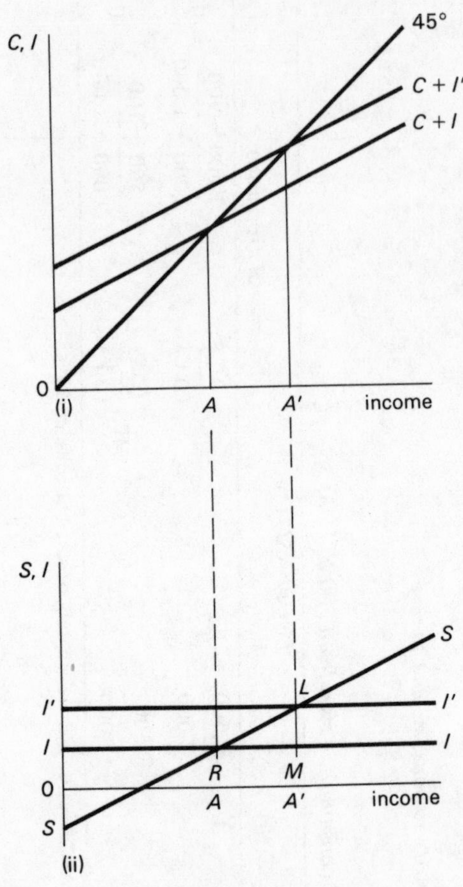

Figure 7.7 *The multiplier.*

ment, the severity of the slump is likely to be greater than otherwise. All this is what might be called the economics of depression, when income is at a low equilibrium level with mass unemployment. But the multiplier can also work upwards in the reverse direction. Once a boom gets going, if there are unemployed resources, there may be an upward multiplier effect on income. This can lead to a further increase in investment, raising incomes again and feeding on itself. In such ways the upswings and downswings of the trade cycle can take place.

MORE COMPLEX ECONOMIES

The analysis of this chapter has been very largely based upon a highly simplified model of an economy in which it is assumed that there are only two sectors, households and businesses, and where expenditure on consumption and investment has been regarded as being either dependent on income or independent of it and therefore assumed to be constant. We cannot consider all the implications for the theory of income determination that would follow from more realistic assumptions, but some indication may be given of the major extensions that would need to be made.

THE COMPONENTS OF AGGREGATE DEMAND

The set of assumptions which approximated more closely to the real world would include the following determinants of expenditure.

A Consumption

(1) Past income levels, future income prospects and the distribution of income. Household expenditure is not blindly determined by current income regardless of the past or future. And the propensity to save is, at the margin, greater for high-income groups than for low.

(2) Expectations of price changes. If prices are expected to rise there is an incentive to spend more on consumption out of current income than if they are expected to fall.

(3) The stock of wealth (including debts as negative wealth). The ownership of wealth enables consumption in excess of current income to be made. Moreover, changes in the real value of accumulated assets, for example, when prices change, may affect household savings habits.

(4) The terms and availability of credit. Current consumption expenditure may be financed by credit. For example, the rate of interest charged on hire purchase loans and the ease with which they may be obtained affects the demand for consumer durables.

(5) Goods available. Technological advance can result in new products being offered to consumers. Private consumption expenditure is also liable to be influenced by the selection of goods and services provided by the state (for example, schools and medical services).

(6) The size of the population. A growing population tends to have a larger level of demand than a declining one. Population characteristics such as age distribution and family size may also be relevant.

(7) Psychological factors. This is a complex area for economists. One is tempted to lump together here such things as the reasons which lie

behind the desire to bequeath a fortune to one's heirs and the effects of advertising on mass consumption.

A realistic statement of the determinants of consumption expenditure would not, therefore, be limited to current income. We should note that, in so far as a change may occur in the relationship between any of the above-mentioned factors and consumption expenditure, it will take the form of a change in the propensity to consume. Graphically it will appear as a shift in the consumption (or savings) function, where consumption is associated only with current income.

B *Investment*

An important distinction that first needs to be made is between new investment and the replacement of existing capital equipment as it becomes old and worn-out or obsolete. A large part of total investment expenditure in certain sectors consists of replacement demand, for example, in the vehicle industry. More generally, the principal determinants of investment expenditure are:

(1) Profit expectations. Investment is undertaken by businesses in order to increase output in the future. Hence it will take place if it is expected that sales will grow. Business confidence is, therefore, an important prerequisite for expanding investment. Profit expectations depend upon forecasts of consumer spending and upon changes in productivity such as follow technological advance. Expectations, however, are formulated in the context of the general state of business optimism or pessimism existing at any time. This is liable to be influenced by a variety of social and political factors, including overseas events and even rumours, all of which tend to make investment expenditure highly volatile at times.

(2) The terms and availability of credit. Investment is frequently financed by borrowing so that the market rate of interest which has to be paid on loans, as well as their availability, can be important determinants. For businesses which finance investment out of their own profits, the rate of interest is still relevant, since the opportunity cost of investing in one's own firm is the interest that could be earned by lending to others.

(3) Income. The possibility that income and investment expenditure might be positively associated was mentioned earlier in our discussion of the Paradox of Thrift. In fact, there is evidence that at least a part of investment seems to be determined not so much by current income as by its rate of growth.[9]

There is one matter that should be emphasised here about the determinants of savings and investment. It is that expenditure decisions on each of them are made not only for different reasons, but by quite different persons and institutions. There is reason for thinking that market forces do not quickly and automatically bring about an exact coincidence of the savings plans of households and businesses with the investment plans of businesses. Moreover, since consumption tends to be a fairly steady function of income, while investment demand is (for reasons given above) more unstable, fluctuations in total expenditure are more frequently attributed to changes in investment than to changes in consumption.

AGGREGATE DEMAND IN AN OPEN ECONOMY WITH GOVERNMENT

The final complication with which we must deal is to extend our two-sector economy to include transactions with foreigners and a government sector. The principles of income determination are not fundamentally altered by these complexities, but the components of aggregate demand and the conditions for equilibrium income need to be stated in a different form.

The presence of government affects expenditure patterns in many ways. The structure of taxes can influence both household expenditure and business investment. Transfer payments, such as to the unemployed and the retired, can likewise alter the aggregate propensity to consume of the community. However, it is convenient to regard these aspects of government activity as affecting the spending behaviour of the private sector. If this is accepted, it is the direct expenditure by the government on goods and services which needs to be taken account of. This is quite straightforward to deal with. Government expenditure on goods and services must simply be added to the total of aggregate demand.

International transactions are only a trifle more complicated to incorporate into our scheme. Expenditure by foreigners on exports is just as income-generating for businesses as domestic expenditure on home sales. So exports should be added to total aggregate demand together with government expenditure. Purchases of imports from abroad by a country's residents, however, do not create income in the domestic economy, but in those foreign countries where the imports come from. Imports should therefore appear as a deduction from the total of aggregate demand.

Using the symbols C and I that we have already met, and employing G to stand for government expenditure on goods and services and X and M for expenditure on exports and imports respectively, the aggregate demand for an economy with government and foreign sectors can be written as:

$$AD = C+I+G+(X-M).$$

In words, this equation says that aggregate demand comprises consumption demand, investment demand, government expenditure on goods and services and any export surplus. (The last item can, of course, be negative).

INJECTIONS AND WITHDRAWALS

We must draw one conclusion from this more comprehensive statement of the components of aggregate demand. It is no longer true that equilibrium income occurs at the level where planned savings is equal to planned investment. That formulation applied only to a closed economy without a government.

We can, however, restate the equilibrium conditions for an open economy with a government sector in a comparable form. Let us group together the flows which may be described as leakages or *withdrawals* from the circular flow. They are savings (S), imports (M) and government tax revenue (T). They may be described as withdrawals because they are not spent on domestic output and do not, therefore, generate income. Next, we group together *injections* of expenditure which do add to the flow of incomes. They are government expenditure on goods and services (G), exports (X) and, of course, investment (I).

The condition for income to be in equilibrium remains that aggregate demand (or planned expenditure) is equal to income or output. However, the simple equality of planned savings and investment no longer describes equilibrium. The sum of all injections and withdrawals must be substituted for it. The re-formulated equilibrium condition for an economy with both foreign and government sectors becomes:

$$\text{planned } S + M + T = \text{planned } I + X + G.$$

In other words, if income is to be in equilibrium, then all planned expenditure other than that on domestic consumption (i.e. $I + X + G$) must be exactly matched by withdrawals (i.e. $S + M + T$).[10]

KEYNESIAN ECONOMICS

The analysis in this chapter has been simplified in two ways. One is that it has been very largely based on a hypothetical closed economy without a government. We have shown that this kind of simplification barely affects the major conclusions reached on the determination of national income.

We must end the chapter, however, by drawing attention to a second kind of oversimplification, which is far more serious and far-reaching, if we want to try and apply economic analysis to the world of the present day. A major deficiency of almost all the arguments in this chapter is that they have shown the relationships between the major variables in real terms. This is because we chose explicitly to ignore the question of the general level of prices and, therefore, of inflation.

There was a good reason for this. The theory underlying the material in the chapter is substantially due to the work of the one British economist whose name is widely regarded as the greatest that this country has produced in the present century, if not for a lot longer than that. His name is John Maynard Keynes. Keynes was both an academic and a very practical economist. He taught economics at Cambridge, he advised governments of this and other countries and he even established a reputation as a successful financial speculator on behalf of his college. Keynes, however, died in 1946 and his most important work was done in the years between the two world wars. He was extremely concerned at the economic circumstances that he lived through – the depression of the 1930s, the tragic period of mass unemployment and slump – and this led him to seek to understand the causes of the troubled times. Keynes focused attention on aggregate demand, or rather the deficiency of aggregate demand, as the source of the depression. He showed through his writings a 'new' way of looking at the determination of national income, emphasising aggregate demand, which was influential in stimulating economic policies designed to pull the world out of the great depression and to prevent its recurrence. A whole new school of economics, calling itself Keynesian, grew up on the basis of his theories.

It is a matter of some controversy whether Keyne's influence would have restored the world economy to prosperity, because the outbreak of the Second World War intervened. His views, however, certainly dominated very large sections of academic economics and government policies after the war.

Keynes's ideas were, it must be remembered, largely formulated in a period of extreme depression and of stable and falling prices. They were responsible for a tremendous advance in economic understanding, but they were not intended to be of such a generality that they could explain the course of economic events at all times. The question arises, in particular, as to how far they are of applicability in a period of chronic and accelerating inflation, since they omitted some relationships which were not then considered important. This is a very controversial question indeed – perhaps the most hotly disputed economic issue of our age. We shall not be able to settle it in this introductory book. It has not even been resolved by the most distinguished economists in this or any other country. We must, however, form some acquaintance with the main issues in the debate. They centre on the one feature of the modern economy which was not a major concern of Keynes – inflation, which has since become a world problem. To understand more about the causes and consequences of inflation and its interrelationships with national income and the level of aggregate employment in an economy we shall have to consider one economic institution to which we have paid passing reference only: the nature and significance of money. To this we devote the next chapter.

NOTES: CHAPTER 7

1 We assume also that the supply and demand curves slope up and down respectively.

2 Y is the conventional symbol for aggregate income. I stands for another magnitude, as we shall shortly see.

3 EE cuts the vertical axis at E. The distance OE measures consumption expenditure which is not associated with income but is determined by all the other factors which we deliberately chose to ignore for the time being. See page 128 above.

4 The equation of ON is $E = Y$.

5 Readers of some other texts will note that $S = Y - C$ is a definition, and the proper way of expressing a definition (or 'identity') symbolically is by using a three-bar 'equals' sign $\equiv$. Hence $S \equiv Y - C$ is the correct way of writing this.

6 It also explains the following. (Let S_p, S_r, I_p, I_r stand for planned and realised S and I.) We have assumed $I_p < S_p$, but we know that $I_r = S_r$. However, something must give way, I_p or S_p. In the text we assume consumption plans are achieved, then $S_r = S_p$ and I_r cannot possibly be equal to I_p. Rather $I_r < I_p$. The difference between them is the unplanned reduction in stocks.

7 Two quick proofs of this reciprocal relationship are:
(i) The infinite series $1 + C(1) + C^2(1) + C^3(1) + \ldots$ has the solution $\dfrac{1}{1-C}$ (if $1 > C > 0$). $\dfrac{1}{1-C}$ is, of course, $\dfrac{1}{\text{the MPS}}$.
(ii) The multiplier is $\dfrac{\Delta Y}{\Delta I}$. We know, however, that $\Delta Y = \Delta I + \Delta C$, and therefore that $\Delta I = \Delta Y - \Delta C$. The multiplier may then be written $\dfrac{\Delta Y}{\Delta Y - \Delta C}$ which is $\dfrac{1}{1 - \dfrac{\Delta C}{\Delta Y}} = \dfrac{1}{\dfrac{\Delta S}{\Delta Y}}$. See note 8 for a third proof.

8 This is a third proof that the multiplier is $\dfrac{1}{\text{MPS}}$. In Figure 7.7 the multiplier is defined as $\dfrac{RM}{LM}$, and the MPS as $\dfrac{LM}{RM}$.

9 The hypothesis that $I = f(Y_t - Y_{t-1})$ is known as the accelerator.

10 Formal statements of the multiplier, the Paradox of Thrift, and so on, should also be rewritten for an open economy with a government sector. These are to be found in most intermediate texts in macroeconomics.

Chapter 8

Money

We started and ended the last chapter on notes of caution. We outlined there a theory of income determination, which was called Keynesian, and which showed that the national income in a country would be determined by the level of aggregate demand. Caution was urged on the reader because the theory was presented in a very simplified form. We omitted consideration of a variety of determinants of aggregate demand in order to focus attention on the role of income itself. Consumption, for example, was starkly said to be dependent on income and investment expenditure was regarded, most of the time, as a constant.

We shall not be able to consider all the determinants of aggregate economic behaviour in this book. One factor that has, however, been excluded is so important that it deserves a chapter to itself. It is money. The reason why we have so far left money out of the explanation of income determination is that our emphasis has been more with output than with the general level of prices. The Keynesian theory, which was used as the basis for the previous chapter, was presented very largely in real terms, that is to say, we ignored the implications for total spending that might follow from a change in the value of money, as expressed in changes in the general level of prices.

The justification for such an approach would be that money, *per se*, does not matter. Suppose the general price level doubles overnight and everybody's income doubles at the same time. Do consumers and business men behave in exactly the same way the next day as they did before?

It is a good question, by which we mean, of course, that no one really knows the answer to it! It is possible to argue that economic behaviour might be exactly the same, since real income has not altered. But it is also possible to take an opposite view, because not everyone may fully appreciate that the underlying circumstances are the same at all. There may be some kind of 'money illusion' in the minds of the members of the community which makes them believe, even if wrongly, that they are better or worse off when their money incomes rise or fall. If they believe this to be the case, they may very well behave differently and their changed behaviour can quite easily bring about changes in the real underlying situation.

The question about money and behaviour can be put simply as: does money matter? does it have, as it were, a life of its own? or, is it simply a veil, a way of measuring the value of physical outputs? The question, it has already been said, is not definitively answerable by logical argument. Nor can it be settled once and for all by observations of the facts of the real world, that is, by seeing how people actually behave when prices are changing. Economics is not always capable of giving firm answers on such questions of fact. The evidence is conflicting about the importance of money and there is a great deal of controversy among economists about who is right. Two popular schools can be identified. One are the Keynesians, who attribute a relatively minor role to money, and the other are the Monetarists who, under the leadership of the contemporary American economist Milton Friedman, believe that money matters a great deal.

The Keynesian/Monetarist controversy has probably been the most vigorously debated issue in economics in recent years. It is heavily imbued with political overtones, but the implications for economic policy which would follow from the unlikely event of either side collapsing are substantial. We deal in this chapter with some of the major issues in the controversy. Note, however, that it would be quite wrong to assume that all economists are lined up like armies on one or other side of a battlefield. It would be much nearer the truth to see them sitting in a field at the end of a rainbow stationing themselves at different positions in the spectrum, from infra-red Keynesians to ultra-violet monetarists at the two extremes. But the great majority of economists will be found at fair distances from the polar positions. Indeed, happily, one finds some from each camp shifting positions in the light of argument, debate and evidence. Our modest task in this chapter is to try and understand some of the reasons why they are involved in the controversy at all.

THE NATURE OF MONEY

STOCK OF WEALTH

Money is an asset that individuals and businesses can hold. The first important characteristic to note is that it represents a *stock* of wealth that gives its owner purchasing power over goods and services, factors of production and other things. It is conceptually different therefore from income which, as we already know, is a *flow* of receipts that accrue over time. The distinction between stocks and flows assumes considerable significance in economics. Any asset existing at a moment of time, such as money, or unused goods or materials held by a business or by a household, is a stock of wealth. Such assets must be distinguished from flows of income or expenditure, which take place over a period of time. (We have already noted that *changes* in stocks between two points of time are effectively flows. They are treated as positive or negative investment. See above, page 106.)

FINANCIAL ASSET

A second characteristic of money is that it is a *financial* asset. In this connection, money must be distinguished from physical assets, such as capital equipment and stocks of real goods and services.

There is a range of financial assets, of which money is but one. The distinguishing feature of a financial asset is that it gives its possessor a *claim* to something of value. The deed denoting ownership of a piece of real estate or a house is a financial asset, quite distinct from the property itself. A life assurance policy is a financial asset. So are shares in joint stock companies, securities issued by the government in return for money borrowed from the public and even the IOU held by the winner of a backgammon game.

These financial assets have value because they are claims to something else. The paper on which they are written is intrinsically virtually worthless, unless they happen to be old collector's items. The value of a particular financial asset is not, however, related only to the underlying real asset it represents. This is obvious when it is realised that some financial assets do not represent claims to any real physical assets at all. Some government securities were issued many years ago to raise finance to pay for the waging of wars. The guns and battleships that were purchased have long since ceased to exist. Yet people still hold some of these securities, such as 'consols', the most famous of all, which were first issued in the eighteenth century. They are still of value, not because of the physical assets that they represent, but because the government still honours its obligation to pay an annual sum, the interest, to any persons or institutions who hold consols and other government securities. The statement at the beginning of this paragraph that financial assets are valuable because they are claims to something else remains true, though in the case of government securities such as consols it is the claim to a fixed annual income that gives them value.

Money is a financial asset which shares one feature with government securities. It does not represent any particular physical asset. In another way, however, money is very different from such securities. It does not give its owner any income. You do not receive any interest from anybody on the £5 note you hold.

Money, government securities and all financial assets, however, have one much more important feature in common. They are negotiable, that is to say, they can be sold and exchanged for other things – goods and services, factors of production, or even for other financial assets. Indeed, in the case of financial assets like government securities, shares in joint stock companies and deposits in building societies, they have value which reflects the advantages that accrue to their owners, such as the right to receive periodic income. There is a market for such financial assets and we shall look at it again later in the chapter.

Money, however, as already stated, possesses no rights to income or to the ownership of physical assets. Its value stems solely from its negotiability, from the fact that it is acceptable in settlement of debts. This is one of the prime characteristics of money, which performs a number of functions.

THE FUNCTIONS OF MONEY

Three chief functions of money are usually distinguished. It acts as a medium of exchange, a store of value and a unit of account.

(1) MEDIUM OF EXCHANGE

Most transactions involving the purchase and sale of goods, services and factors of production are made through the medium of money. The existence of money avoids the need for direct barter of goods against goods. If you have a radio you wish to exchange for a camera, you will find it much easier to make an indirect sale for money, which you then use to buy a camera, than to advertise in the hope that you will find someone with exactly the opposite complementary wants to your own. Finding such a 'double coincidence of wants', as it is called, can be a lengthy, if not impossible, task. It is rendered unnecessary by money which acts as a medium of exchange.

This prime function of money is of outstanding importance in the process of production. It means that a business can pay its workers with money, which can be used to buy varieties of goods and services, instead of having to pay them with bricks, steel tubes, or whatever the company happens to produce. It is not surprising, therefore, to learn that economists regard money as a vital 'lubricant' in the economic system, allowing specialisation to a high degree by avoiding the need for individual workers (and businesses) to be paid in quantities of their own physical outputs.

To the man in the street, what he regards as money is probably just the notes and coins which he can use to buy whatever he needs. To the economist, money is both these things, but it is something very much more as well, and consists of anything which acts as a medium of exchange by being immediately *acceptable* in settlement of debts.

(2) STORE OF VALUE

Money performs a second important function in addition to acting as a medium of exchange. It is an asset which can be used to store wealth over time. This function of money derives in the main from the fact that payments for goods or services, including those for factors of production, are not always made immediately the purchase is made. Workers are rarely paid daily, even if they are on daily rates of pay. Many goods are sold on credit to households and businesses. Gas and electricity bills are sent out quarterly, cars may be bought on extended hire purchase payment systems over one or two years, houses are often paid for over periods as long as twenty to thirty years and businesses usually trade with each other by allowing a variable time for the settlement of accounts. The function money performs as a store of value is simply that it allows households and businesses to store the debts that they owe, or are owed, until the payments are made or received. This function derives from the existence of time-lags between the transactions in goods and factors and the payments for them.

(3) UNIT OF ACCOUNT

The final function of money, not unrelated to the last, is that it aids economic calculations. Economic decision-making would be difficult and imprecise if there were no money to act as a unit of account. Consider a business firm, for example. It needs to decide regularly what operations to undertake, how much to produce, whether to switch to different products, how many workers to employ, whether to engage in capital investment, even perhaps whether to close down altogether. Proper decisions can be made about such matters only if a firm can estimate the effect of any of its decisions on sales and profits. Calculations for these purposes are made in money terms and it is unthinkable that complex businesses could be run efficiently if there was no monetary unit of account in which they could be made. In a similar way, the existence of money aids households to make sensible decisions on spending and assists governments to compare alternative ways of raising revenues to cover intended expenditures.

LIQUIDITY

Money, we have seen, is a financial asset which performs a number of functions. It is able to do so for a particular reason, which has been implied, but not yet specifically mentioned. This is that money is the most *liquid* of all financial assets. Liquidity is a technical term of particular relevance to money's function of acting as a medium of exchange. In so far as all financial assets are, as previously pointed out, negotiable, this means that they may be exchanged for other financial assets. To an extent, therefore, any financial asset is capable of being used in settlement of debts. If I decide to buy a new car, for example, I may not have enough money to pay for it, but I may have some other financial assets, such as shares in a joint stock company that I can sell and use the proceeds to settle the bill for the car. However, there are two specific disadvantages to paying in this way rather than for cash. In the first place it takes time, and in the second place there is some uncertainty about how much my shares will actually fetch in the market when I sell them. There is even a risk that they will prove worthless.

There is neither delay nor uncertainty in the case of money. I can use it immediately in the settlement of any debt. I know all the time how much of it I have and that it will be an acceptable means of payment. It is true that the prices of the goods I may want to buy with money are liable to change, but that is a different matter. Ten pounds is ten pounds is ten pounds, whereas ten shares in a joint stock company may be worth £10 today, £11 yesterday and only £9 tomorrow.

This feature, which is the advantage that money has over all other assets, is known as its liquidity. Assets are said to be more or less liquid according to the speed with which they can be used for the settlement of debts and the certainty about their money values. We shall return to this subject shortly when looking at the reasons why people hold money at all. Meanwhile, we may conclude that money is the one riskless asset that is perfectly liquid, in the sense that it is immediately acceptable for the settlement of debts. Indeed one definition of what constitutes money is that it is any perfectly liquid asset. Note, incidentally, that there are many other very liquid assets, such as deposits in building societies, which can be drawn on at short notice by account holders. They are known as 'near money'.

THE DEMAND FOR MONEY

Now that we know what money is, we can ask the question why individuals and businesses want to hold it. Put like that it sounds a rather silly question. Of course people want to hold money, it is valuable. However, money, as we saw earlier, is only one of a range of financial assets.

Two characteristics distinguish money from other financial assets:

(1) it is perfectly liquid and (2) it does not yield any income to its owner. When someone holds money rather than other financial assets, therefore, he or she is opting for liquidity rather than an income. Now the question looks quite different. Why should anyone choose to sacrifice a stream of income in the form of annual payments from the profits of companies, interest from the government, and so on, in order to have a stock of money?

Three reasons are usually given for holding money. They are related to the functions that money is said to perform and are known as the transactions, precautionary and speculative motives.

(1) TRANSACTIONS MOTIVE

The first reason why people want to hold some of their assets in the form of money is simply in order to make everyday transactions. The need for a stock of money stems from the fact that receipts of both households and businesses do not usually match their payments in terms of time. A typical wage-earner, for example, is paid only once a week or once a month, but needs to pay out general living expenses continually during each period between pay-days. Some of his payments may be fairly regular, such as the daily fare for his journey to work or his quarterly fuel bill. Others may be irregular, such as a visit to the circus or repairs to a washing machine. Many payments and receipts of businesses are not synchronised, too. Workers have to be paid before goods are sold and materials have to be bought in before production can begin. Both households and businesses therefore, have a need for money to pay for these kinds of transactions.

The transactions demand for money depends on the presence of time-lags between the flows of receipts and payments that occur in the normal life of a household or a business. We can go further and say that the greater the frequency of receipts and the closer they match payments, the smaller the demand for money for transaction purposes. Moreover, the institutional and conventional arrangements for settling accounts in the economy are relevant to the demand for money. The growth of credit cards has reduced the need to hold large quantities of notes and coins for individuals and any easing or tightening of the credit allowed by businesses to each other will affect the cash requirements of businesses.

(2) PRECAUTIONARY MOTIVE

The second motive for holding money is barely more than an extension of the first. The difference between the transactions and the precautionary demands for money is that the former is a response to known needs and the latter to unknown. No one, individual or business, can be absolutely certain of all its cash requirements in the future, because we happen to live in an uncertain world. So, there is a precautionary demand for money, which people and institutions wish to keep as a safeguard against unforseen events.

The size of the precautionary demand for money, then, is related to uncertainty and, in particular, to the community's expectations about the future. The uncertainty can be about real events, such as the likelihood of being laid off work due to sickness, or it can be about financial matters. Doubts about future prices, for instance, may affect the precautionary demand for money.

(3) SPECULATIVE MOTIVE

The idea of price expectations, mentioned in connection with the precautionary demand for money, is of much greater importance for the speculative motive. In order to understand the rationale for holding money for speculative purposes it is necessary to go back to the idea of a sacrifice being made when money is held rather than any other financial asset. The opportunity cost of having money in the bank is the income that would accrue from lending it. However, there are two possible motives for buying assets for profit, only one of which is to receive income as, for example, interest or dividends from companies. The second motive is related to the capital value of the asset. People who buy securities may also be fortunate enough to make a capital gain if the price of the securities rises. If people think that the price of an asset is likely to rise, they will buy it for this reason. However, sometimes prices are not expected to rise, but to fall. Capital gains may still be made. In such circumstances the action of a speculator is to sell securities while the price is high and buy them back when the price has fallen. If he behaves in this way he will make a capital gain, just as if he buys on a rising market. But during the time that the speculator is waiting for prices to fall, he may very well increase his holdings of money, the one asset that by definition cannot change in money value.

The speculative demand for money is, therefore, related to expectations about future prices. In inflationary conditions, for example, if people expect prices to rise, and especially if they expect the rate of inflation to accelerate, they will tend to increase their spending before prices rise and, in consequence, to hold less money, which will lose its value. There is one important kind of asset that should be mentioned in connection with the speculative demand for money: securities that yield a fixed rate of interest (as distinct from a variable return, for example, with the profits of a business). Consols, mentioned earlier, are securities issued by the British government and are such fixed interest securities. The holder of consols is assured of £2.50 per annum for every *£100's worth* of them in his possession. It is a kind of IOU; a promise to pay, not a capital sum, but an annual interest. This is what gives it value. The *£100's worth* is italicised because the value mentioned is related to what is known as the *nominal* value which may or may not be its market value. It is quite likely to have been the value of the securities when they were first issued.

If the market rate of interest happens to be 2½ per cent at the time the government needs to borrow money, then it would have to offer £2.50 interest for every £100 it borrows simply in order to attract funds from other borrowers. However, the market rate of interest, as we shall see later, varies with supply and demand conditions. The piece of paper called '£100's worth' of consols may not even have the nominal value written on it. It may merely state that the holder is entitled to receive £2.50 every year from the government. It would, therefore, be worth £100 while the market rate of interest is 2½ per cent.

Suppose, however, that the market rate of interest rises from 2½ to 5 per cent, because of a generally increased demand by borrowers. If the government wants to borrow another £100 it would need to offer £5 per annum and the *new* security would be worth £100. What would have happened to the value of consols? They would, of course, have fallen in value. More precisely their value would have been halved. If the right to receive £5 per annum is worth £100, the right to the £2.50 per annum (on consols) would only be worth £50. As a matter of fact, interest rates have risen so much in recent years that consols have dropped in price to less than £20 per nominal '£100's worth', implying a rate of interest over 10 per cent.

The point of this rather lengthy explanation should now be clear. There is an inverse relationship between the price of fixed interest securities and the market rate of interest. If the rate of interest is high they will be worth less than if it is low. It is the inverse relationship between these two variables that makes possible capital gains on fixed interest securities and to that extent, therefore, affects the speculative demand for money. If speculators believe that the rate of interest is going to fall they can switch from money into fixed interest securities. If they think the rate of interest is going to rise, they will hold money rather than bonds, which will fall in price if and when the rate of interest moves upwards.

It is important not to overemphasise switching between money and fixed interest securities and giving the impression that these are the only assets in a speculator's portfolio. It has already been explained that there are many kinds of financial assets, with different degrees of liquidity and rates of return. Speculators in financial assets are liable to rearrange their holdings of all of them in anticipation of any price changes. It is the expectations about future price movement which cause switching between money and other assets that we need to emphasise under the head of the speculative demand for money.

THE SUPPLY OF MONEY

We have another stage to pass before we can return to the question of how important money is. We know what is meant by money, what functions it performs and what motives lie behind the demand for it. We need only to know where it comes from. In other words, what is the supply of money?

Let us start with the man in the street. To him, the supply of money comprises the notes and coin in circulation. These are certainly money. They fit our definition because they are immediately acceptable for the settlement of debts. In primitive societies money took somewhat different forms. Valuable goods like gemstones and even cattle performed money's functions. The more portable, durable and divisible they were, the better they served the purpose. Intrinsic value was never necessary so long as the tokens conventionally used were readily acceptable in society as a means of payment. Indeed, some things could even be *too* valuable to make good money, because they were too risky to carry about.

In complex modern societies forms of token money persist in the shape of notes and coin, but there is another quantitatively more important part of the money supply that fulfils the functions of money extremely well and is, therefore, included by economists in the total. We refer to deposits held in bank accounts. These are the most commonly used means of making financial transactions by businesses, but are widely used also by households. Current accounts carry no interest and are immediately usable. About half of bank deposits in Britain are, however, interest-bearing. They are true deposits (or deposit account balances) and may not always be withdrawable in full on demand. Anyone who has a bank current account has only to write a cheque (which is merely a standard form of a letter to his bank) instructing his banker to pay a certain sum to someone to whom he owes money for any purpose and the payment will be made without any need for transfers of notes and coin.[1]

THE BANKING SYSTEM

Since bank deposits are a major part of the money supply it is necessary to make an excursion into the nature and behaviour of banks. This is a technical subject and our excursion will be brief. (Readers are advised to refer elsewhere for detailed information about the banking system.)

The basic principle by which banks operate is, fortunately, simple enough. Banks are financial institutions whose objective is to make profits by making loans. They are able to do so very largely because people and institutions find it convenient to keep money on deposit in banks.

The business of banking may be illustrated by assuming a very simple economy in which there is but a single bank. Table 8.1 sets out the balance sheet of such a bank, which has just received a deposit of £10,000 in coin from a merchant. The two sides of the account show its assets of £10,000 of coin in the vaults and its liabilities of £10,000 to the merchant, who may, in principle, come at any time to take his coin back again.

Table 8.1 *Assets and liabilities of a bank before deposit creation*

Liabilities		*Assets*	
Deposits	£10,000	Coin	£10,000
	£10,000		£10,000

Issue of banknotes

The first observation to be made about the importance of banks in the supply of money is that the banker probably gave the merchant a receipt for his £10,000. Such a receipt, if signed by a reputable banker of good standing, constituted a claim, or financial asset, which could be negotiable, that is, exchangeable in settlement of debt. It is, in fact, a kind of banknote. If you look at a pound note you will see it is no more than a promise signed by the chief cashier at the Bank of England to pay the bearer on demand the sum of one pound. Early bankers were in fact responsible for the introduction of banknotes. The system persists to the present day, though private commercial banks are no longer allowed to issue banknotes in England. This is now the prerogative of the Bank of England.

'Creation' of bank deposits

There is a second and crucially important way in which banks are responsible for the supply of money. It arises from the fact that cheques drawn on bank accounts are acceptable for the payment of the great majority of debts. Since cheques are acceptable, bank deposits are, by definition, money as far as economists are concerned.

Let us look again at the balance sheet in Table 8.1. It shows that the bank has £10,000 in its vaults which appears also as a debit on the liabilities side of the account, representing the debt to a customer. Suppose, however, to make the example more realistic, the £10,000 was not deposited by one person but by 100 people depositing £100 each. Why should the banker keep £10,000 worth of coin in his vaults? The only reason his customers deposited money with him was that they had no immediate need for cash. If the bank examines past records of drawings on cash it will find that only a proportion of depositors want their 'money' back at any one time. It would be quite safe to keep a proportion of the total liabilities in cash, basing the proportion on past experience.

Let us suppose that the bank finds that, on average, it is safe to keep enough coin in the till to meet 10 per cent of total liabilities to depositors. What can the bank do? It has £9,000 more coin than is really needed. It is earning no interest either. Hence it would be an idea to lend it to people who want to borrow for various purposes. If the bank does this, it can make a profit by charging interest on loans.

What the bank does is indeed to make loans. But it does not need to lend out coin. The existence of the cheque system, whereby people can make payments to each other simply by writing cheques, means that it is sufficient for the bank to lend merely by opening accounts in the name of borrowers. Thus loans can be made, in effect, by creating deposits in favour of persons and institutions to which the bank lends money.

If a bank works to a 10 per cent safety rule and has £10,000 worth of notes and coin in the vaults, it will be able to make loans to the value of £90,000. The situation after the loans have been made is depicted

Table 8.2 *Assets and liabilities of a bank after deposit creation*

Liabilities		*Assets*	
Deposits	£100,000	Coin	£10,000
		Loans	90,000
	£100,000		£100,000

in Table 8.2. The bank's total assets and liabilities are now £100,000. It has liabilities to all depositors, who have the right to draw coin of £100,000, and it has assets equal to exactly the same amount – £10,000 of coin, and £90,000 of credits representing loans made.

The simplicity of the arithmetic in the last paragraph must not be allowed to obscure the importance of the result. The bank has actually *created* money, as a result of carrying on its commercial operations of borrowing and lending. The power of banks to create money is limited by the size of the safety rule to which they adhere.

In our example, the safety rule takes the form of a ratio of coin (or cash) to deposits, of 10 per cent. This allows the bank to create deposits equal to ten times the cash base it holds in its till. This credit-creating power is sometimes known as the bank credit multiplier. As can be seen from the example, the multiplier is the reciprocal of the cash ratio $\left(\frac{1}{0.1} = 10\right)$.

In the modern world there is, of course, more than a single bank. This limits the credit-creating powers of any one of them, but it does not affect the multiplier for the banking system as a whole. A more important modification is that banks do not deal in only two assets, coin and loans. They have a whole range of financial assets to choose from. In practice, they do hold cash and make loans (or advances as they are sometimes called), but they also use part of the funds at their disposal to purchase securities of one sort or another. These other assets vary in two important ways: their liquidity and their profitability in terms of the income that they yield. It is beyond the scope of this book to describe them in detail. Suffice to say that the art of banking has been described as maintaining a nice balance between profitability and liquidity – ensuring that there is enough cash to meet normal demands and enough loans at profitable rates of interest. A bank's ability to achieve this target is greatly helped by the existence of the range of financial assets available. Some highly liquid assets, like loans made literally on a day-to-day basis, provide almost as much security as cash itself. And there are other short-, medium- and long-term assets circulating in the money market. A sensible banker has a spread of assets in his portofolio. The only general statement that can be made about them here is that the higher the yield of an asset, the greater the risk likely to attach to it.

The final limitation on the commercial banks' power to create money through lending to depositors is due to the activities of the government. We shall consider the control that 'the authorities' can exercise over the money supply when dealing with economic policy in the next chapter.

THE PRICE OF MONEY

We have one last question to deal with before returning to consider how important money is. We have to say something about the price of money.

In one sense, of course, the price of money is an utterly trivial question – in money terms a pound is always worth a pound. However, in terms of opportunity cost which is, as we learned earlier, what economists are most concerned with, the price of money is a real one. It is the rate of interest that is forgone when one holds money rather than income-yielding assets. It is the interest that one receives or pays when money is lent or borrowed. We should not, therefore, be at all surprised to be told that both the supply and demand for money are affected by the rate of interest. While this statement is certainly true, it does not follow that the rate of interest is *determined* by the supply and demand for money and by nothing else, though certain schools of thought have emphasised this approach in the past.

Most prices, as we know, are determined by a variety of factors. Even the price of a simple commodity like an ice cream is determined by many variables, including its cost of production, the utility derived from ice cream, the level and distribution of income, the size and age structure of the population, the weather, and so on. The rate of interest is certainly influenced in part by the supply and demand for money, but it is affected by other variables too, because it is the price not only of holding money, but of borrowing and lending for a wide variety of purposes. Some of these are 'real' factors, for example, the demand to borrow by a business for capital investment in plant and machinery. Others are monetary such as the demand to hold cash rather than other financial assets.

THE RATE OF INTEREST

It is difficult, some might even say dangerous, to offer an elementary explanation of the determination of the rate of interest. The forces that are involved are too complex to deal with adequately in a brief introductory book. However, with the warning that the student will have to learn a great deal more about the subject in his later studies in economics, we prefer to embark on an admittedly oversimplified explanation rather than leave the subject completely obscure.

The rate of interest, expressed as a percentage, can be viewed as a reward for lending and as a cost of borrowing what may best be described as loanable funds. We can assemble some of the main constituents of the two sides of the market by considering why there are lenders and borrowers.

Demand

Two major sources of the demand for loanable funds may be mentioned. The first and more important consists of investment demand by businesses. As previously mentioned, capital investment is a time-consuming operation. A stream of yields appears only when time has elapsed after a decision to build a new factory or install a machine has been taken. Funds are needed in the meantime to enable investment projects to be undertaken. Capital is, as we know, a factor of production and it is possible to construct a demand curve for loanable funds, derived from the productivity of investment, in a manner broadly similar to the demand for labour as a factor of production described in Chapter 5.

Imagine all the investment opportunities available to a business. They could be arranged in rank order according to their productivities. Some might yield 2 per cent, others 3, 5, 10, 20, 30 per cent, and so on. The importance of the rate of interest as a determinant of the demand for loanable funds for investment is not difficult to see. If the rate of interest happens to be, say, 10 per cent, then this represents the cost of borrowing money to finance it (or the opportunity cost of not lending it for a firm providing its own finance). All investment projects yielding more than 10 per cent return on capital invested will in this case be worthwhile.[2] If the rate of interest is below 10 per cent, more investment projects will appear profitable; if the rate is above 10 per cent, fewer of them. In other words, there will be a demand curve by borrowers for investment as a function of the rate of interest and it will slope downwards to the right (as *DD* in Figure 8.1).

In addition to investment demand by businesses we can discern a demand for loanable funds by households who may wish to spend on consumption in excess of their current income, for example, to buy consumer durables on hire purchase. This demand would also be

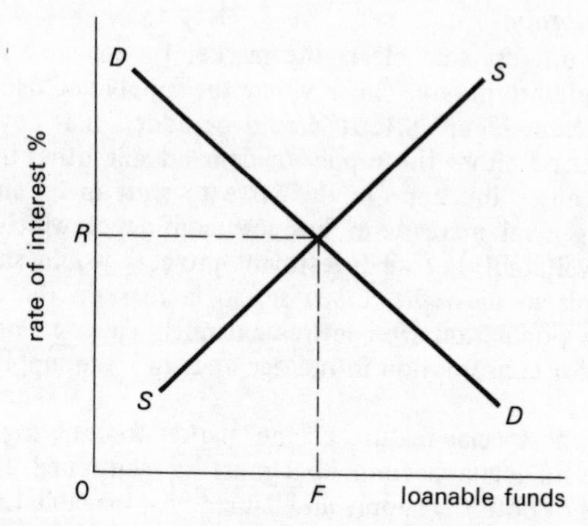

Figure 8.1 *Determination of the rate of investment.*

expected to be inversely related to the rate of interest. The higher the rate the lower the demand, and vice versa. The sum of business and household demands might, therefore, be represented by the curve *DD* in Figure 8.1.

Supply

The supply curve, *SS* in Figure 8.1, is drawn as upward sloping. This implies that the amount of loans that individuals are prepared to make rises the higher the rate of interest. In so far as lending involves the sacrifice of present for future consumption, it seems reasonable enough that the relationship should be of this kind. It assumes that, *ceteris paribus*, people prefer consumption now than in the future and, therefore, need to be paid interest in compensation for not consuming now. Moreover, the greater the compensation (the rate of interest earned) the larger the sacrifice people may be prepared to make and the greater the supply of loanable funds.

One source of loanable funds is, therefore, individuals prepared to consume less than their current income in exchange for interest. A second source consists of businesses offering funds on the market instead of investing them in their own businesses. Some further supply may comprise dishoardings of cash balances that either households or businesses are induced to make. A final source of funds of special significance are any increases in the quantity of money, including new bank loans, which, we have seen, are a form of money creation. Such changes in the money supply assume importance in connection with government macroeconomic policy. They will be dealt with in the next chapter.

Market Equilibrium

The rate of interest that clears the market for loanable funds is, as usual, the equilibrium rate. This is where the supply and demand curves intersect, *OR*, in Figure 8.1. It should be added that any change in a determinant on either the supply or demand side other than the rate of interest causes the appropriate curve to shift in its entirety. For example, a general increase in business confidence which raised the expected profitability of all investment projects would shift the *DD* curve upwards to the right. Likewise, an increase in the expectation of life of the population after retirement might cause greater provision to be made for consumption in old age and shift the supply curve also upwards.

There is one special feature of the market forces lying behind the supply curve for loanable funds that must be mentioned. It is that the determinants of both the supply and demand for loanable funds include not only the rate of interest, but also the level of income. This fact implies that it is not possible to conclude that it is necessarily the rate of interest that equates supply and demand. The equilibrating agent may at times be, not interest rates, but the level of income.

It makes a great deal of difference whether income or the rate of interest changes. Let us reconsider one of the components of the supply of loanable funds: household income in excess of consumption. This is, it may be recalled, no more than what we defined as saving in Chapter 7 ($S = Y - C$). We put forward quite a different sequence of events then. A rise in the propensity to save brought about a fall in income. This was the phenomenon of the 'Paradox of Thrift'. The reader is advised to return to this section (pages 138–9) to remind himself of the argument, which may be summarised by saying that the rise in the propensity to save increases withdrawals from the circular flow of income and exerts downward pressure on national income.

We are, therefore, in a state of uncertainty about the effects of a change in the propensity to save. On the one hand it can be argued that it tends to lower interest rates and increase investment. On the other hand, it can lead to a fall in incomes and consequent decline in the level of total saving. In both cases savings and investment are equated, but in the first situation it is the rate of interest that does the trick, while in the latter it is the level of income. It is important to know which way the economy works, because the implications of the two paths to equilibrium are different in a way that might be highly significant. The level of investment rises if interest rates play the key role; it does not do so in the second case. All that happens then is that the level of income falls.

The answer to the question about the effects of a rise in the propensity to save is that a great deal depends on the responsiveness of the supply and demand for loanable funds to changes in the rate of interest. If responsiveness is high, then the postulated increase in savings propensities will tend to force interest rates down. Moreover, if investment responds to interest rate changes rather than to other factors (such as income changes), the downward multiplier effect of the extra savings of Chapter 7 will not take place (or will be to an extent muted).

In terms of the diagram of Figure 8.1, the argument of the previous paragraph can be expressed as being about whether the supply and demand curves are relatively steep or relatively flat. It is not possible to give a very general statement about their real shape because the evidence is not clear and it is highly likely that the degree of responsiveness of supply and demand for loanable funds varies at different times. We cannot take the matter much further here. It is important, however, to point out that the appropriate macroeconomic policy to deal with output and inflation hinges critically on whether interest rates or income levels are the more important determinants of agreggate expenditure and whether changes in expenditure such as in the propensities to save and invest work their way through the economy primarily via variations in interest rates or via incomes. It seems likely that both income and interest rates are important but at times the former and at other times the latter may be dominant. The critical question is 'when?'. We shall consider these matters again in Chapter 9.

Real and nominal rates of interest

One aspect of interest rates that needs attention is the effect on them of changes in the general level of prices. Although we did not draw attention to it earlier, the absence of a clear label on the vertical axis of Figure 8.1 makes the analysis of the diagram ambiguous. There are two possible signs that could be fixed to the axis, according to whether we are measuring the rate of interest in nominal or in real terms, that is, by allowing for inflation.

If we are talking about the nominal rate of interest, then we must take account of the difference between it and the real rate. The distinction can be made clear by an example. If inflation is proceeding at a rate of 10 per cent then a money rate of interest of 15 per cent implies a real rate of return to a lender of 5 per cent.

The introduction of the rate of inflation to an extent complicates the analysis. However, one can expect that if people anticipate a certain rate of inflation to occur they will allow their behaviour to take their expectations into account. This applies on both the supply and demand sides. Exactly how behaviour will be affected depends on all the circumstances of a particular case. However, it may be said that, as a general rule, expectations of increases in the general price level would tend to push up nominal interest rates; though real rates, adjusted for inflationary expectations, may not be affected.

The structure of interest rates

A final point must be made, that our discussion in this section has been conducted as if there were only a single rate of interest, whereas it is common knowledge that there are many different rates ruling in markets where loans are made. Three principal sources of such differences may be suggested. In the first place, loans vary in the degree of risk that attaches to them. Risk differences may be due in turn to the nature of an investment project, the reliability of the individual borrower, the kind of market that the final product will sell in and similar factors. Different rates of interest in these cases would presumably carry risk premiums reflecting the relative uncertainty in each case. A second cause of interest rate differences might be variations in the periods before loans are due to be repaid. By and large, the expectation here would be for loans of short duration to carry lower interest yields than those of long term, because funds are at risk for longer. A third cause of interest rate differentials might be that the capital market is imperfect, in the sense that there are barriers to the movement of funds from sectors where interest rates are high to those where they are low. This explanation parallels that given for the persistence of wage differentials (see above, pages 93–4). Barriers may be institutional, due to information deficiencies or to the presence of monopolistic tendencies on either the supply or demand side.

There is only one other observation to be made about the existence of a wide range of interest rates for loans of different types, risk and duration. It is that businesses in the financial sector of the economy will tend to adjust their portfolios of assets to take account of any changes which affect the structure of interest rates.[3] The implications of this statement are quite considerable, but cannot be pursued further at an introductory level.

THE IMPORTANCE OF MONEY

We are at last in possession of sufficient information about the nature, supply and demand for money to bring this chapter to a close by returning to the question asked at the beginning. Does money matter? Since we are going to give two answers to the question, it would be better to state in advance that there are really two admittedly related questions in one. The first is whether the quantity of money is an important determinant of the price level and the second is whether it also exerts a significant influence on the level of real activity in the economy – on the level of national income and employment. We can make a first approach to answering these questions if we think of the national income or output as comprising a volume of physical goods and services valued at their money prices and asking how the quantity of money affects the valuation.

Reverting to symbols in order to reach one of the most celebrated equations in economics, we can denote the average price level by the letter P. The volume of output is the same as the total number of transactions that occur when the goods and services are brought and sold. We denote these by T. So we can interpret PT as a measure of the value of national output – the number of transactions that occur over a period of time multiplied by the average price level.

There is another way, however, of valuing national expenditure (which we know is the same as the national income or output). Since national output consists of goods and services valued in money terms, it can be expressed as the total amount of money in the system multiplied by a factor representing the number of times that it is, on average, used – termed its velocity of circulation. If we denote the quantity of money by the symbol M and the average number of times it is used by the symbol V, we can measure the value of national output – alternatively as the product of M times $V - MV$.

Both methods of valuation are definitively true. We can, therefore, put them together in what is sometimes known as the 'equation of exchange'.

$$MV = PT$$

THE QUANTITY THEORY OF MONEY

The equation of exchange does no more than describe two ways of valuing the national output. It does, however, employ a different approach from the one referred to as Keynesian, which was used in the last chapter. Both are concerned with aggregate demand. The Keynesian analysis stresses the determinants of *real* output, while the equation of exchange concentrates on the *nominal* value of national income and the general level of prices.

The role allotted to money in the equation $MV = PT$ provides the basis for what is known as the quantity theory of money. The feature which turns the definitionally true equation into a theory of the determination of the money value of output is the nature of V. Specifically, if the velocity of circulation is predictable, the quantity of money, M, assumes a deterministic role. Early statements of the quantity theory of money stressed the tendency for the velocity of circulation to be constant. If V never changed then an alteration in M would necessarily be reflected in a change in the nominal value of output, PT.[4]

The first question to ask about the quantity theory is whether or not V might be stable. Under certain conditions, it could be argued, V and M might change in opposite directions to each other. Keynes suggested that, in depressed conditions such as existed in the 1930s, this might indeed be what would happen. An increase in the quantity of money might in such circumstances even induce an opposite downward movement in the velocity of circulation. In other words, people would not spend the extra money. It would pile up in their bank accounts. MV would not change if M went up and V went down to cancel it out. Monetary changes would be unimportant.

Reasoning of this kind led to a disregard for the importance of the quantity theory of money. The evidence showed too that the velocity of circulation was not stable, but appeared to vary over the business cycle and, secularly, with structural changes in the banking and financial system.

However, events of recent history led to the reformulation by Friedman of a 'modern' quantity theory which does not depend on V being stable, so long as it is predictable.

The question of whether the reformulated quantity theory of money is sufficiently supported by evidence is a complex and highly controversial one with which we cannot attempt to deal adequately in this introductory book. However, it may be said that the debate hinges, to an extent, on whether economic behaviour is such as to make V reliably predictable. This in turn rests on whether it is possible to identify and quantify the factors on which V depends.

The determinants of the velocity of circulation may perhaps best be understood by recalling the nature of the demand for money, discussed earlier in the chapter (see above, pages 154–8). Given the money supply, the lower the demand by the community to hold money balances, the faster money circulates and the greater the value of V, and vice versa. All the determinants of the demand for money are, therefore, liable to affect also the velocity of circulation. They include the frequency with which payments are made and the more closely they match receipts, the rate of interest and expectations of future price changes.

These are difficult matters. They are also controversial. The evidence can be interpreted in more than one way and different schools of thought emphasise their preferred determinants of the level of output and prices. Economists adhering to the school described as Monetarist stress the critical role of the quantity of money for the nominal value of national income. Keynesian economists, in contrast, while not denying the relevance of monetary forces entirely, emphasise rather the other determinants of real aggregate demand, discussed in the last chapter. The crucial issue, where the two schools differ, relates to the sensitivity of the spending habits of households and businesses to changes in the money supply and other variables.

We cannot pretend to try and resolve the controversy here. But it is possible to argue that there might be a sense in which both Monetarists and Keynesians could both, paradoxically enough, be right – but at different times, or in different circumstances. Take, for example, the question of whether an increase in the quantity of money raises the value of national income. In periods of depression, it might seem plausible that the creation of additional money might be quite ineffective. At the opposite end of the trade cycle, in contrast, during periods of booming activity, it is equally plausible that such increases could well lead to rising nominal output by causing inflation. The former would be described as the Keynesian case, when newly created extra money was not spent but piled up in bank balances. The latter would be the Monetarist case, where excessive increases in the quantity of money showed up in inflation of the general price level.

A second explanation of how the two views of the way in which the economy functions could both be correct is that they might refer to different time periods. Economic behaviour does not always alter overnight. Changes in incomes or in the quantity of money, for example, take time before they are effective. Short-run and long-run consequences might, therefore, be very different. Few Keynesians would deny that continued increases in the supply of money would eventually affect economic behaviour. At the same time, few Monetarists would claim that a change in the money supply instantly affects spending. A part of the debate is, therefore, about how long the time-lags are, as well as whether they may sometimes be too long for comfort. One of the most frequently quoted statements of Keynes himself is that 'in the long run we are all dead'. He made this remark precisely because he wanted to emphasise short-run effects. But it can provide a clue to the resolution of some controversial issues, when two economists are engaged in disputes with different time-periods in mind.

OUTPUT AND INFLATION

There is a final important question about the effects of a change in the quantity of money that was deliberately avoided in the previous section. It is whether such a change which affects the nominal national income is a real or only a monetary one. In terms of the quantity theory of money, given V, does an increase in M leading to a rise in MV cause a change in the real volume of output (T) or merely in the general price level (P)? All we have said so far is that it may cause PT to increase.

The question can be answered only if we leave the determination of aggregate demand on one side and look at what may be happening on the supply side of the economy. To throw light on the matter Figure 8.2 has been constructed. The diagram depicts four positions of the aggregate demand curve, AD, and two aggregate supply curves, labelled AS and AS'. The latter show the quantity of output that businesses wish to supply at different average general price levels.

Consider, first, the aggregate supply curve AS and the aggregate demand curve AD. Suppose there is an increase in aggregate demand. It can be seen quite clearly that there will ensue a rise in the general price level. The reason can be traced to the fact that the aggregate supply curve is vertical at levels of output above OF. A possible explanation for the curve having this shape is that OF is 'full employment income'. If so, increases in demand cannot, by definition, raise physical output. The full effect must, therefore, be seen in rising prices, or inflation.[5] An increase in aggregate demand from AD^2 to AD^3, on the other hand, produces no upward pressure on the price level, because the aggregate supply curve is horizontal.

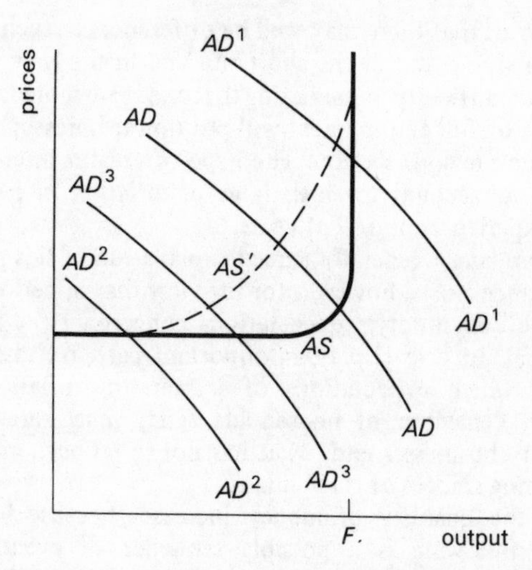

Figure 8.2 *Output and the general price level.*

The argument of the previous paragraph is capable, therefore, of showing that an increase in aggregate demand, brought about by an increase in the quantity of money (or by any other means), may sometimes push the price level up. At other times, the effect is seen, not in changing prices, but in the real volume of output. The decisive factor is the shape of the aggregate supply curve. In the case we have dealt with, the curve *AS*, changes in aggregate demand are inflationary only at output levels above full employment, *OF*. Suppose, however, the aggregate supply curve does not look like *AS*, but like *AS'*. In other words it slopes generally upwards, rather than having horizontal and vertical sections. If that is the case, then upward pressures on prices would not be confined to income levels greater than full employment, but would be much more general.[6] It is obviously important, therefore, to establish the slope of *AS*. Unfortunately, it has to be admitted that the aggregate supply curve has not been definitively plotted by economists. But in the face of the coexistence of high rates of inflation and high unemployment in the 1970s, it would appear that the curve does slope upwards over quite a substantial range.

Money and the price level

It remains to try and make clear the relationship between the quantity of money and the price level that has been referred to, *en passant*, in the previous sections. It is not easy to generalise. We have already suggested that the effect of changes in the money supply depends on the extent to which the economic behaviour of households and businesses is affected by it; that there may well be differences in such behaviour in boom and in slump and in the short run and in the long run. There is relatively little difficulty in predicting that excessive monetary expansion in conditions of full employment will put upward pressure on prices, as we saw in the previous section. The issue of greater interest is, rather, how one is to account for high rates of inflation in periods of low output, as experienced in recent years.

There is no single generally agreed explanation of this phenomenon. Wide acceptance exists, however, for the view that in periods of chronic inflation, the community's expectations concerning the future course of the general price level play an important part. We discussed earlier the way in which expectations of accelerating inflation affect the consumption behaviour of households. They must surely affect also investment by businesses and, what has not so far been mentioned, the wage bargaining stances of trade unions.

Suppose the quantity of money increases because banks expand credit. The following is a possible sequence of events. Businesses may immediately increase their investment expenditures in anticipation of selling more output. They may, therefore, take on more labour leading to a fall in the level of unemployment in the short run. What happens next depends on the response of trade unions to the new situation. This, it may be argued, depends in turn upon their expectations of the future level of prices. If the unions think that the rate of inflation is going to accelerate they may make such wage demands as would keep their living standards from falling in real terms. Such action effectively pushes up the price and depresses the demand for labour. The unemployment level may then rise again and output fall back to levels existing before the increase in the money supply.[7]

Cost and demand inflation

The argument of the previous section should have suggested that inflation is a *process*, which involves rising prices and rising wages. Indeed, one of the best definitions of inflation is no more nor less than a sustained rise in the general price level. Inflation proceeds over time and it is common to observe a game of leap-frog in motion with prices and wages vaulting upwards over each other. It is not so long since debates were common as to whether the prime cause of inflation was to be found in an increase in aggregate demand or whether there were other factors which raised costs of production and led to higher prices. The controversy was largely a sterile one in as much as increases in costs and in aggregate demand accompanied each other so regularly that the attribution of a causal role to either was difficult to establish. It is no more possible to give a definitive answer to the question most of the time than it is to decide whether the proverbial chicken did or did not pre-date the egg.

There are periods when one can observe an outstanding rise in costs, especially when they originate from overseas, such as the fourfold rise in the price of oil that followed the move by the OPEC countries in 1973. But, most frequently, one observes the shifting of both demand and supply curves. Trying to identify either as *the* prime cause of inflation is not a very rewarding task.

HOW MUCH DOES MONEY MATTER?

This chapter has been concerned with the question of the importance of money as a determinant of economic behaviour. At the end of it we have to admit that there is at present no general agreement about the answer to the question how much does money matter. The subject is highly controversial and we tried to identify major areas of disagreement between the two major schools of thought, Monetarists and Keynesians, though there are also several intermediate positions adopted by economists.

We might attempt to sum up the debate by pointing out first that there is no dispute about the fact that there is a clear correlation between the quantity of money and the level of business activity in the economy. There is no disagreement to speak of, either, about whether changes in the quantity of money can exert influence. The debates are about *how important* a factor money is and whether the observed statistical association is basically a causal one – whether, that is, money changes *cause* income changes or the causal link runs the other way round, from income to money.

Both Keynesian and Monetarist economists study the components of aggregate demand; the former stress the way in which real output is determined; the latter emphasise nominal output. The debate between them ought, in principle, to be resolvable by the facts – by how the economy does behave. The evidence from economic history is not, however, sufficiently clear to settle the controversy. Until agreement can be reached on the responsiveness of aggregate demand and supply to changes in the money supply and in the rate of interest, differences will continue.

It is difficult for any economist writing at the present time to give a totally balanced presentation of the views of different schools on the central issue of the importance of the quantity of money. We suggested earlier that the effects of changes in the money supply may vary in the short run and the long run and in conditions of chronic inflation and depression. There is also a possibility that there may be an asymmetry in the effects of *in*creases and *de*creases in the quantity of money. Not every economist would agree with these statements. The causal chains through which monetary changes work are complex. There are critical time lags involved in the processes and many of the key relationships are, as already stated, unproven.

One must, however, take some stance on the importance of money if one is to make any recommendations for the conduct of macroeconomic policy, to which subject we now turn.

NOTES: CHAPTER 8

1 If the payee has an account at the same bank as the payer it is obvious that there is no need for more than a pair of entries in the bank ledger, one credit and one debit. But even if there are several banks in the economy, it may be appreciated that, for the banking system as a whole, transfers may cancel out and only book-keeping remains to be done.

2 Investments yielding 10 per cent will also be marginally profitable in the sense that they yield the opportunity cost of capital.

3 Portfolio adjustments might also be expected to follow changes in income, wealth or price expectations.

4 An alternative approach asks whether the proportion of money income that the community wishes to hold as transactions balances, symbolised by k, is constant. V is then the same as $\frac{1}{k}$.

5 Note, incidentally, a relatively small area of income around OF where the curve is not quite vertical. This could reflect bottlenecks appearing as full employment is approached.

6 To the extent that increases in aggregate demand are not effective in increasing output, the Keynesian version of the multiplier (see above, pages 139–42) needs modification to allow for its stopping short due to inflation.

7 A more extended explanation of the role of price expectations in the generation of inflation, using Phillips curves, is given in the next chapter (see below, pages 182 ff.).

Part Four

ECONOMIC POLICY

Chapter 9

Economic Policy: I Macroeconomics

The UK, in common with all modern countries, delegates to its government certain powers which influence many aspects of economic life. We shall examine in this and the next chapter the main reasons why this is so, referring in the process to some of the ways in which the British Government tries to exercise control over the economy. The reader should be warned in advance that this is the most controversial part of the book. Economists differ from each other in their policy recommendations for several reasons. They have different views on how the economy works, largely because the evidence is capable of varied interpretations. They disagree about the most efficient policy instruments that can be used to achieve given objectives. Finally, we must recognise that economists are also citizens and they differ on the appropriate goals to adopt because they have different political views on the kind of society they want to live in.[1]

The choice between alternative economic policies is an immensely complex matter. Reaching decisions on the best policy to adopt in any situation is, moreover, further complicated by the fact that even agreed policy objectives can conflict, in the sense that the closer we get to one target the farther we may find ourselves from another. For example, a distribution of income which society regards as equitable might have undesirable effects on economic incentives. If there were such a conflict, the question would have to be asked of the relative importance of the two goals. Or, to pose it more appropriately, we might think of a 'trade-off' between equity and incentives, so that a decision could be made about how much it would be worthwhile sacrificing of one for the sake of the other. Sometimes, there may be no choice. At other times there may be and an answer to the question cannot be given without involving political attitudes.

We shall look separately at the subject of macroeconomic and microeconomic policy formation in this and the next chapter. We begin with the former for no other reason that that it follows more naturally from Chapter 8.

THE GOALS OF MACROECONOMIC POLICY

The first need is to set out the principal goals of macroeconomic policy. Three primary targets are usually distinguished:

1 Economic growth
2 Full employment
3 Price stability

A fourth goal, which is sometimes included, relates to the balance of payments. This may at times be of great importance, but it is, however, more appropriate to regard it as a *secondary* than a *primary* goal because it is sought after, not so much for its own sake, but because a country's balance of payments can act as a serious constraint on the achievement of one or more of the other goals.

(1) ECONOMIC GROWTH

The desire to achieve a high rate of economic growth sometimes appears to be almost the only fundamental target for a country to aim at. 'League tables' comparing growth rates of different countries are often constructed and simplistic conclusions drawn that the countries at the top of the league are, so to speak, winning some kind of race. It is certainly true that growth is usually accepted as a laudable objective, but the implication that the sky is the limit is hardly justified.

In the first place, economic growth is not wanted for its own sake but in order to raise living standards. In this respect the reader may remember that the growth rate of national income may not mirror precisely at all times the growth of living standards. The reasons were discussed at some length in Chapter 6 (pages 107–12) and will not be repeated here. It may be recalled, however, that it is necessary to take account of such matters as population changes, the distribution of income, leisure and other categories excluded from the national accounts. Moreover, it has to be recognised that there are costs of economic growth. Three major costs may be distinguished. (a) Growth is sometimes accompanied by an increase in economic 'bads', such as pollution and spoilation of the physical and social environment. (b) In so far as growth in future years requires capital investment in the present, it is likely to involve a sacrifice of present consumption in order that resources may be devoted to the production of capital equipment. (c) To anticipate a later conclusion, economic policies to promote economic growth may involve the sacrifice of other objectives, such as price stability or a more desirable income distribution.

A final aspect of the nature of the goal of economic growth that must be mentioned in any discussion of economic policy is that there is no known and certain way to promote growth. It is easy enough to state the obvious – that the national income will rise faster the greater the supply of all the factors of production and the more efficiently they are employed. It is a good deal harder to find ways of implementing it. How does one make managers more efficient or make labour more productive, for example? Is competition important? What is the quantitative contribution of education and training? These are leading questions, to which even leading authorities are uncertain of the answers.

(2) FULL EMPLOYMENT

The objective of keeping unemployment low is so widely regarded as being desirable that politicians almost always pay at least lip service to it. Yet as a goal it is almost inevitably a rather vague one.

Quite apart from the fact that every country has some 'unemployables' who are incapable of work, no one seriously believes that the rate of unemployment either could, or even should, be reduced to zero. A certain amount of temporary unemployment is inevitable if an economy is to grow and change its structure. Frictional and structural unemployment are the names given by economists to what are the minimum levels that have to be tolerated in the short and long run if workers and firms are to shift jobs and industries as technological and other changes call for the expansion of some sectors of the economy while others are contracting.

The unemployment target is often expressed as a percentage of the total labour force out of work. Such a figure can be misleading because the total numbers are ambiguous. They are commonly restricted to those persons actively seeking work (and registering at employment exchanges for the purpose). But this number is likely to vary with the state of the labour market. When unemployment is high, for example, some potential workers, married women for instance, may not bother to register.

An alternative target runs in terms of the ratio of the numbers of unemployed to the numbers of job vacancies. If the only unemployment is structural, this ratio should in the long run be approximately equal to unity, though if expanding sectors are less labour-intensive than contracting ones the short-run ratio may be higher. If there is a deficiency of aggregate demand in the economy the unemployed should outnumber the vacancies, and vice versa. Even equality between vacancies and job seekers may be unsatisfactory for the individuals concerned. If there are 1,000 unemployed shipbuilders on the Clyde, it is no comfort to know there are vacancies for 1,000 shorthand typists in London. Government policy to improve job and geographical mobility, both of workers and of industry, is usually undertaken for this kind of reason.

(3) PRICE STABILITY

Curiously enough there is nothing obviously and inevitably unsatisfactory about price instability itself. Yet inflation, which is a particular form of price instability, has in popular belief come to be thought the scourge of our times. Is there any substance to the belief?

The first thing to be said is that a kind of price instability is regarded, similarly to a certain degree of unemployment, as being part of the cost of economic advance. Prices act as signals reallocating resources as technological and other underlying factors change and a degree of variation in prices is, to an extent, helpful.

The price instability that causes concern, even alarm, is not, however, of relative price movements in individual sectors but of the *general* price level. It is inflation – creeping, persistent, accelerating – that is the butt of current onslaught. On the face of it we might wonder why? We argued earlier that if prices doubled overnight and everyone's income and assets doubled at the same time, real underlying economic circumstances need not have changed at all.

The point of repeating this illustration is that it focuses attention on *why* circumstances are not precisely the same when the price level changes. There are three principal reasons. The first two concern the allocation of resources and the third, the size of the national income.

Consider first the distribution of income before and after the doubling of the general price level. It is surely most unlikely that every single person would receive twice as much as he did before. Some individuals would perhaps only get a 50 per cent rise while others got 150 per cent or more. Although *total* personal income doubled, there would be gainers and losers. In inflationary conditions, this is what generally happens. We can identify the gainers as those whose incomes keep ahead of prices and the losers as those whose incomes lag behind. At different times the gainers and losers may vary, but the former include those with substantial market power, such as businesses selling goods where demand conditions facilitate upward price adjustments, or labour in strong trade unions. Individuals whose incomes are fixed in money terms, for example, widows living on annuities or recipients of state security payments which are not revised upwards to allow for rising prices, are obvious losers.

Inflation affects the value of assets as well as incomes. Holders of cash balances lose, by definition, while owners of assets the prices of which rise faster than the general level are gainers. An obvious example of the latter is houseowners. Between 1970 and 1979 average house prices roughly quadrupled, while the index of retail prices only tripled. Creditors tend also to lose, relative to debtors, in so far as debts fixed in money terms are easier to repay with depreciating currency.

Inflationary circumstances distribute resources in ways other than would occur if prices were steady. This is particularly important when price rises are substantial or accelerating and when uncertainty about future inflation rates is great. Lending becomes risky, especially for long periods. So, too, does borrowing in the face of uncertainty about future costs of production. Productivity may then be adversely affected. Inflation stimulates the acquisition of assets like works of art, coins, stamps and wine, rather than productive investment, as individuals search for safe hedges against rising prices. The result of inflation may therefore be to impede economic growth and affect total national output.

A complete answer to the question of whether inflation really is the scourge it is often accused of being must, therefore, take account of both its real and its distributive consequences. We cannot make any generally useful assertions about whether the latter are equitable or not any more than we could conclude that the redistribution that would be involved if inflation were halted overnight would or not be fair. We should minimally know the financial circumstances of gainers and losers to offer an opinion; even then we should find it difficult to avoid making political value judgements. It must be remembered that continuing inflation tends to become accepted as a fact of life, with the result that arrangements are made by which an increasing number of incomes are more or less automatically adjusted to the cost of living.

The argument that the real rate of economic growth is held down by inflation (which also affects a country's international competitiveness) is a potentially serious one. In cases of 'moderate' inflation the issue is debatable. When the rate of inflation is *accelerating*, there is less doubt about it. Moreover, it is necessary to take notice of an extreme case. Occasionally the rate of increase in prices has reached runaway proportions, as in Germany after the First World War and Hungary after the Second. When such hyperflation, as it is called, sets in, prices jump astronomically, even hourly. All faith in the currency is lost and people resort to barter, with commodities like cigarettes and coffee assuming money's role as a store of value. This can bring the economy to a state of virtual collapse and call for draconian measures to restore confidence.

In cases where the rate of inflation is moderate and economic growth not affected, we may conclude that a stable price level might be preferable to one that was rising, but that there is no compelling reason for giving the conquest of inflation absolute priority over other objectives of economic policy. The issue is perhaps best put as a question asking what are the benefits of reducing the rate of inflation by a certain amount and what are the costs, in terms of sacrifices of other objectives which might have to be borne to achieve it. This leads us to consider whether there are any 'trade-offs' whereby inflation can 'buy' any economic advantages. This is one of the central problems in macroeconomic policy of the present day.

UNEMPLOYMENT VERSUS INFLATION

The expression 'trade-off' is no more than an application of the notion of opportunity cost to economic policy. When economists talk about a trade-off between inflation and unemployment, they imply that there may be a conflict of objectives and that a choice may have to be made between them. In other words, a reduction in inflation could 'cost' more unemployment and vice versa.

The first question that must be asked is whether there is or is not such a trade-off at all. Discussion of this crucial issue cannot be conducted without reference to the work of the New Zealand economist, the late A. W. Phillips, which has been so influential that some simple facts to which he drew attention have become known as the 'Phillips curve'.

Phillips was interested in the historical relationship between wages, prices and unemployment in Britain over the period 1861 to 1957. The close association that he observed between wage rates and unemployment is illustrated by the curve *PC* in Figure 9.1. The statistics suggested

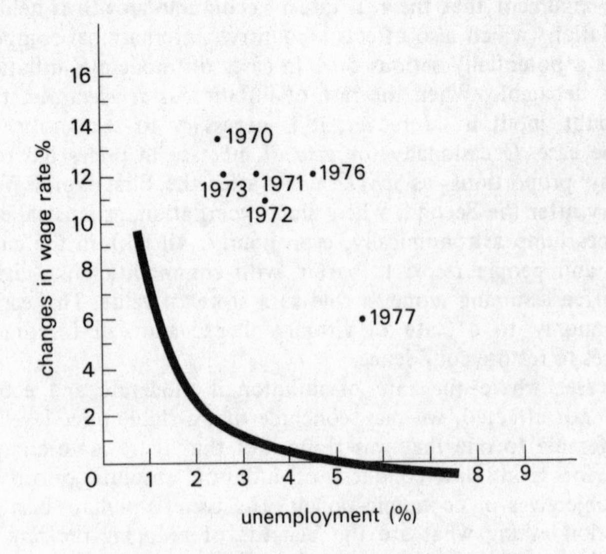

Figure 9.1 *The Phillips curve (1861–1957).*

Source: Phillips, A. W., 'The relation between unemployment and rate of change of money wage rates in the UK, 1861–1957', *Economica*, n.s., vol. XXV, no. 100 (1958).

that the strength of the excess demand for labour explained both the level of unemployment and the rate of inflation. They also implied that, for policy purposes, a trade-off existed and that it was a fairly stable and predictable one. As can be seen from the graph, unemployment tended to be low when price increases were high and vice versa. Interest attaches to the point where the Phillips curve cuts the horizontal axis – around 5½ per cent, which is the unemployment rate at which price stability would appear to occur. It should be added that this result carries with it the implication that about 5½ per cent unemployment is the rate to ensure stability in wages as well as prices, if there are no increases in productivity. Historical trends show, however, a tendency for productivity to rise over time. The conclusion should be amended to allow for this. Assuming an annual average increase in productivity of about 2 per cent for example, price stability could be maintained if wage increases were held around 2 per cent per annum and the associated unemployment rate became a little under 2½ per cent.

Work along the lines of Phillips's study was soon under way in other countries, where reasonably stable relationships between inflation and unemployment were found. However, after the mid-1960s the nature of the relationship appeared to change. Ten years later, predictions from the old Phillips curve differed so greatly from the facts that the curve began to be described as dead. The observed associations between the rate of change of prices and the level of unemployment for some recent years are shown in Figure 9.1 as single points marked with dates. They are well off the original curve. To show the utter failure of history to repeat itself, one can even refer, for example, to the year 1974, when unemployment was standing at 2½ per cent and wages were rising at about 30 per cent (so far off the curve it cannot be shown on this graph). According to Phillips's calculations wages should have been rising by no more than 5½ per cent at this level of unemployment.

What had happened to the Phillips curve? Had it disintegrated, or were the recent observations points on one or more new Phillips curves to the right of the old, that is, had the curve shifted, temporarily or permanently?

It is an important question. Disintegration would imply the disappearance of any trade-off between unemployment and inflation. Shifting, in contrast, would imply a trade-off, but a different one – specifically, that price stability could be bought only at the cost of higher unemployment levels than previously.

The new observations relate, of course, to the period of the 1970s discussed previously, when high unemployment coexisted with high rates of inflation (see pages 120–1). A great deal of work has been done to try and identify the causes of the changes in the situation and effectively, therefore, to discover what happened to the Phillips curve.

Numerous theories have been put forward to explain the new relationship. It has been suggested that the higher levels of employment associated with given rates of inflation might be due to increased trade union power, higher rates of social security payments and the narrowing of wage differentials, which price unskilled workers out of the market.

THE ROLE OF EXPECTATIONS

One explanation requires special attention. It calls for the introduction into the analysis of the expectations of the community about the course of future rates of inflation.

The proposition is that the association that Phillips found derived from experience of periods when the general level of prices was fairly stable. In an inflationary age, in contrast, it is argued, people do not ignore the fact that prices are rising. They come to expect them to continue to do so and they incorporate their expectations of future price movements into their behaviour. The argument applies both to businesses and to labour. Consider the attitude of trade unions to wage negotiations (and assume for simplicity that there are no changes in productivity). If unions expect the price level to rise by, say, 10 per cent, they need to achieve a 10 per cent wage increase to maintain the standard of living of their members. If businesses have the same expectations, they will also expect to be able to raise prices by 10 per cent. They will, therefore, be prepared to grant 10 per cent wage increases. A 10 per cent inflation rate ensues.

Price expectations can be incorporated into the type of diagram used by Professor Phillips by the expedient of drawing, not one, but a set of, short-run Phillips curves, each of which corresponds to a belief held at a particular time about future movements in the general price level. The original Phillips curve assumes that the price level is not expected to change (dubbed therefore 'naive' in an inflationary age). It is PC^1 in Figure 9.2. Each of the other curves is drawn on the assumption of different price expectations, which are built by labour into wage bargains in order to maintain constant *real* wages in the face of rising prices. PC^2, for example, is the curve pertaining to an expected inflation rate of 10 per cent. It is the curve that shows the relationship between inflation and unemployment when the community expects inflation to run at a 10 per cent rate. PC^3 and PC^4 are the short-run Phillips curves corresponding to 20 per cent and 30 per cent inflationary expectations.[2]

The diagram may be used to illustrate the situation described above of continuing 10 per cent inflation. If the community expects the price level to rise by 10 per cent, then the Phillips curve applicable to its behaviour is PC^2. Suppose that the economy is at full capacity output, which corresponds to a level of frictional and structural un-

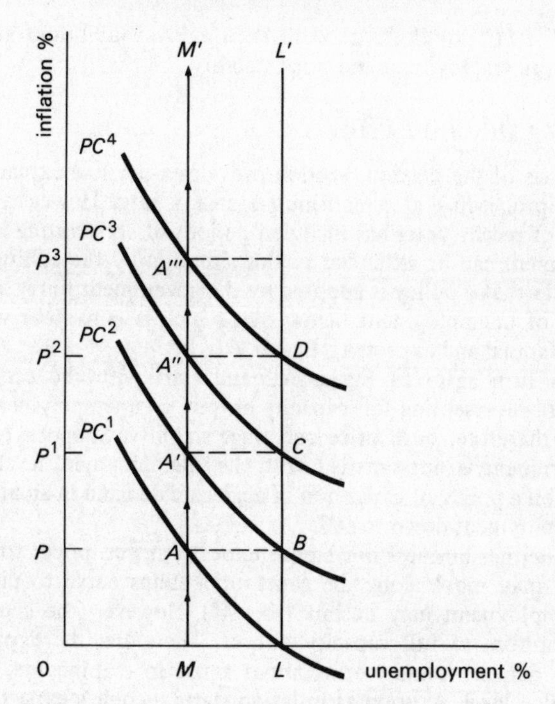

Figure 9.2 *Shifting short-run Phillips curves.*

employment equal to *OL*. Labour seeks a 10 per cent wage increase to keep real incomes constant, because it expects prices to rise by 10 per cent, and both take place. Let us draw a vertical line through *L* (*LL'*) to show the level of unemployment associated with full capacity output, but which, as we shall see, might be associated with a range of rates of inflation. The economy will be in equilibrium at *B* in the diagram, where the short-run Phillips curve (PC^2) cuts the line *LL'*. This position is consistent with expectations of the price level rising by 10 per cent and with those expectations being realised. Indeed, if expectations continue unaltered, the economy may rest at an equilibrium position, such as *B*, with continuing inflation of 10 per cent. If no outside influences to act as disturbances occur, one might expect such to be the case. Expectations may not unreasonably be related to past experience.

Note, however, that all the points of intersection of short-run Phillips curves with *LL'* are positions where expected and actual inflation rates are the same. Each shows a different rate of price increase. The economy could be at rest at any of the points *B*, *C* or *D* with inflation proceeding steadily at the rate corresponding to the Phillips curves PC^2, PC^3 or PC^4. It could even enjoy equilibrium at *L*, representing full employment and price stability.

ACCELERATING INFLATION

The analysis of the previous section provides a possible explanation of inflation proceeding at a continuous steady rate. However, the experience of recent years has included periods of *accelerating* inflation. The argument can be extended to this situation by the addition of an assumption that a policy is adopted by the government to try and bring the level of unemployment below that which is consistent with zero inflation (actual and expected), that is, *OL*.

Let us turn again to Figure 9.2 and start with the economy at position *L*, representing full capacity output, an unemployment rate of *OL* and, therefore, both price and wage stability. Suppose, now, that the government is not satisfied with the unemployment level *OL* and embarks on a policy of expansion of aggregate demand in an attempt to get unemployment down to *OM*.

Since neither business nor labour expects, as yet, prices to rise, the economy may move along the short-run Phillips curve to position *A* and unemployment may decline (to *OM*). However, the economy is, by assumption, at full capacity output. Therefore, the expansion in aggregate demand cannot bring about a rise in real income, but only in the price level. As soon as inflation starts, people's expectations of continued price stability are liable to be revised. If we suppose that the rise in prices is 10 per cent and that rate is expected to persist, then labour will need to bargain for 10 per cent wage increases in order to maintain *real* wages. The relevant Phillips curve is no longer PC^1, but PC^2 (expectations of 10 per cent inflation). The economy moves to position A'.

If we assume that the government continues to try to keep unemployment down to *OM*, it will need to induce a further expansion in aggregate demand to enable business to pay the wage increases demanded by labour (which were not expected). The same argument applies again, that output cannot be raised beyond full capacity, so the effect of the increase in aggregate demand can only be seen in further rises in the general price level. Let us suppose that this is another 10 per cent, so that prices rise 20 per cent above the original level. When this happens, it will become apparent to trade unions that wage increase of 10 per cent was insufficient to maintain constant real wages. They therefore bargain for a further 10 per cent wage rise, making 20 per cent in all. The short-run Phillips curve, PC^3, corresponding to inflationary expectations of 20 per cent, then comes into play (replacing PC^2). The economy moves to position A''. But this is not a position of equilibrium and the level of unemployment *OM* can only be held if aggregate demand is yet further expanded. Such an expansion would cause the price level to rise yet again, bringing forth expectations of even higher inflation. If labour continues to bargain to maintain real wages, the Phillips curve shifts upwards once more, and the economy moves towards A'''. The time path of the economy, when the government follows a policy which allows aggregate demand to expand in order to keep unemployment down to OM, can be viewed as follows: ever-upwards movements vertically along MM', with the short-run Phillips curves shifting also upwards as expectations of accelerating rates of inflation replace each other.

The critical elements in the explanation of accelerating inflation described in the previous paragraph are (1) the incorporation of price expectations into bargaining over real wages and (2) the policy of trying to hold the level of unemployment below that which is associated with full capacity output and price stability. The analysis follows from the assumptions. It is another matter whether it is also a valid description of economic behaviour in this, or any other, particular country. On this question opinions vary. Figure 9.2 can, however, aid understanding of three possible situations: (1) accelerating inflation corresponding to upwards movements along MM', as just described; (2) a choice of stable rates of inflation at different points on LL' at full capacity output and unemployment equal to OL (including zero inflation at L); and (3) a choice between unemployment and inflation involving a movement along a Phillips curve.

The key question is which of the three alternatives represents the real situation? It is one of fact, but there are many opinions on the matter. We may illustrate two extreme views with the use of Figure 9.2. The school of thought which believes that a trade-off exists assumes that it is possible to move along a Phillips curve, sacrificing price stability for lower unemployment levels, or vice versa. Such a possibility is denied by those who argue the opposite view, that the Phillips curve shifts upwards as expectations are revised in the light of experience of inflation. For them, the long-run Phillips curve is vertical, along LL' (or possibly MM' with continued expansion of aggregate demand). There is no possibility of a trade-off according to this argument. One simply cannot reduce unemployment in the long run without accelerating inflation.[3]

An intermediate position is a trade-off possible in the short run but impossible in the long run. This was, as a matter of fact, described at the start of this section on accelerating inflation, where the economy started at position L and moved, in the short run, to the left along the Phillips curve PC^1, as aggregate demand was expanded to reduce unemployment, but entailing higher prices. It was attainable in the short run only until the Phillips curve shifted to PC^2 as a result of incorporating revised expectations about the future of the price level. Without further expansion of aggregate demand, equilibrium would have settled at *B*, with continuous 10 per cent inflation of wages and prices.

The importance of the previous analysis for macroeconomic policy is considerable. If there is a real possibility of trade-off, in the short or in the long run, between unemployment and rising prices, then there is a choice facing the government about how much inflation it is worth tolerating in order to secure a given level of unemployment. However, if no trade-off exists, there is no point in trying to keep aggregate demand at a level that keeps unemployment below that associated with full capacity output, unless one is prepared to tolerate accelerating inflation. In the long run even this may prove impossible.

UNEMPLOYMENT AT FULL CAPACITY OUTPUT

The conclusion reached in the previous paragraph hinges to a considerable extent on the meaning given to the phrase 'the rate of unemployment compatible with price stability and full capacity output'. This rate has been termed the 'natural' rate of unemployment, but it may be defined as the rate at which there is no unemployment caused by a deficiency of aggregate demand; that is, all unemployment is frictional or structural.

From a policy point of view, concern is minimal if this level of unemployment associated with full capacity output is relatively low and stable. However, if it is high, and especially if it is rising, problems arise because, by definition, frictional and structural unemployment is not curable by expansion of aggregate demand. In practice, it is difficult to know what the level of structural unemployment is that cannot be cured by expansionary policies. The evidence is not easily interpreted, but there are reasons for believing that the rate may have been rising in recent years as a result of technological advance. This would follow if expanding industries have been less labour-intensive than contracting ones. More unskilled workers (or workers with the wrong skills) would then have been released than could be absorbed by capital-intensive new industries.

In circumstances of this kind, the most effective means of reducing the level of unemployment would lie in the direction of policies aimed at increasing labour mobility, for example, retraining programmes and subsidies in support of geographical mobility, when expanding and contracting sectors are highly localised far apart from each other.

This is a very controversial policy area and an emotive one because of the human misery that is associated with heavy unemployment. The advocates of maintaining high levels of aggregate demand argue that it is worth risking a certain amount of even accelerating inflation to keep the economy right up to full capacity output so that new industries are continually encouraged. Those opposed to this policy are not necessarily any less concerned with the social costs of high rates of unemployment. They press the more strongly for policies related directly to increasing mobility simply because they regard this, structural, unemployment as being unalterable by the expansion of aggregate demand; that is, they do not believe in the existence of a long-term trade-off whereby the government can 'buy' less unemployment with higher inflation.

We cannot pursue the matter further here. There are distinguished economists on both sides of the fence as well as many adopting intermediate positions. It is, however, a relevant point of departure for the examination of the alternative instruments of macroeconomic policy between which governments can choose.

THE INSTRUMENTS OF MACROECONOMIC POLICY

We have deliberately chosen to lead into the discussion of the alternative instruments of economic policy on a controversial note in order to emphasise that a major reason why policy recommendations among economists differ is disagreements about some important aspects of exactly how the economy functions. Different schools have their own ideas of the determinants of economic behaviour and prescribe accordingly. Until we improve our understanding of the nature of certain economic forces, we have to live with this state of affairs.

With this realistic, if discouraging, opening, we may consider that the authorities have a number of alternative instruments that can be employed to achieve the macroeconomic targets of economic growth, full employment and price stability. Three groups are usually distinguished: fiscal, monetary and prices and incomes policies.

(1) FISCAL POLICIES

Fiscal policy is the term given to measures which aim at the control of aggregate demand by budgetary means. It developed from a Keynesian view of how the economy works, which was described in Chapter 7. Governments using fiscal policy to counteract depressions, for instance, adopt budget *deficits*, increasing spending and/or reducing taxation to add to overall purchasing power. Figure 9.3 illustrates the technique of fiscal policy to counteract a depression due to a deficiency of aggregate demand. Government expenditure is added to the consumption and investment expenditure of the private sector. Aggregate demand is pushed up from $C+I$ to $C+I+G$ leading to a rise in

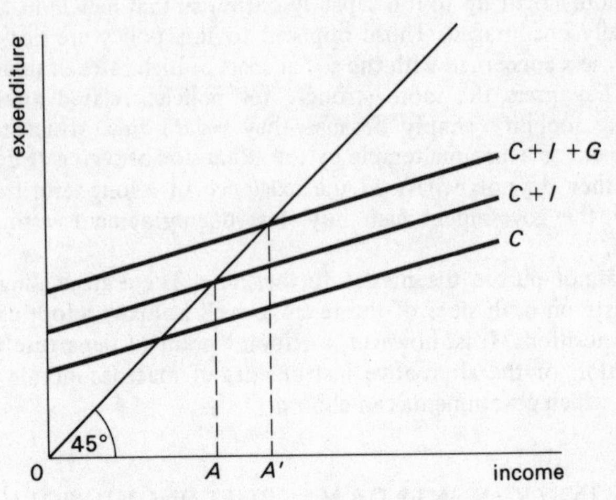

Figure 9.3 *Fiscal policy.*

income, through the action of the multiplier, from *OA* to *OA'*. In boom conditions, fiscal policy takes the form of budget *surpluses* to reduce the pressure of total demand.

Fiscal policy may call for discretionary decisions to alter the size of government income and/or expenditure. But it is important to note that most tax systems contain some so-called 'built-in stabilisers'. For example, progressive income taxes have the property that their yield automatically increases as income rises and vice versa. It is true that some other taxes work differently, for example, those fixed in money terms (like TV licences and the duty on alcohol and tobacco). However, it has been estimated that the net effect of inflation is to raise government receipts in the UK. This is known as 'fiscal drag'.

In addition to changing direct demand by the government, fiscal policy also includes budgetary changes aimed at altering private expenditure on consumption and investment by varying the structure of the tax system, for example, by shifting tax rates on lower and higher income groups, who tend to save different proportions of their incomes.

We shall return to consider the merits and demerits of fiscal policy after we have dealt with alternatives. It may be said now that fiscal policies were extensively used in the earlier postwar years, but that it is debatable whether their effects were on balance stabilising or destabilising. The reason for the debate is largely that it is difficult to know how the economy would have behaved had there been no fiscal intervention by the government.

(2) MONETARY POLICY

Fiscal policies are particularly suitable for dealing with depressed output and employment in times of falling (or stable) prices. They have been criticised as being inapplicable to inflationary periods and, in particular, to occasions characterised by the coexistence of high inflation and high unemployment in the 1970s. The monetarist school of economics, whose views of the way the economy works underlines much of Chapter 8, developed largely as a reaction to what were regarded as the deficiencies of Keynesian emphasis on fiscal policy.

Monetary policy attempts to influence aggregate demand, employment and the price level by controlling the quantity of money and interest rates. The institution which is used to operate monetary policy for the government is the central bank – in Britain this is the Bank of England. Its activities are to a considerable extent technical and the reader is advised to seek full explanations of these elsewhere. However, the mechanism is important and we must briefly explain the basic principles by which a central bank can implement monetary policy for the government.

It will be recalled, from Chapter 7, that the main component of the money supply in a country consists of the deposits of commercial banks. It will also be remembered that these banks keep to a safety rule that requires them to hold a certain proportion of their assets in liquid form, described as 'cash'. It must now be added that the commercial banks' cash base includes balances in accounts at the central bank. These are available for use (in the same way as are the commercial bank deposits by individuals) to settle their debts to other banks, to members of the public and to the government.

The central bank is able to exert pressure on commercial banks' lending activities (and, therefore, on their deposit-creating powers), in so far as their liquid cash base can be varied. One of the ways of doing this is known as 'open market operations'. This is a technique whereby the central bank buys or sells securities on the open market. If, for example, it is desired to reduce the supply of money, the central bank sells securities. These are bought by members of the public, who pay for them by writing cheques on their bank accounts in favour of the government. This has the effect of reducing the size of the commercial banks' balances at the central bank, that is, their cash base. It therefore depresses their cash ratio and, if this was held at the limit of the safety margin, will put pressure on them to make fewer loans. Bank deposits therefore tend to fall. The opposite procedure is adopted if it is desired to increase the quantity of money. The central bank then buys securities on the open market, adding to the cash base of the commercial banks.

The Bank of England

The way in which the Bank of England controls the money supply in this country is a good deal more complicated than that implied by the simplified process described in the last paragraph. A major reason for this is that the commercial banks hold more than the two kinds of assets, cash and loans, implied in the illustration. Their assets cover a wide range of financial securities of differing degrees of liquidity (and profitability). They include some very highly liquid loans made 'overnight', or 'at call', as well as others like Treasury Bills which are short-term government securities, repayable three months after issue. The commercial banks maintain what they regard as balanced portfolios of assets and the fact that they hold those of different kinds suggests an alternative technique of monetary control which is employed. Certain of its liquid assets can be specified and the banks required to maintain a minimum ratio of them to their total deposits.[4]

Other techniques of monetary policy are used in this country. Calls are made for the banks to place deposits in frozen accounts at the Bank of England. These are known as 'Special Deposits' and may be altered by the Bank from time to time. Alternatively, the banks may be asked, formally or informally, to restrict their lending operations in periods of monetary restraint.

All the policy instruments described so far are related to control of the quantity of money directly. They may also, however, be directed towards interest rates, which may influence spending. For instance, an increase in the money supply might succeed in pushing the rate of interest downwards, thereby encouraging investment (and perhaps even consumption) expenditure. The opposite consequences for interest rates might follow if the quantity of money were decreased. The Bank of England can also try to influence interest rates directly in a number of ways. The best-known of these makes use of what is called the minimum lending rate (MLR), the rate of interest at which the Bank is always prepared to make loans to City institutions. When this policy instrument is used, as a matter of convention, changes in MLR announced by the Bank of England tend to filter quite quickly through to other market rates of interest.

Economists who favour monetary rather than fiscal policies to control the economy stress the inadequacies of the latter. They are inclined to view aggregate demand as responsive to monetary forces, both to the quantity of money and to the rate of interest, and they are sceptical of the power of fiscal policy to deal with the twin aims of full employment and inflation.[5] Special criticism is given to the effects on the private sector of fiscal policy which takes the form of budget deficits. The so-called 'crowding out hypothesis' is a contention that increases in government expenditure tend to push up interest rates and, as a result, merely succeed in replacing private expenditure which is, as it were, crowded out. An associated criticism is that government borrowing to finance expenditure in excess of taxes is inflationary. Attention is directed to the public sector borrowing requirement (PSBR) which can increase the liquidity of the banks and feed inflationary increases in the money stock.[6] All this implies that the Keynesian multiplier analysis (see above, pages 139–43) may exaggerate the effect of fiscal policy on real national income if a part is reflected only in rising prices.

(3) PRICES AND INCOMES POLICIES

Economists of what might be described as a middle-of-the-road school believe that both fiscal and monetary policies should be used in pursuit of the economy's macroeconomic goals. Some hold that a prices and incomes policy can provide useful support. This applies particularly in cases of cost inflation. But it is also thought that such policies could influence inflationary expectations and, in the short run at least, temper any accelerating tendencies.

Prices and incomes policies set targets, or guidelines, for price and wage increases designed to reduce inflation. At the most ambitious level they may aim to keep the growth of money national income in line with productivity. If trade unions and businesses can be induced to lower expectations about future inflationary rates, it may be argued, this could ease the task of controlling the money supply without adversely affecting either output or employment.

The evidence of the success or failure of past attempts by UK governments to set guidelines for wage and profit increases and maximum prices for products is that they have been more successful in the short run than in the long run. Pressure on wage rates tends to build up while income policies are in force, only to be released, sometimes with a bit of a bang, later on. Such policies also have other drawbacks. For trade unions, they interfere with the process of free collective bargaining. They also tend to affect wage differentials, in so far as lower-paid workers are treated relatively favourably and skill premiums fall. The last effect may also be seen as indicating a distorting influence on the way in which prices serve as resource allocation devices. If *relative* prices are held more or less constant, the price mechanism is impeded in its allocative function of directing resources into their most profitable uses. Finally, it should be added that total enforcement of prices and incomes policies is difficult, if not impossible, to achieve. Black markets are encouraged by maximum price controls and individual groups in strong bargaining positions tend to be treated as 'special cases'.

THE BALANCE OF PAYMENTS

Before turning to discuss the controversial issue of choice between policy instruments, it is necessary to refer to the balance of payments, which was mentioned earlier as sometimes acting as a constraint on a country's macroeconomic policies.

We learnt, in Chapter 6, that the balance of payments is an account of the international transactions made between the residents of a country and the rest of the world over a period of time. These transactions comprise payments and receipts for visible and invisible imports and exports and flows of funds for investment. It is important to examine the principal factors on which the size of these flows depends. Three determinants may be distinguished: (1) incomes, (2) prices and (3) rates of interest.

The influence of each of these determinents on the balance of payments may most simply be explained in the context of a world in which there are only two countries. Let us call them H, standing for the home country, and R, standing for the rest of the world. First, changes in incomes affect the balance of payments because a part of income is normally spent on imports. Consider the position from the viewpoint of country H. If incomes rise (or fall) in H, its residents will tend to spend more (or less) on imports. If incomes rise in R, on the other hand, this carries the implication that foreigners will buy more goods and services from H, whose exporters thereby benefit from increased sales.

Secondly, relative prices affect a country's balance of payments in so far as demand and supply of internationally traded goods are responsive to price changes. If, for example, inflation is proceeding more rapidly in H than in R, this means that H's general level of prices is rising relative to that of R, making its exports and its domestically produced goods less competitive with R's.

Thirdly, relative interest rates affect the flows of funds for investment purposes on the capital account of the balance of payments. If rates of interest in H fall relative to those in R, funds will tend to flow from H to R in search of the highest rates of return.

The effect of relative prices on the size of trade flows needs further elaboration. In so far as a rise in the price level in H causes the *volume* of exports to fall, it does not follow that their *value* will also be lower. The value of exports is price multiplied by quantity ($p \times q$). The reader will recall that the effect of a fall in the price of a good on total outlay by consumers depends on the elasticity of demand for the product. The same is true of the value of exports and imports after reductions in their prices. In order to know the balance-of-payments effect of relative price changes, we need information on the elasticities of demand for traded goods. The numerical values of such elasticities are, of course, empirical matters. Provided the elasticities are, however, large enough, changes in relative prices will lead to changes in the values of imports and exports in the same direction as volume changes. If this is in fact the case, it follows that relatively more rapid inflation in H than in R would lower the values of H's exports and increase the value of its imports, thereby tending to bring pressure on H's balance of payments.

EXCHANGE RATES

It is necessary to add an important qualification arising from the fact that each nation values its goods and services in terms of its own national currency. There is, then, a question of the *rate of exchange* between currencies. £1 may sell, for example, for $1.00, $1.50, $2.00, or whatever the rate of exchange happens to be. Since the rate of exchange is a price, we should not be surprised to learn that the dollar–sterling rate is liable to be affected by the supply and demand for dollars, that is, the quantities offered and demanded at different exchange rates.

Let us continue the same example and assume that H's currency is sterling and R's is dollars. We can identify the sources of supply and demand for dollars to include the following. The demand for dollars comes from importers in H, who need foreign exchange to buy R's exports. The supply of dollars comes from exporters in H, who wish to convert the proceeds of their sales to R into their own currency (pounds).[7]

We must now reconsider the effects of a rise in the rate of inflation in H when the rate of exchange is brought in as a variable. The rise in prices in H relative to R is in domestic prices, *expressed in sterling.* It will not necessarily be reflected in prices *converted into dollars.* This depends on the sterling–dollar exchange rate used for conversion. The rate may be unchanged or variable. If it is fixed, domestic and foreign prices move together. Any change in the sterling prices of H's imports or exports will be accompanied by exactly equivalent price changes in terms of dollars.

The rate of exchange may, however, be allowed to vary with changes in the supply and/or demand for dollars. If so, we must examine the way in which these forces affect the exchange rate. Let us look, first, at the effect on H's exports. The fall in demand for H's exports following their price rise means a fall in demand for sterling to pay for them. *Ceteris paribus*, lower demand tends to bring price down. The price of sterling on the foreign exchange market is the number of dollars it is worth. Hence a fall in its price simply means that it is worth fewer dollars. This can be described as a downward movement in the exchange rate, or a *devaluation* of sterling. The argument can be clarified with an example. Suppose H exports cars priced at £4,000 each. When the exchange rate is £1 = $1, the dollar price of a car, for importers in R, is $4,000. Assume that inflation raises the price of H's cars to £5,000 each. The dollar price will change by an amount depending on the sterling–dollar exchange rate. If the value of sterling falls to £1 = $0.80, the car would still be priced at $4,000.

The supply and demand for foreign exchange can, therefore, affect the size of currency flows through variations in the exchange rate. Such movements may offset changes in domestic price levels in different countries – that is, the rate of exchange can act as an equilibrating force.[8] In our example, relatively rapid inflation in H tends to make exports less competitive, but the devaluation of sterling tends to offset this price disadvantage and thereby helps maintain, or restore, equilibrium on the balance of payments.

There are, moreover, similar forces acting on the import side. Inflation in H makes foreign goods relatively cheaper and domestic consumers tend to buy more imports in consequence. However, devaluation of sterling tends to counteract the relatively lower *dollar* price of imports, making foreign goods dearer in terms of *sterling*.

Provided the elasticities of demand[9] are great enough and other conditions are favourable, the rate of exchange can maintain equilibrium in currency flows and automatically offset disturbances which would put the balance of payments of a country under pressure. However, freely fluctuating exchange rates may be considered undesirable. This is, in fact, one of the reasons why the balance of payments has been described as sometimes acting as a constraint on domestic economic policy. Countries may take steps, alone or in collaboration with others, to stabilise their exchange rates. Indeed, internationally agreed fixed rates of exchange operated for many years (see below, pages 198–9).

Exchange rate stability has been considered desirable for a variety of reasons, including questions of national prestige. But a major objection to very volatile exchange rates is the fear that they might inhibit international trade in goods and services. An exporter who is worried that the rate at which he can convert foreign earnings into his own currency might move unfavourably, for example, may perhaps decide not to export at all.

Capital flows

The argument has a certain validity.[10] Exchange rates have occasionally passed through periods of great volatility, such as when there have been runs of so-called 'hot money' away from a country in which confidence has suddenly dropped. Heavy selling of a currency tends to lead to large falls in its exchange rate. We should look into the capital account of the balance of payments for sources of large changes in the supply or demand for foreign exchange. As mentioned earlier, there we find flows of funds for investment seeking the highest return on capital. Such flows are sensitive to interest rates in the money markets of different countries. They are also liable to be affected by expectations of movements in the rate of exchange itself. If, for example, dealers anticipate that the value of sterling *vis-à-vis* the dollar is likely to fall, they tend to sell sterling and buy dollars before the devaluation takes place. Such a switch of funds would, *ceteris paribus*, bring about the very devaluation expected. Anticipation of a rise in the value of sterling could have the opposite effect.

Speculation can be soundly based, reflecting expert views on the basic soundness of an economy, the likely future course of inflation, productivity and international competitiveness, and so on. It may also, however, be based on unreliable, flimsy evidence or political fears. Panic can occasionally set in and lead to large-scale flights of short-term capital away from a currency, putting immense pressure on its exchange rate and causing serious economic consequences. This is the type of instability that governments particularly try to avoid by insulating the exchange rate from the free play of market forces.

BALANCE-OF-PAYMENTS POLICIES

We may now return to the policy question with which we began. The reason why the balance of payments can act as a constraint on domestic economic policy is that countries try to ensure that international currency flows are kept roughly in balance, at least over a reasonable period of time. This implies the necessity to prevent any sustained reduction in the flow of receipts, relative to payments, for any purpose which would depress the exchange rate. We may distinguish four basic policy options for the government of a country under balance-of-payments pressure: (1) use up reserves of foreign exchange and/or obtain loans from abroad, (2) take action designed to alter domestic incomes, prices and rates of interest, (3) use the exchange rate as a corrective mechanism and (4) intervene directly in international markets.

(1) USE OF RESERVES AND FOREIGN LOANS

The first alternative is to use up reserves of foreign exchange and seek loans from other countries (and international organisations), thereby increasing the supply of foreign currencies to offset a downward pressure on the exchange rate. These can be no more than relatively short-term solutions. Reserves are limited and foreign loans will not be indefinitely forthcoming, unless other action is also taken.

(2) DEFLATION

The second set of methods is aimed at domestic incomes, prices and interest rates. A country suffering from balance-of-payment pressure would be called upon to reduce aggregate demand, lowering incomes and, therefore, the demand for imports. It would also try to lower its domestic price level in order to promote the sale of exports and to make home production more competitive with imports. Finally, it could also seek to raise the rate of interest in order to attract flows of capital into the country in search of higher earnings. Deflationary fiscal and monetary policies may aid in bringing down incomes and prices and in raising interest rates, but they are likely to be resisted internally in so far as economic growth might be inhibited and if the level of unemployment is already high. However, if a country in this situation does nothing about its balance of payments, some or all of these consequences may ensue naturally from the operation of market forces. In particular, falling exports and rising imports lower the national income (refer back to Chapter 7, pages 145–6, if you have forgotten why), thereby tending to restore equilibrium to the balance of payments.

(3) EXCHANGE RATE VARIATIONS

The third solution is to use the exchange rate as an instrument to reduce the imbalance between international flows of payments and receipts. Devaluation is normally called for when there is an excess of demand over supply for foreign exchange.[11] The mechanism by which exchange rates operate has already been explained. Its efficiency depends, as we saw, on the responsiveness of exports and imports to price changes. There is, however, one important consideration that has not yet been mentioned. In so far as devaluation increases the domestic prices of imported goods, it raises the level of home costs and prices, thereby reducing its effectiveness. Strict accompanying monetary and fiscal policies may be needed to inhibit such inflationary effects of devaluation.

The extent to which exchange rate variation can be used *as a policy instrument* depends on whether the rate of exchange is fixed or flexible, that is, allowed to vary with the forces of supply and demand in the market. During much of the nineteenth and twentieth centuries exchange rates were fixed by the operation of what was called the gold standard. Under this system, countries maintained a stable price of gold in terms of their own currencies. This effectively fixed the rates of exchange between the currencies of all countries on the gold standard. More recently, since the early 1970s, most nations have adopted variable exchange rates, though governments nevertheless continue to exercise some influence on the rate of exchange by intervening in the market – buying and selling foreign currencies.

(4) DIRECT INTERVENTION

The final set of policy instruments available to one country suffering pressure on its balance of payments involves direct interference with international transactions. Attempts to cut expenditure on imports, for example, can be affected by the imposition of tariffs (import duties) and quotas. Exchange controls can also be used to restrict the outflow of foreign currency for travel, investment, and so on. Taxes and subsidies can encourage exports and the production of substitutes for imports. Direct intervention of these kinds has two signal disadvantages. In the first place, it interferes with the international division of labour whereby countries specialise in the production of goods and services for which their particular endowments of factors of production best suit them. Students may recall the discussion of the principle of comparative advantage and the gains from specialisation and trade that it can create (see pages 27–9 above).

The second disadvantage of direct controls is that they may lead to retaliation. When a country restricts imports, this necessarily means a fall in exports for others, who may retaliate. Tariff wars can ensue. The resulting proliferation of 'beggar-my-neighbour' policies may be self-defeating all round and depress the volume of world trade.

We may close this discussion of international economic policy by emphasising the interdependence of nations. They are bound together as a result of international flows of payments and receipts for all purposes. Movements in incomes, prices and interest rates in one country have inevitable repercussions on others. If one country suffers balance-of-payments pressures and its exchange rate falls, at least one other country 'enjoys' a rise in its exchange rate which, it is important to add, may not always be viewed as an advantage, since it reduces the competitiveness of its exports in world markets.

Countries have, therefore, profound interest in each other's economic development and policies and in maintaining a high volume of world trade. A number of international organisations have been set up at various times to try and co-ordinate the aims and objectives of nations in the interests of all. The best known, on a broad front, are the International Monetary Fund and GATT (the General Agreement on Tariffs and Trade), but international co-operation also takes place on a smaller scale, such as by members of the EEC in the Common Market.

THE CHOICE OF POLICY INSTRUMENTS

We turn back from balance-of-payments problems to consider the difficult question of how to choose between the three major sets of policy instruments: fiscal, monetary and prices and incomes policies. This is a highly controversial matter, as must be clear from the way attention has been drawn in this chapter to alternative views of the manner in which the economy functions. Different policy recommendations are, at least in part, attributable to varying beliefs about the causes of economic events and the sensitivity of economic behaviour to different stimuli as well as about the length of time that policy instruments take to work.

MONETARISM VERSUS KEYNESIANISM

As we have pointed out, economists are often grouped into two leading schools of thought on macroeconomic policy, Monetarist and Keynesian. So long as it is not forgotten that many individuals stand in intermediate positions, such a simple division may help in understanding the principal differences in the basic attitudes of the two schools.

They start from a common agreement that it is important to emphasise. The statistics of past history show an unquestionably high correlation between changes in the quantity of money and changes in the money value of national income, in many countries and at many times. A major point of difference between Monetarists and Keynesians, however, relates to the nature of the *causal* chain between money and income. For the former group the causal sequence goes from money to income, that is, changes in the quantity of money *cause* changes in income. Keynesians, in contrast, do not deny that this may sometimes occur, but they believe the causal chain is frequently the reverse, that is, that changes in income *cause* changes in the quantity of money. The statistics cannot prove conclusively that either side is correct.[12]

The importance of money to the policy prescriptions of the two schools arises from the fact that they have different views of the sensitivity of certain key categories of economic behaviour to changes in the quantity of money. They would move much closer to each other if it could be established that savings and investment were highly sensitive to changes in the rate of interest (Monetarism), or were mainly determined by other factors, such as income and the state of business confidence (Keynesianism).

Many of the controversies encountered in the last two chapters reflect these basic differences about how the economy works – for example, whether there is, or is not, a trade-off between unemployment and inflation in the short and in the long run; whether inflation is always due to an excess of aggregate demand or can arise from the cost side; when changes in aggregate demand lead to changes in output or in the price level; how much unemployment is purely structural and, therefore, incurable by increasing aggregate demand; whether expanding public expenditure raises incomes or merely 'crowds out' private investment expenditure; and so on.

One important aspect of the choice between policy instruments is how long they take to work. Two kinds of time-lag are involved: those delaying the implementation of policy and those delaying its effectiveness. The preference of Monetarists for monetary policy partly reflects doubts about the speed with which fiscal policy changes may be made. Although there are some built-in stabilisers in most tax systems, discretionary fiscal policies can take time for evidence to be collected, interpreted and acted upon by policy-makers. Moreover, given the delays in the production of some essential data, the policy needs of the moment may turn out to be quite different from those indicated by recent history. When it is recognised, too, that there are sometimes important errors in the data themselves, it is fair comment that the economic forecasting essential for proper policy decisions is far from perfect. Monetarists, therefore, tend to prefer reasonably straightforward non-discretionary rules relating to the rate of growth of the money supply, which should be designed to lead to price stability and the steady growth of output in line with long-run productivity trends. Keynesians, in contrast, are more concerned with the time-lags after policies have been put into effect. There seems little doubt, for example, that contraction of the money supply works a good deal more quickly on the level of output and employment than it does on the price level. The reluctance of Keynesians to rely on monetary policy as the sole instrument for the control of inflation reflects concern for the short run, when output falls well before the price level is brought down.

It must be added that there is a certain fundamental difference between Monetarists and Keynesians on the question of whether the economy contains sufficient self-correcting mechanisms. The former school believe that it does and, moreover, that there is little hope or point in trying to rush them, because any attempts in that direction often turn out to be ineffective or, worse, counter-productive. Keynesians, in contrast, do not deny that, given enough time, economies will solve many of their own problems. They could hardly argue otherwise. Every slump in history has eventually been followed by a boom. The Keynesian emphasis is, rather, on the short-term costs, both economic and social, of inaction. It seeks to avoid years of low-capacity output which has, arguably, been amenable at times to government intervention.

Finally, one is forced to admit the existence of different political and philosophical stances between schools of economists about the role of government and the priority that should be given to economic growth, price stability, full employment and the distribution of income. Economists are citizens and it is unrealistic to imagine that they are never influenced by personal political views. Monetarist policies tend to be attractive to political conservatives, who are less tolerant of government influence in the economy. Keynesian solutions, on the other hand, appeal more to those who are relatively optimistic about the effects of giving power to the state.

In conclusion, it must be said that it is virtually impossible for any living person to be totally objective about these controversial matters. The author is alive and well and the reader is entitled to know his position in so far as it affects the presentation of the problems of macroeconomic policy. To end, therefore, with a personal view, I would submit that the differences between Keynesians and Monetarists are often exaggerated. Both schools recognise the key role of aggregate demand, but have different views on how and how much to try and regulate it. One suspects that policy disagreements would be greater in periods of inflation than in those of heavy depression. Hence, were there a repetition of the extremely low output, production and employment on the scale of the 1930s, many Monetarists and Keynesians would welcome both fiscal and monetary expansionist policies. In the inflationary conditions experienced since the 1970s, the contrast between the policy recommendations of the two schools is greater. However, both agree that inflationary expectations may play a key role in the inflationary process. This has led a number of economists of both persuasions to see some place for prices and incomes policies, at least occasionally and, in the short run, specifically in order to exert influence on such expectations. There is agreement, too, on the desirability of increasing mobility in the economy to counteract structural unemployment that accompanies technological advance. Extremist views will doubtless continue to be heard on both sides, but if we can improve our understanding of the way the economy works they are likely to move closer together. For the present, we have to live with the debate continuing.

NOTES: CHAPTER 9

1 For a careful discussion of the problems of economic policy formation, see Hartley, K., *Problems of Economic Policy* (Allen & Unwin, 1977), chs 1–3

2 They are known by the clumsy title of 'expectations augmented Phillips curves'.

3 The argument of this section is based on the assumption that expectations are based on past experience. It is not the only possible one. If businesses and workers correctly anticipate all future price changes, aggregate demand cannot increase employment even in the short run. All the economy can do is to move up (and down) LL' in Figure 9.3. This is the implication of adopting what have been called rational expectations, when the community is so well informed that it anticipates all relevant changes before they occur.

4 The ratio of liquid 'reserve assets' (as they are called) to total deposits could, in principle, be varied in accordance with policy needs. This technique is not used in the UK.

5 There is, however, doubt about the extent to which the Bank can control the *real* quantity of money (that is, the money supply adjusted for changes in the price level) unless it can also control inflationary expectations.

6 Public sector borrowing may be inflationary when it raises the liquidity of the banks. But the evidence is that by no means all of PSBR borrowing is of this kind.

7 Importers and exporters in R will demand and supply sterling; the former to purchase H's exports, the latter to convert the sterling proceeds of their sales to H into their own currency.

8 According to the Purchasing Power Parity theory of exchange rates, a given percentage change in relative domestic price levels is fully reflected in percentage changes in the rate of exchange between domestic and foreign currencies.

9 Elasticities of supply are also relevant, as readers of more advanced texts will find out.

10 Market forces can provide means of reducing the risks of suffering from exchange rate movements. 'Futures' markets exist where one can buy or sell foreign currency for delivery at a future date, but at a price stated at present.

11 If the elasticities (of demand and supply) are extremely low, revaluation upwards might be a remedy.

12 See below (pages 244–5) for an explanation of the difference between statistical correlations and causes.

Chapter 10

Economic Policy: II Microeconomics

We have considered, in the last chapter, problems of macroeconomic policy. It is the turn of microeconomics and we now deal with policy issues relating to the allocation of resources. Some of these have already received attention in earlier parts of this book and we shall be referring back to them. The reader is also advised to refresh his memory of the concluding sections in Chapters 3 and 4 before reading further.

THE GOALS OF MICROECONOMIC POLICY

Two microeconomic policy goals may be distinguished, equity and efficiency.

(1) EQUITY

It is important to emphasise, at the outset, that microeconomic policy is no less controversial a subject than is macroeconomic policy. It is obvious that this is so when the subject of equity is being considered. Equity means fairness and is a matter of personal opinion. One simply cannot decide which of a number of distributions of income, or wealth, is the more equitable, for example, without involving preferences for some individuals over others. The question whether one wishes to favour rich, poor, young, old, sick, healthy or industrious people is an ethical and political one. It is not one on which economists are necessarily better judges than other people. The role of the economist is to make clear the distributional effects of particular economic policies, not to choose between them; though as a citizen every economist will have his own views.

It must be stressed that the goal of equity is not the same as that of equality, which would imply that everyone should be treated equally. Equity, on the other hand, is a much more complex matter. There are many considerations which are relevant to the question of whether a situation is fair. Two are worthy of special mention: the criterion of need and that of reward. They may give rise to major problems when a policy results in a districbution of income which is fair by one standard but less so by the other. The question whether the highest incomes should go to those with the greatest needs or to those who work hardest is an ethical one, though it has important economic implications, for example, for the size of the national income which is available for distribution.

(2) EFFICIENCY

The goal of efficiency might seem, at first glance, much less troublesome. However, this is not the case as readers who recall the argument of Chapter 4 will appreciate. A very concise summary of that argument is that it is not possible to assess the efficiency of the allocation of resources in a market economy independently from equity, because the forces of supply and demand are affected by the distribution of income. People have different tastes and demand for different goods and services varies with income. Consequently, two or more distributions of income can produce different collections of goods and services, through the working of the price mechanism. It was argued in the previous section that we cannot choose objectively between one distribution of income and another from the viewpoint of equity. It follows, therefore, that we equally cannot unequivocally prefer the combination of goods and services produced with one distribution of income to that with another.

Efficiency, like equity, is not a simple concept. In the sense it has been used so far, an efficient set of goods and services means a set that best satisfies consumers. Efficiency is also relevant to production techniques. This can best be understood by ignoring the problem of the first paragraph of this section and assuming it has been decided which goods and services shall be produced. Efficiency can be brought in at this level by declaring that goods should be produced in the most efficient manner, that is, employing the most efficient techniques. Production methods will be efficient if it is not possible to produce more of any goods without producing less of any others. (The economy will be on the production frontier, as in Figure 3.4 in Chapter 3.)

Choice of techniques necessarily involves consideration of the prices of factors of production. For example, in so far as relative scarcities lead to the price of capital being low relative to the price of labour, it would be efficient to adopt capital-intensive production techniques. However, factor prices cannot be discussed without recognising that personal incomes depend upon them. Hence, we may see that income distribution impinges on even this aspect of efficiency. A complete discussion of microeconomic policy, therefore, requires consideration of all interactions between equity and efficiency. It will necessitate also accepting that the two criteria may suggest conflicting actions. We may leave this on one side for the moment.

THE PRICE MECHANISM AND MARKET FAILURE

There is no single correct way to approach the subject of the efficiency and equity of the allocation of resources. However, the UK is an economy where major sectors are in private hands, so that the forces of supply and demand result in the production and distribution of goods and services. It has been argued several times previously that a case can be made for approving the allocation of resources brought about by a pricing system. We start by summarising the argument briefly. We then examine the main reasons why a completely free market system may fail to operate ideally, repeating some earlier considerations and adding some new ones. Finally, we describe the various instruments of microeconomic policy available to deal with market failures of different kinds.

The case that a freely working pricing system might bring about a satisfactory distribution of resources was set out in Chapters 3 and 4. It is the so-called case for *laissez-faire*, that self-interest drives individuals in such a way that state intervention is unnecessary. It is not a case that is accepted in its entirety by anyone, but it has certain merits which deserve consideration. Moreover, the analysis provides a starting point for the identification of particular reasons why the market fails to operate ideally. Such an anatomy of market failure may then form the basis for the analysis of the case for intervention.

THE CASE FOR *LAISSEZ-FAIRE*

We might summarise the case as follows.

If we assume that consumers always adjust their expenditure on goods so as to maximise their satisfaction, given their tastes and the relative prices of the goods and services available to them, then we may infer that the price that is paid at the margin (that is, by a consumer who finds it just worthwhile buying one more unit of a product) is a measure of the satisfaction he derives from a good. In other words, price measures marginal utility.

We now add the further assumption that producers always maximise their profits, given the prices of the factors of production and consumer demands. Producers find their optimum outputs where the marginal cost of producing a good is equal to the marginal revenue received from selling it. Provided each producer can sell as much as he wants at the market price, marginal revenue must be equal to price. Therefore, we can conclude that the market brings about equality between price and marginal cost. In other words, the cost of producing the 'last' unit of each good is exactly the same as the satisfaction that it brings. If output were smaller, marginal cost would be less than marginal utility, so that an increase in production would be valued by consumers at a figure in excess of the extra cost that would be involved in producing it. Conversely, if outputs were larger than at the point where marginal cost equals marginal utility, a reduction in output would bring a larger fall in costs than in benefits.

Moreover, we must remember that costs are real opportunity costs, measuring the sacrifices of goods not produced. Hence, provided marginal cost equals marginal utility in every market, no reallocation of resources between products can bring about a better pattern of production. Prices, acting as signals, direct resources to the uses which maximise the satisfaction of consumers. In such circumstances, provided the system works reasonably speedily, it might be argued, interference with the freedom of the market mechanism to work towards the best allocation of resources is unnecessary.

THE RELEVANCE OF *LAISSEZ-FAIRE*

In Chapter 3 we examined the way in which the price mechanism functioned through the interaction of supply and demand. Towards the end of that chapter we set out six conditions which should obtain if a market system is to work efficiently. Let us remind ourselves of these conditions. They can provide a basis for the understanding of micro-economic policy. For a pricing system to lead to a satisfactory allocation of resources, it was said that:

(1) markets must be efficient in the sense that buyers and sellers are well informed and supply and demand must respond reasonably quickly to price changes;
(2) buyers and sellers must aim at maximisation of satisfaction and profits;
(3) there must be effective competition of both sides of the market;
(4) the distribution of income and wealth must be 'optimal',
(5) the only goods and services must be those that benefit individuals as individuals;
(6) the social, legal and institutional framework must be regarded as satisfactory.

THE CAUSES OF MARKET FAILURE

The analysis of the previous section was designed to set out the assumptions necessary for the price mechanism to allocate resources ideally. We next examine the case for *laissez-faire* from a critical viewpoint. Analysis of market failure may appear destructive. Its importance lies in the identification of causes for criticism and in the provision of a framework for the discussion of microeconomic policy. If a doctor knows the causes of a disease as well as being able to recognise it, he will be more likely to cure it than merely to relieve its adverse symptoms.

There are a number of different ways of grouping together the causes of market failure. The fivefold classification chosen here involves certain overlaps but happens to suit our circumstances.

(1) The distribution of income and wealth.
(2) Market imperfections.
(3) Time-lags.
(4) Private versus social values.
(5) Paternalism.

(1) The distribution of income and wealth

The first reason for questioning the allocation of resources brought about by a freely working market system is that the distribution of income and wealth, within which the price mechanism works, may be regarded by society as less than satisfactory. We shall not waste space by repeating the full argument. It was stated at length earlier in the book and summarised at the beginning of this chapter. We know that market forces can result in a different selection of goods and services for each alternative distribution of income and wealth.

The price mechanism, of course, affects income distribution through the operation of markets for factors of production. We saw in Chapter 5 how these work. The demand for a factor, such as labour, reflects its productivity. Its supply represents the numbers of persons offering their services at different wage rates. Equilibrium obtains in each market at a price which equates supply and demand so that there are no unsatisfied buyers or sellers of labour services.

The question of whether the distribution of income resulting from the operation of the price mechanism is equitable and efficient is not, as was argued earlier, one to which an answer can be given objectively. It is a matter of opinion and personal value judgements are inevitable. We can, however, indicate the ways in which certain social and institutional arrangements may affect supply and demand in the market. They suggest some of the reasons why personal incomes differ and allow us to take better-informed stands on whether we approve or dissaprove of the results.

Explanations of income differences were dealt with in Chapter 5, so we need only summarise them here. First, an individual's income may accrue from more than one source – for example, a wage from employment, interest or profits derived from the ownership of capital, and so on. One cause of different incomes is, therefore, to be found in the fact that some people have more sources than others. This is particularly important because wealth is, by and large, more unevenly distributed than is earned income. Secondly, money wages are sometimes low or high because there are non-pecuniary advantages and disadvantages of different occupations. Thirdly, individuals vary from each other in a great many ways which influence their productivity and, therefore, their earnings. Some of these characteristics, such as ability and personality, may affect work drive or taste for risky, high-paid employment. It is not within the competance of economists to know how far they are innate or produced by the environment. For policy purposes, however, it may be useful to know how far they are within or outside an individual's control. No one can do much about his age, sex or race, for example. Other characteristics are, however, more capable of influence, if not always by the individual himself, at least by government action. The most important illustration of a quality which affects skill and earnings is the education and training a person has received. A fourth cause of differences in incomes is the existence of various barriers which hinder the movement of individuals from low- to high-paid occupations. Such barriers may be geographical. They may reflect the time needed to acquire new skills for workers in industries contracting as a result of economic progress. They may be merely informational barriers, which prevent everyone knowing where there are job vacancies paying relatively high wages. Fifthly and finally, it must be recognised that labour markets are not all perfectly competitive. Wage negotiations are conducted by trade unions and employers' organisations which possess varying degrees of monopoly power. The result is that wages for comparable skills may differ by occupation and by industry.

We conclude that there are many possible explanations for uneven distributions of income in a country at any time. They are complex and usually difficult to unravel; particularly so because the available statistics are not entirely reliable. Much of the data comes, for example, from tax returns; not the most credible source! There are also problems in interpreting the statistics, allowing for under-recorded income, fringe benefits, part-time employment, and so on. It can be said only that unless we can identify (or be prepared to guess at) the causes of differences in incomes between persons, we shall find it difficult to decide whether we regard the distribution itself as being unsatisfactory or not, and what to do about it. For instance, if we find a man to be low paid because he chooses a job he likes we shall probably be less concerned than if his low income is due to being disabled.

(2) Market Imperfections

It was explained earlier that our fivefold analysis of the causes of market failure contained some overlaps. We have already seen in the last section that imperfect competition may be a cause of income differences. However, there is a special reason for considering market imperfections in their own right.

The basis of the argument was that explained in Chapter 4 and the reader is urged to refer back to pages 72 ff. for a full statement. It should be recalled that one of the necessary conditions for *laissez-faire* to bring about an efficient allocation of resources is that output should be 'optimal', in the sense that marginal cost equals marginal utility at the margin of production. Prices, acting as signals, perform the function of achieving this automatically under conditions of perfect competition. However, when markets are less than perfect, producers are price-makers rather than price-takers. Marginal revenue is less than price. A profit-maximising monopolist produces output where marginal cost is equal to marginal revenue. This is, in consequence, where marginal cost is less than marginal utility. The situation was illustrated diagrammatically in Figure 4.11, which showed that a profit-maximising monopolist produces less than 'optimal', perfectly competitive, output. In addition to this kind of resource 'misallocation' that may accompany less than perfectly competitive markets, it was shown in Chapter 4 that firms in monopolistic conditions may also be less subject to competitive forces inducing them to keep their costs to a minimum. The present of such 'X-inefficiency', as it is called, when managers are shielded from competition, is a second reason for treating imperfect competition as a separate cause of market failure.

When we were discussing the relevance of income distribution to the efficiency of a market system we emphasised the importance of trying to identify the causes of whatever was regarded as unsatisfactory. The same is true here. It is essential to know the reasons why a firm possesses monopoly power to be able to decide what, if anything, could or should be done about it.

A useful approach to this question in any particular case is to ask why competition is not perfect, that is, why there is not a large number of firms in the industry producing an identical product. The answer may be the existence of barriers to the entry of other firms so that one, or a few of them, can hold and maintain a dominant position in the market.

It is necessary to understand the nature of the different kinds of barriers to entry before one can properly discuss microeconomic policy in this area. The sources of power that a firm may have in a market are many and varied. They may stem from the ownership or control of the supply of a raw material, from rights, such as patents, acquired by law, from the fact that the products of a firm are differentiated in the minds of consumers, or from geographical isolation, which can turn a small shop into a local monopoly. There is, however, another source of monopoly power which has important implications for policy. It is the power which stems from the existence of economies of large-scale production. Such economies of scale arise usually from technological factors making highly capital-intensive methods the cheapest way of producing a given output. They constitute barriers to entry of new firms as effectively as any other circumstance.

The importance of identifying the source of monopoly power in individual cases may now be understood. For example, if a monopoly rests on the possession of patent rights, a firm could be forced to allow others to engage in production under licence. If monopoly power in another case is due to consumers believing, unjustifiably, that the products of the firm are different from those of other firms, because of advertising or other cause, a remedy might lie in improving information services available to the community.

It would be possible to multiply examples of alternative solutions to monopoly problems by reference to different causes of monopoly power. But there is one particular kind of entry barrier that we have already noted has special implications for policy. When a monopoly is based on economies of large-scale production, we are faced with a problem which calls for a quite different approach. The reason is that such a firm, if it operates efficiently, must be the lowest-cost producer. Any attempt to break its power by easing entry for other firms would fail in one vital respect. Two or more firms sharing the same market would necessarily face higher costs of production than a single firm, often known, therefore, as a 'natural monopoly'.

The situation is illustrated in Figure 10.1. This diagram is similar in every respect, save one, to the standard diagram of monopoly in Figure 4.11, explained earlier. The distinctive feature of Figure 10.1 is that the cost curves of the monopolist continue to decline until they cut the demand curve. The profit-maximising monopolist would produce output *OA* compared to an 'optimal' output of *OB*, where marginal utility is equal to marginal cost. The cheapest way of producing *OB* output is, however, for a single firm to do so.[1]

We see, therefore, that special policy problems are likely to arise when monopoly power rests on technical factors giving rise to economies of large-scale production. Breaking up such a monopoly is liable to raise costs of production. Preferred solutions might then lie in finding ways of inducing a monopolist to expand output. Even this kind of policy would be deficient, however, if there is suspicion of 'X-inefficiency' being present, raising the firm's cost curves (without altering their downward tendency). Public policy to deal with natural

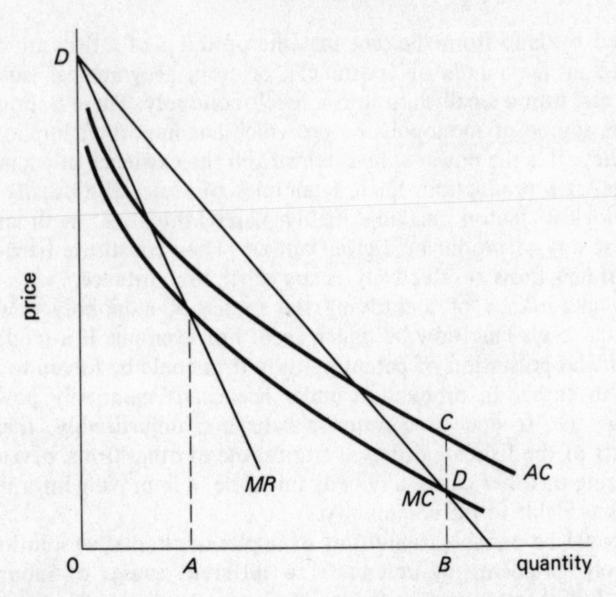

Figure 10.1 *A 'natural' monopoly. Costs decline until market demand is satisfied.*

monopolies is therefore particularly awkward.[2] State regulation, or even nationalisation, is often proposed for them, for example, in the power and transport industries. Government ownership or control does not of itself dispose of their basic economic problems. We return to this matter below. (See pages 221–3.)

(3) Time-lags

The third cause of market failure is more straightforward than the first two. The essence of the case for *laissez-faire*, with which we should by now be familiar, is that market forces by themselves lead to a satisfactory allocation of resources. However, it is in the nature of things that supply and demand do not respond instantaneously. They take time to work. The question is whether they work fast enough or need to be speeded up. We might note, first, that there is another overlap here with the last cause of market failure. The longer the time allowed for market forces to work, the easier it is for firms to enter industries where a monopoly is active. Patents run out, information spreads and monopoly power tends to wane.[3]

At the microeconomic level, the relevance of time-lags must be viewed sector by sector. One example may be given where the price mechanism is often judged to take too long to work by itself and government intervention is common. It is agriculture.

Many agricultural products characteristically operate in conditions both of inelastic demand and of inelastic supply. Demand is not very responsive to price changes for certain basic foodstuffs, such as bread. The same is true of a number of agricultural raw materials because they form very small proportions of the total cost of a finished product. (Think, for instance, of the price elasticity of demand for corks by wine importers.) On the supply side, price inelasticity stems often from high storage costs and the existence of time-lags between planting and harvesting. They can be as long as seven years (for a rubber tree), and can lead to low elasticity of supply in response to price changes.

When a market operates in conditions of great inelasticity of supply and demand, there is a tendency for prices to fluctuate substantially with quite small changes in demand or supply. The analysis was illustrated with the aid of a diagram, Figure 4.8, in Chapter 4. Readers are referred back to remind themselves of the argument. The conclusion reached there was that not only prices, but also farm incomes, tend to fluctuate more than may be justified. Farmers are inclined to be relatively well off when harvests are small and badly off when they are large.

We should be used by now to the idea that the best way of tackling each of the various symptoms of market failure is one that is related to its proximate cause. Excessive fluctuations due to the vagaries of the weather are examples of cases where it is clearly impossible to change climatic conditions. Government intervention in agriculture, therefore, tends to be of price support kinds aimed at stabilising farm incomes. Time-lags in other cases may be more effectively dealt with directly. For instance, labour mobility may be speeded up by state-aided training schemes in new skills and firms may be assisted financially to relocate themselves in areas where unemployment is relatively high.

(4) Private versus Social Values

The next cause of market failure is linked to the fifth condition listed above on page 207 for the price mechanism to work efficiently, namely, that the only goods and services should be those which benefit individuals as individuals. If this is so we might reasonably expect the total satisfaction of the community to be the simple sum of the satisfactions of all the individuals in it. However, this is not always the case.

Let us once again remind ourselves that price acts in a market as a signal of both the marginal benefit to consumers and the marginal cost of production of a good. Under the 'right' circumstances, as we have seen, the marginal cost to society of resources employed in producing a good is equated to price, which itself is a measure of the marginal utility, or benefit, that it gives.

Implicit in the argument is the idea that the price paid by a consumer for a good is a measure of the satisfaction which he gets from it. Provided the person buying a product is the only one benefiting from the purchase and that the producer of a good is the only one who has to bear the costs of producing it, the price mechanism cannot be faulted on this count. For certain goods and services, the individuals buying and selling them are the only ones involved in costs and benefits. For other goods, however, price does not indicate benefit or cost *to society*, although it might perfectly well measure utility and cost to the private individual.

Let us take an example of two goods. Compare a service such as smallpox vaccination with one like a visit to a greyhound race meeting. When someone pays to attend a race meeting, the only consumer benefit we can reasonably expect to accrue is that to the person who goes there. This we term *private benefit*. In fact this private benefit is all that is likely to accrue here. No one other than the individual concerned derives satisfaction from his visit to the races as a rule.

In contrast, consider the case of a smallpox vaccination, the benefit deriving from which extends beyond that rendered to the person vaccinated in so far as it reduces the risk to other people of contracting the disease. In this case we say that there are what are called *external*, *spillover*, or *neighbourhood* effects, and that *social benefits* are greater than private benefits. Consequently, if the output of race meetings is expanded to the point where the marginal utility to the individual paying for the service is equal to the marginal cost of providing it, the price mechanism will result in exactly the 'right' numbers of race meetings. But if the same policy is applied to smallpox vaccinations, output will be expended only up to the point where marginal utility *to the person vaccinated* is equal to marginal costs. Output, however, will be too small, because the amount spent by individuals on vaccination does not fully measure the benefit deriving to *society as a whole*. In other words, marginal utility to society (called marginal social benefit) exceeds marginal cost of production.

External effects are probably quite widespread throughout the economy, although they may be difficult to quantify. Moreover, while social benefits can be *greater* than private benefits (as in the case of smallpox vaccinations) they can also be less than private benefits, when expenditure by a private individual reduces, thereby, the satisfaction of someone else. If, for instance, I build a tall house next to yours and block your view, or smoke a cigarette in a confined space, you may suffer.

The examples given so far relate to consumption. Equally well, externalities can be on the side of costs. If a business starts a training school for its employees, some trained personnel may leave and work for other businesses, which may profit from lower costs without fully paying for them. If a fish cannery starts up next to a perfumery, the latter may be forced into making special expenditures to prevent fishy smells affecting its perfume.

Public goods. There is one special case involving external effects which is of great importance. This occurs with what are known as *public goods*, which have marginal social costs approaching zero.

A classic example of a public good is a lighthouse. Once built, the marginal cost of maintenance is very low, and it costs no more to shine for a thousand ships than for a single one. To put the matter in another way, a product may be called a public good if, when one person has more of it, there is no reduction in the quantity available for everyone else. Consider a television programme, which costs as much to put on the air for one viewer as for a million. Compare it with a private good, such as the egg I had for breakfast. When I ate it, there was nothing edible left for anyone else.

Public goods are sometimes termed *collective consumption goods* to include education, health, defence, and so on. We must be careful to distinguish the technical meaning of the term public good from its occasional loose use to describe any goods and services that governments happen to provide.

A freely working price mechanism will not secure the production of the 'right' amount of public goods, because if marginal cost is zero, then only a zero price is appropriate, and no business will produce goods to give away free. The state may, therefore, decide to intervene, as in the case of goods with some external effects, to encourage or discourage production by means of taxes or subsidies where there are net social benefits or detriments. On the other hand, the government may prefer to deal with the situation by making rules, such as the law that motorists must have insurance to cover third parties who may be hurt through no fault of their own.

There are three major problems to be solved where there are goods for which private and social costs differ.

(*a*) How to quantify the benefits and costs, including all external effects, in order to decide how many should be produced.
(*b*) How to decide whether they should be produced by the state or by private enterprise.
(*c*) How to decide on the best price at which the goods should be sold.

To solve the first problem, elaborate statistical exercises to measure social costs and benefits (known as social cost-benefit analyses) are often undertaken. The second is mainly a political matter, and resembles the problem of whether natural monopolies, dealt with earlier, should be nationalised. The third problem also contains political difficulties. If marginal cost of a public good to the individual is zero, then the only efficient price is also zero – that is, the products should, perhaps, even be free.

(5) Paternalism

The final set of reasons for doubt about whether a free market would result in an ideal allocation of resources stems from the last of the conditions listed on page 207 for a *laissez-faire* market system to work reasonably well: namely, that the social, legal and institutional framework must be satisfactory. There is one aspect of this condition of particular concern. It is related to the rights of the individual to make decisions for himself. We are not concerned here with the spillover effects of a person's behaviour on others (which was dealt with under the head of private versus social values) but with the freedom of the individual to look after his or her own best interests.

Sometimes societies take the view that the state should adopt a paternalistic role, like a father who prevents his child from injuring itself and forces it to do things which it would not choose to do itself, but which are beneficial. Interfering with the freedom of adults is, of course, a very different proposition from that of directing children. Hence, feelings run high on the question of how far the state should limit personal freedom. Nevertheless, there are activities where it is widely accepted in many societies that individuals may not be able to make the best decisions for themselves. For example, it is argued that a person may not realise that certain drugs are habit-forming or injurious to health or that driving on bald tyres increases the risk of accidents. Even if he is aware of the dangers, a man may choose to ignore them and a paternalistic state may deem it right to stop him injuring himself. No wonder strong opinions are heard on this subject!

A less controversial example of paternalism arises from the observation that human beings appear to be somewhat myopic. They tend to pay less attention to the future than perhaps they should, or at least as much as they might wish in later life they had done. Hence, if the state forces people to save, for example, during their working life to provide for a degree of comfort in old age, they may be happier in the long run. Similarly, since the pleasure one can get from reading 'good' books or hearing 'good' music cannot necessarily be fully anticipated before the event, the government may decide to subsidise public libraries and the arts.

Strict paternalism probably accounts, too, for at least part of government expenditure on education, since the beneficiaries (the pupils) are not normally the purchasers (the parents) of education services.

We may also include under the paternalistic heading those actions of a government which are sometimes described as 'non-economic'. Society, through its government, prohibits certain types of trade which might other wise be carried on between willing parties. For example, you cannot buy the services of an expert to take your exams for you. Nor can you pay or be paid to commit murder, or deal in slaves. These and other activities are taken out of the marketplace by governments seeking to provide what is currently believed to be a 'civilised' environment. Even defence expenditure is sometimes included in this category, although it might equally well be considered a public good, since defence cannot be provided for one citizen without also being available for another.

THE INSTRUMENTS OF MICROECONOMIC POLICY

The discussion of microeconomic policy in this chapter has been fairly theoretical. We have sought to set out the case for and against a system in which the allocation of resources is determined by market forces, in order to provide a framework within which particular problems of economic policy may be discussed. There are a great many such problems and we shall discuss a few of them to illustrate some general principles. This section describes the chief instruments of microeconomic policy that are available to governments.

It is useful to distinguish two very general approaches to policy when the market system is regarded as having failed. One is to try and make the market work better and the other is to replace it. The former approach accepts the signalling value of prices, while admitting that the prices ruling in free markets do not always succeed in bringing about an ideal allocation of resources. The latter approach implies that the price mechanism has failed so seriously that it should not be tampered with, but replaced by an alternative allocative mechanism.

IMPROVING MARKET EFFICIENCY

Let us deal first with policies aimed at trying to make the market system work better. Two kinds of policy instruments may be distinguished. The government can attempt to influence market prices or it can introduce rules and regulations aimed at improving the framework within which the market operates.

Pricing policies

In certain circumstances, the most effective means of improving market allocations may be through the price mechanism itself. The best way of explaining why is by illustration. Take the problem of pollution, for example. As argued in the section on social versus private costs, the presence of externalities carries the implication that market prices fail to take account of social considerations which do not directly enter into the private cost calculations of suppliers. Specifically, private costs ignore any detriment to the environment from pollution, which may incidentally affect consumers and/or producers.

Taxes and subsidies. One solution to this problem might be for the government to estimate the external costs imposed on others by the producers who are responsible for pollution and to levy taxes on them equal to the excluded costs. The effect would be to change the price received by such producers, so that it reflects the full social costs of their actions and not merely private costs. Their maximum profit output should, in consequence, fall, thereby reducing the level of pollution.

Taxes may, thus, be used to influence resource allocation while retaining the basic market system. It should be added that this form of intervention will work satsifactorily if production decisions are sensitive to price changes and if the state can make reasonably reliable estimates of social costs. The sensivity of production decisions to changes in price is an important issue. If the supply curve is inelastic, such a policy is hardly likely to succeed. (Refer back to Chapter 4 if you need reminding of the meaning of the elasticity of supply and of how to use supply and demand analysis to predict the effects of the imposition of a tax on a commodity.) However, there is more to it than that. The nature of the tax itself is relevant. For maximum effectiveness the tax should be linked to output, because the object of the exercise is to induce producers to recalculate the profitability of different levels of output when full social costs are included in the price they receive. A tax which took the form of a licence fee and was not, therefore, directly related to output would be barely effective. It is true that a business might cease production entirely if the license fee absorbed its whole profit. However, if it was smaller, output could be unaffected (though profits lower), since there is no change in receipts, at the margin, from *additional* sales. The way to affect production is to use the tax to reduce the profitability of each unit of output, thereby changing financial incentives for producers.[4]

Pollution is only an illustration of a case where taxes may be used to try and correct deficiencies of the market. There are many others. Taxes may, in principle, be imposed anywhere in order to make price reflect full social costs. They may, for example, be levied on goods, such as tobacco, which are believed to be harmful to health, reflecting a paternalistic cause of market failure. Taxes may also be used in the factor, as well as in the goods, market to improve the distribution of income. Progressive rates of income tax, which absorb higher proportions of the income of the rich than of the poor, usually have this aim. Taxes on wealth may have similar objectives.

Finally, we should make reference to negative taxes or, as they are usually called, subsidies, which can perform similar functions of encouraging production where social benefits exceed private benefits and a free market supplies insufficient quantities. Subsidies to the arts, universities, housing and many other goods and services are often justified on such counts. Subsidies may also encourage factor mobility, when certain regions in a country are relatively heavily depressed. They can be used, too, to improve the distribution of income, where individuals at the bottom of the scale are not liable to tax and cannot, therefore, benefit from low tax rates.

Price controls. It would be wrong to leave the subject of state intervention using the price mechanism without adding that taxes and subsidies are not the only means of trying to affect output and/or consumption decisions. Price controls may achieve similar ends. The authorities may stipulate either maximum or minimum prices. The former have the effect of changing the demand curve facing a producer (making it perfectly elastic at the maximum price). They might, for example, be used to try to stimulate output from a monopolist. Legally fixed minimum prices affect the supply curve (making it perfectly elastic at the minimum price). They could be adopted, for example, to establish a floor to wages in conditions where free market forces would otherwise cause hardship.

Figure 10.2 illustrates the use of price controls. In the absence of intervention, the market settles at an equilibrium price of *OP* and quantity of *OE*. If a maximum price is set at *OP* max., the market will only supply *OC*. This may be the desired price, but it is important to note that there will also be an unsatisfied demand (*CF*) at the legal maximum price. In the absence of intervention, the presence of excess demand over supply would tend to force price upwards. Here it is prohibited. If nothing further is done, one might not be surprised, therefore, to find queues or black markets developing (as, for example, with cup final tickets). Hence price controls are often accompanied by procedures for the orderly allocation of scarce supplies (for example, residence qualifications for council houses or ration coupons for food in wartime).

Minimum prices create parallel but different problems. In Figure 10.2, if the legal minimum price is set at *OP* min., there will ensue an excess of supply over demand, of *AB*. In a free market, economic forces would tend to lower price. This is excluded here, so one must expect some output to be unsold. Suppose, for example, the market was for unskilled

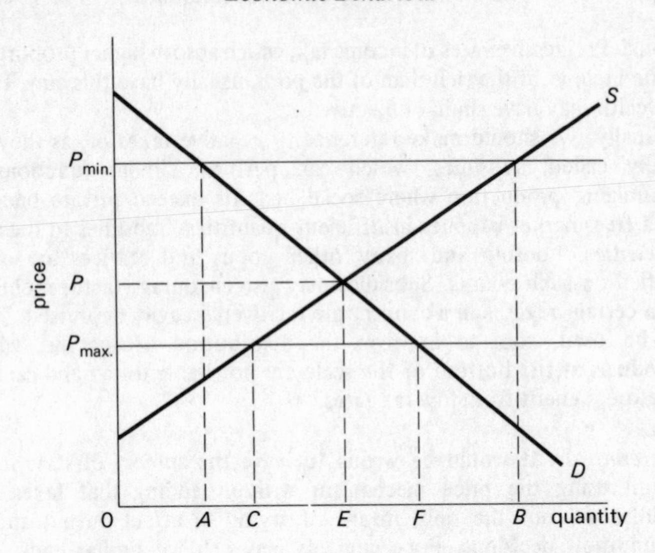

Figure 10.2 *Price controls effecting market equilibrium.*

labour and the minimum price was introduced by the government to put a floor to wages. Unemployment, however, would *ceteris paribus*, tend to occur. (*AE* fewer workers would find jobs than if wages were allowed to fall to the equilibrium level.) It would, therefore, be unwise to introduce such a measure without recognising its full implications.[5]

Rules and regulations

We turn next to consider how the state can exert influences on markets by means of rules and regulations. These can take the form of absolute prohibitions and compulsions or more general measures affecting the legal and institutional framework within which the price mechanism works.

Rules of absolute prohibition or compulsion may be resorted to when supply and/or demand is insensitive to price, when alternative policies are impracticable or very costly, or when the allocation of resources brought about by market forces is considered so unsatisfactory that nothing less will do.

It may be helpful to give a few examples of this type of intervention. Certain kinds of pollution may be absolutely prohibited, where the effects would be extremely serious or where the cost of measuring pollution and monitoring a system of taxes would be very expensive. Bus lanes may be barred from private motorists; factory building may be forbidden in highly congested areas; the import of animals carrying health risks may be banned; and so on. Absolute prohibitions, of course, deprive individuals of freedom of choice. In some cases, compromise solutions of partial bans may be appropriate – for example, the division of trains into compartments where smoking is, or is not, allowed.

The examples given in the previous paragraph are of rules declaring activities illegal. There is no clear dividing line between them and measures of compulsion. For example, the law requiring employers to adopt policies of equal pay for men and women can be seen also as a ban on pay discrimination by sex. However, there are certain policies which force people to do things that they would otherwise not. It is compulsory for children to attend school; for restaurants to register with health authorities; for visitors to some countries to be vaccinated or innoculated; for motorists to take out third party insurance policies to cover innocent accident victims; for employees to pay social security contributions because they may not otherwise make provision for their old age.

The state may pass laws, or establish institutions, designed to affect the framework within which markets operate in order to improve their efficiency, their fairness, or both. There are many possible illustrations – for example, the laws governing the sale of goods, advertising, hire purchase contracts, patents, copyrights, compensation for loss of job, and so on.[6] Institutions set up by the state to exercise influence on market behaviour include the Monopolies and Mergers Commission, the Restrictive Practices Court, employment exchanges, industrial and rent tribunals, training boards, and so forth.

We could continue at great length to give examples of the rules and regulations that have been introduced to try and remedy defects of particular markets. The only general comment an economist might make would be to emphasise that, in so far as there is any interference with the forces of supply and demand, one should look for effects similar to those discussed earlier in connection with price controls. This should by no means be taken to mean that any intervention is necessarily undesirable, but that it may need accompanying measures for the allocation of supplies as well, of course, as ensuring compliance.

STATE CONTROL OF PRODUCTION AND DISTRIBUTION

There are certain economic activities where the market may be regarded as so inadequate for the production and distribution of goods and services that the government may decide to take them on itself. Such a decision may, of course, be made on purely political grounds, for example, when nationalisation is proposed because of dissatisfaction with the ethical basis of a capitalist system. Public co-operation may, however, be a solution for particular problems arising from market failure, leading to partial state ownership and control of sectors of the economy. It is, in fact, a common feature of the economies of many Western countries that public goods like lighthouses are operated by government agencies. State corporations in Britain run natural monopolies such as electricity and railways. The government also undertakes the provision of the armed forces, police, schools, hospitals and a variety of social services.

State control, it must be emphasised, does not, by itself, solve economic problems. They do not go away when an industry is nationalised. They are, however, put into a new context, in that allocation decisions are, to a greater or lesser extent, taken by government or its agencies instead of by private producers and consumers in the market. The need for appropriate output and pricing policies remains. The real cost of production need not be materially affected by changes in ownership.

State control may be of production and distribution or confined to either of these. For example, the government may wish in the case of health services to be supplier and distributor. Alternatively, in the case of the provision of motorways, the state may decide how much should be spent on them and where they should be located, while leaving the construction of the roads themselves to private businesses. The extent of desired involvement varies with circumstances and there is little general guidance that economists can offer on the matter. One consideration is, however, worthy of mention. It concerns the question of freedom of choice. A decision may have to be taken on whether consumers should be allowed to purchase for themselves goods or services similar to those provided by the state. This is, of course, an issue with heavy political overtones. For instance, should individuals be free to buy medical care at their own expense at higher levels than are available on the national health service? Or, to give another controversial example, should parents be allowed to buy, for their children, standards of education different from those in state schools? There can be no objective answers to questions like these. They are matters of personal opinion, though one relevant economic argument may be that competition may help maintain standards.

There is one final, and also controversial, economic aspect of state-provided services. How should their costs be covered? Many methods are possible, but the discussion can be simplified by first considering two extreme solutions: (1) services may be provided free and (2) those who use them may be charged for doing so. This is another area which runs into deep political waters, especially when charges for social services are under discussion.

Let it be emphasised that the real costs have to be borne by someone. Free provision simply places the burden on general taxpayers, instead of on consumers if charges are levied by use. The pros and cons of the alternatives must sensibly be weighed case by case. For goods which are clearly consumed collectively, there is no practical method of financing them other than from central funds. Defence expenditure on armies and equipment is an obvious case in point, where it is widely accepted that the cost should come from general taxation. No one seriously suggests, either, that the police can or should have their costs paid for by the individuals who use their services! However, the question of the proper way to pay for state education and health is much more controversial. On the one hand, are those who argue that free provision encourages abuse of the system. On the other hand, there are those who contend that charging discourages the use of services by those in greatest need. One can also identify intermediate cases, like the provision of motorways or bridges, where charges to cover the whole or part of costs may be levied on users but where the administrative costs of charging are not negligible. Arguments can only be sensibly assessed in the context of particular cases. One should add, moreover, that the proper price to charge is not necessarily that which just covers cost if there are important externalities present, giving benefits to those other than to direct consumers. (For instance, users of minor roads benefit from reduced congestion when a new motorway is constructed.)

THE CHOICE OF POLICY INSTRUMENTS

We conclude this chapter by putting forward a suggested approach to decision-making on questions of policy which appears logical. It involves a four-step procedure.

Step 1 Identify the general cause of market failure, that is, whether due to dissatisfaction with income distribution, market imperfections, time-lags, externalities, or paternalism.
Step 2 Identify the *proximate* cause of the situation deemed undesirable, that is, determine whether, for example, monopoly power is based on economies of scale or product differentiation.
Step 3 Identify the alternative policy instruments which could be employed to try and remedy the defect under consideration.
Step 4 Quantify all the costs and benefits of each alternative policy (including that of non-intervention), taking account of all side-effects and political practicalities.

The last step is a formidable one that may be extremely difficult and costly to carry out. However, unless some attempt is made to quantify, even approximately, the costs and benefits of alternative policies, it is hard to know which to select. No one should pretend that there exist identifiable optimum solutions to the problems of economic policy. Personal and political attitudes are unavoidable and there is usually too much uncertainty about the precise effects of different policies to allow full assessments to be made. The four-step procedure suggested above is supposed to be no more than a guide to clear thinking on policy alternatives. It certainly should not be taken to imply that the best solutions can be simply discovered.

One implication of the procedure deserves, however, to be amplified. Step 1 might be thought to indicate that it is possible to isolate a single cause of market failure in particular cases. This is unlikely. A market may fail for several interconnected reasons and it may be hard to unravel them. For example, consider the case for intervention in the housing market. Is it justified on grounds of income disitribution (that the poor cannot afford decent housing)? On grounds of paternalism (that people do not sufficiently realise the benefits that accrue from living in 'better' housing)? On grounds of imperfect competition (that there are monopoly landlords and builders who keep the supply down to push the price up)? On grounds of delays and time-lags (because it takes so long for a significant increase in the housing stock to materialise)? On grounds of external spillover effects (on neighbours living next door to families in 'substandard' housing)? It is easier to pose questions like this than to answer them. That is no reason, however, for not asking them at all, nor for failing to try and assemble whatever rudimentary evidence one can, to help in making sensible decisions. There is often a wide range of alternative policies available.

To continue with the previous example, suppose the main cause for dissatisfaction with the working of market forces in housing was that it was believed that the poor could not afford to pay for adequate accommodation. A first step would be to try to discover the income levels of families living in inferior housing. If it was found that they were indeed very poor, one might at least consider a policy which raised their incomes, but left them the choice of how to spend it in ways that maximised their satisfaction, given their varying needs and tastes. One could compare this policy with another which subsidised housing directly and which might perhaps be justified by the advantages accruing to the children of such families. Alternatively, the proximate cause of concern might have been a fear of monopolistic landlords. This, too, could be checked by sample surveys and, if confirmed, might suggest a policy of rent controls. It would then be necessary to consider side-effects, such as the possibility of a reduction in the supply of rented accommodation.

EQUITY VERSUS EFFICIENCY

The consideration mentioned in the last sentence should remind us that policy instruments can have undesired side-effects. This may make choice difficult. It may be made more so because the goals of equity and efficiency may be conflicting ones. For example, the tax system may affect incentives as well as redistribute incomes. One often hears the argument that progressive taxes cause people on high rates of pay to work less hard. If true, this is an important consideration for policy-makers. However, it must be pointed out that the evidence on the effects of high marginal tax rates on incentives is far from unequivocal. On the one hand, it appears that some people do work less hard when tax rates are increased. But, on the other hand, there are others who work harder, in order to earn the same pay *net* of tax as they did previously. In the present state of knowledge, therefore, it cannot be concluded that raising rates of tax on the community as a whole has incentive or disincentive effects on balance.

One might perhaps close with an admission. Attempts to achieve a perfect allocation of resources are doomed to fail. We might, therefore, better concentrate on trying to make improvements to present situations. Then, we might end up with an economy that is at least second rather than third, fourth or fifth best, or even worst!

COMPARATIVE ECONOMIC SYSTEMS

Economic policy has been discussed in this chapter in as detached a manner as possible. It should be emphasised, however, that any writings on this subject must reflect the personal opinions of an author. There is no better way to appreciate this remark than to read widely, which the reader is advised to do.

Policy recommendations can be seen as arising from basic political attitudes towards state intervention. Those who see great virtues in a freely working price mechanism stress the advantages it confers. Self-interest supplants government. The market is cheap and impersonal. Price is the same for every person who enters the market, regardless of sex, race or religious belief. The price mechanism works continuously, reflecting changes in supply or demand, while planning decisions take time to be put into effect. Moreover, the ballot-box provides only an infrequent opportunity for consumers to express approval or disapproval of what planners achieve.

Those who are less fearful of state intervention, in contrast, stress the causes of market failure – the long time prices take to work, the desirability of redistributing incomes, the prevalence of monopoly, and the divergences between private and social costs which result in an imbalance between private and public sectors, typified by too many cars and too large classes in schoolrooms.

There are obvious weaknesses on both sides. No one seriously argues that 100 per cent *laissez-faire* or 100 per cent state control is ideal for an economy. Indeed, it is perhaps remarkable how central planners in some communist countries appear to realise that prices can play an important role in a socialist state, without private ownership of the means of production. At the same time Western economies tolerate considerable interference in economic life. Britain has a mixed economy with private and public sectors, which may confirm that there is merit in both.

NOTES: CHAPTER 10

1 Total costs for a single firm are *BC* times *OB*. They would necessarily be greater if the market was shared with one or more other firms. The reader can prove this for himself. Suppose the market was shared between two firms of equal size having the same costs. Average cost of each firm would be half *OB* times the vertical distance between the point on the quantity axis bisecting *AB* and the average cost curve directly above it. Total cost is given by the rectangle formed by this distance times output. If you measure the size of the total cost rectangles they must be greater than the rectangle *OB* times *BC*, representing the total cost of the single firm monopolist.

2 Not least because the sale of 'optimum' output (*OB*) at a price equal to marginal cost (*BD*) would involve losses (of *CD* per unit).

3 There is parallel here too with a basic issue of macroeconomic policy: that of the time for any self-correcting mechanisms in the economy to work to ensure full employment. (See above, Chapter 9, page 201.)

4 Note that the social optimum is not necessarily to reduce pollution to zero, but to a level where the full social costs are equal, at the margin, to benefits provided by the goods produced.

5 For a detailed discussion of government prices policy see Mitchell, J., *Price Determination and Prices Policy* (Allen & Unwin, 1978).

6 For a discussion of the links between economics and the law see Oliver, J. M., *Law and Economics* (Allen & Unwin, 1979).

Part Five

THE NATURE OF ECONOMICS

Chapter 11

The Methods of Economics: Tools and Techniques

The reader who has reached this last chapter will, hopefully, have found out for himself the answers to the questions what do economists do and how do they go about their job. This is the best way to learn. But the student may find it useful to have the main ideas of the methods of economics now brought together.

THE SOCIAL SCIENCES

Economics belongs to the group of subjects known as the social sciences. The term includes sociology, social psychology and political science, and the subjects share two important characteristics. They are 'social' and they are 'scientific'.

(1) 'SOCIAL'

The subject-matter of the social sciences is human behaviour, past, present and future. There is no point in trying to define the boundaries of each subject. They overlap and cannot be defined precisely. It was once fashionable to consider the merits of alternative definitions of economics in textbooks. But the only faultless statement reached was the uninformative 'economics is what economists do', so that the matter is hardly worth pursuing. The different disciplines encompassed by the social sciences complement each other. One can better predict total British output next year, for example, if a forecast includes the incidence of strikes and political changes as well as variables like productivity discussed in this book.

(2) 'SCIENTIFIC'

Students used to debate whether economics was a science. The question is no more fruitful than that of comparing alternative definitions of economics. A subject is a science if it uses scientific methods. The essence of a scientific approach is that it involves confronting theories with evidence, before incorporating them into the main body of learning. The method contrasts with the no less respectable one which involves emotions and impressions. Consider, for example, the statement that Shakespeare was a better writer than Tolstoy. There is no objective set of facts other than people's opinions against which to test it.

In economics, in contrast, there is plenty of scope for comparing theories with facts. Chapter 1 opened with a discussion of family budgets and a theory was advanced that high housing expenditure in London was partly attributable to high incomes there. We examined statistics of household expenditure to see whether they did, or did not, support the theory. We were, in a rudimentary way, checking a hypothesis against the facts. To the extent that economics proceeds in this manner it is valid to describe the subject as being a science.

THE BRANCHES OF ECONOMICS

There are a number of ways of dividing economics into different branches.

(1) MICROECONOMICS AND MACROECONOMICS

A clue to this distinction is suggested by the words themselves: *micro* (small) implies a close look at each part of the economy; *macro* (large) implies viewing the economy as a whole. More generally, microeconomics can be said to be the study of resource allocation and includes the analysis of price and output determination in individual markets by supply and demand. Macroeconomics deals with the determination of national income, total employment, the general level of prices and other *aggregate* economic behaviour. The distinction between them should not be exaggerated. A full understanding of the way the economy functions necessarily involves microeconomics and macroeconomics.

(2) POSITIVE AND NORMATIVE ECONOMICS

Almost everybody has views on the rights and wrongs of some economic policies, like those concerned with inflation, growth and taxation. Indeed, a major reason for studying economics is to acquire a better understanding about the way the economy functions so that opinions on policy matters may be better informed.

It is important to distinguish between understanding how the economy works and making policy prescriptions. The former involves positive economies, while the latter is likely to include questions labelled normative. The difference between positive and normative statements is one that is, in principle, straightforward, though it is not always simple to apply in practice. Normative statements involve moral or ethical value judgements; positive statements do not. The distinction can be clarified by saying that positive economics deals with questions of what *is*, was or will be, while normative economics concerns what we think *ought* to happen or to have happened. A few examples may be useful. 'Income tax ought to be lower', 'the price of houses is too high' and 'the rate of economic growth is too low' are all normative statements. 'Income tax lowers the number of hours worked', 'rent control results in a fall in the supply of rental housing' and 'lowering interest rates leads to a rise in the rate of economic growth' are all positive statements.

Positive economics is, therefore, a subject from which personal opinions are excluded. It is studied in a detached manner and the conclusions of positive economics may be regarded as objective. In so far as positive statements relate to the real world, they are, moreover, testable in principle against facts. This is no more than what was described in the previous section as scientific method – confronting theory with evidence. The reason why the three illustrative statements in the last paragraph are positive ones is that they can, in fact, be tested against the facts. Empirical evidence can be collected to try to determine whether taxation lowers the number of hours worked, whether rent controls reduce the supply of rental accommodation and whether reductions in the rate of interest raise the rate of economic growth. Such tests can be carried out without involving any value judgements about whether rent control, longer hours or economic growth are desirable or undesirable.

Two observations about the nature of positive economics should be made. First, positive statements about the real world must only be testable *in principle*. They do not have to be capable of positive proof. If, after examining the available evidence on the subject, we come up with the conclusion that we do not know whether taxation causes a reduction in hours worked, this does not turn the statement into a normative one. Secondly, positive statements are not necessarily concerned with the real world, but can take the form of conditional theorising of the form 'if the rate of interest rises, then, *ceteris paribus*, the demand for money will fall'. Such a statement may be made about a hypothetical economy. It may or may not apply to a real situation because the other things held constant, by the *ceteris paribus* assumption, may change in the real world. (For example, incomes may change as well as interest rates.) The statement is nevertheless a positive one because no moral value judgements are needed to make it.

It should be noted that certain kinds of judgements may be needed in order to interpret evidence about the real world so as to determine whether it does or does not support a hypothesis. The facts we need are not always available in the precise form required and we may have to exercise judgement about their meaning. Such judgements do not, however, involve moral issues.

The professional job of an economist is a positive, not a normative one. Ideally, one hopes that no economist is influenced in his work by his opinions as a citizen. It does not follow that an economist should not therefore concern himself with questions of economic policy. When he does so, however, he should limit himself, *qua* economist, to their positive aspects. If, for example, he is asked a normative question, such as 'Is taxation too high in Britain?', his reply should be: 'If you tell me what you regard as being too high, I shall try and give you an answer.' If the question is then rephrased into a positive one, for example, 'Does the present tax system cause fewer hours to be worked than if it were lower?', he can reply to it in a professional manner.

We could summarise the role of the economist as one which keeps personal opinions on one side and is concerned with discovering the causes of economic behaviour of individuals, businesses and the economy as a whole. It would be unrealistic to leave this topic without admitting that value judgements cannot, in practice, be totally excluded from economic analysis. Willing though we may be to try to detach ourselves from all conceivable influences, we can hardly hope to be 100 per cent successful. A completely objective statement of the way an economy behaves would require asking an enormous number of questions about it. Only some occur to us, those which our background and training suggest may be useful.

(3) ECONOMIC THEORY AND APPLIED ECONOMICS

The final distinction between branches of economics relates to positive statements about behaviour which are testable. Economic theory is concerned with the derivation of hypotheses and applied economics with testing them. Consider the following example.

Abstract reasoning might lead to the hypothesis that the demand for houses is determined by their price. This conclusion may then be confronted with evidence. Such a method is known as a deductive one. It is to be contrasted with an inductive method, where the facts to be explained are examined first, and a theory is then designed to fit them. Both methods are used in the physical sciences. An example of inductive reasoning could be the theories offered to account for phenomena like pulsars *after* they have been observed. An example of deductive methods could be those which led physicists to predict the existence of new particles *before* they were identified.

Most work in modern economics is probably best described as being a mixture of inductive and deductive methods. Theories are continually developed by being put to tests which often reveal new evidence suggesting ideas for the improvement of the theories, and so on.

ECONOMIC MODELS

The economist usually sets to work by constructing a simplified model of an economy, or part thereof, that he wishes to analyse. A model is merely a fashionable word to describe a hypothesis about the determinants of economic behaviour. It must contain three elements:

(1) *dependent variables*, the behaviour to be explained;
(2) *independent, or explanatory, variables*, the determinants of behaviour;
(3) *behavioural assumptions*, the nature of the causal relationship between the explanatory and dependent variables.

In Chapter 4, for example, we used what we may now recognize as a simple model to analyse the demand for ice creams. There was one dependent variable, the number of ice creams demanded per unit of time; one independent variable, the price of ice creams; the behavioural assumptions included the hypothesis that consumers always tried to maximise their satisfaction in deciding how many ice creams to buy.

The world is a complex place and it would be virtually impossible to analyse all explanatory variables at the same time. The economist therefore concentrates on certain of them and excludes others in an attempt to identify causal relationships between them. Variables are termed *endogenous* and *exogenous* according to whether they are or are not determined within the model. Abstracting from excluded variables is made by the use of a *ceteris paribus* assumption.

Abstraction may be justified if an explanatory variable is of minor importance, if its influence does not change during the period under consideration, or if it is one which economists are not competent to study. Models of the demand for ice creams in the first week in July, for example, generally do not include the price of wafer buscuits, the size of the population, or the weather, for these three reasons. All are potential determinants of demand but unlikely to vary in their influence during so short a period as a week. Abstractions can result in a useful model if it turns out to describe behaviour in the real world. If it fails to pass this test, better models will be called for.

Improving a model may involve the addition of more explanatory variables, for example, adding consumer's income to the determinants of the demand for ice creams. It may, however, merely involve a reformulation of the relationship, perhaps by including a time-lag between dependent and independent variables.

If behaviour takes time to adjust to new situations (for example, if expenditure varies more closely with previous than with current income), the model can reflect this. The most useful models are those which contain precise quantitative relationships. For example, a model which states that price rises cause demand to fall is less helpful than one which says that a 10 per cent price increase will lead to a 15 per cent fall in demand. Finally, it must be pointed out that economic models can be expressed in several different ways, verbally, graphically or algebraically. Graphs can be used, as we have done in this book, when only two variables have been involved, and we shall deal with algebraic formulations shortly.

EQUILIBRIUM MODELS

The ice cream demand model which has been used for illustrative purposes contains one dependent variable, the demand for ice creams, and one independent variable, the price of ice creams. It would be more useful if it could predict the price of ice creams as well as the demand for them. The model could be extended to do just this. We recall from our study of the nature of markets that price depends on supply and demand and that quantities supplied and demanded depend on price. We know, too, that equilibrium is defined as existing in a market when the quantities demanded and supplied are equal.

These pieces of information can be put together to construct a model of the market for ice creams. The model contains three interdependent variables, supply, demand and price. If the relationships between them can be expressed quantitatively, the model can be used to determine market equilibrium price and quantity. Such a procedure involves finding the values of all three variables when supply and demand are equal. It is called finding a *solution* to the model.

Three ways can be used to solve a simple model of this kind – using supply and demand schedules, graphs or algebra.

(1) Solutions using schedules

Let us suppose that we have the information contained in Table 11.1 about the quantities of ice creams supplied and demanded at a range of prices. All that we need to do to solve the model is to find the price at which the quantities supplied and demanded are equal. By inspection of the table, it is seen to be a price of 40 pence, which leads to sixty ice creams being bought and sold.

Table 11.1 *Demand and supply schedules for ice creams*

Price (pence)	*Quantities*	
	Supplied	*Demanded*
10	15	75
20	30	70
30	45	65
40	60	60
50	75	55

(2) Graphical solutions

As we saw in Chapter 4, demand and supply schedules can be plotted on graphs. The data in Table 11.1 have, therefore, been represented in the form of demand and supply curves in Figure 11.1. We know, of course, that equilibrium obtains where these two curves intersect. The values of the two variables at the point of intersection are 40 pence and sixty ice creams, the same solution as given by inspection of the demand and supply schedules.

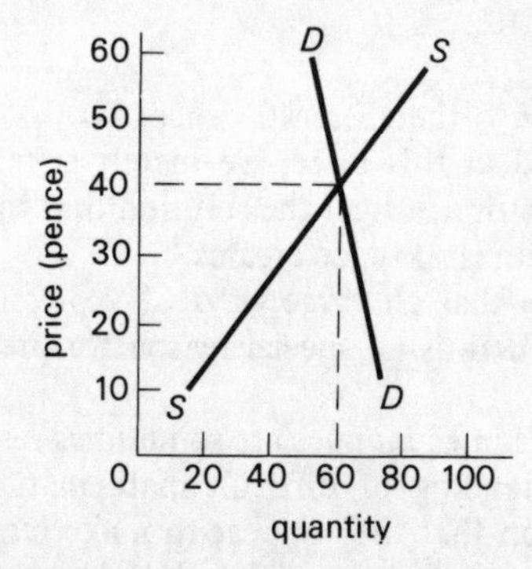

Figure 11.1 Graphical solution of ice cream market model.

(3) Algebraic solutions

Demand and supply curves can be plotted on graph paper from equations expressing the relationship between each of them and price. If we assume that the supply of ice creams is such that the quantity supplied is always equal to one and a half times the price, we can use the symbolic notation of mathematics to write

$$Q_s = 1\tfrac{1}{2}\,p \quad \text{(the supply equation).}$$

If we also assume that the demand for ice creams is always eighty minus half the price of ice creams, we can write

$$Q_d = 80 - \tfrac{1}{2}P \quad \text{(the demand equation).}$$

The symbols Q_s and Q_d stand for quantities supplied and demanded and P stands for price.

These two equations, if plotted, will give the curves of Figure 11.1. But we can solve the model algebraically by using the two equations and adding the equilibrium condition that quantities supplied and demanded must be equal – in symbols:

$$Q_s = Q_d.$$

Using the equilibrium condition we deduce that supply and demand must have the same value if there are to be no unsatisfied buyers or sellers, i.e. Q_s and Q_d in the supply and demand equations must be equal. Therefore, of course, the two equations must also be equal to each other,

$$1\tfrac{1}{2}P = 80 - \tfrac{1}{2}P,$$

which by rearrangement of terms becomes

$$1\tfrac{1}{2}P + \tfrac{1}{2}P = 80$$

$$P = 40.$$

The equilibrium price is therefore 40 pence. To find the quantities demanded and supplied at this price, we merely substitute the value of 40 for P in each equation, to get the solution that the quantity bought and sold in equilibrium is sixty ice creams.[1]

We may conclude that all three ways of expressing the model give the same solution. There is no special reason for preferring one to the others in this case.

Algebraic methods in economics are sometimes resisted because they may require understanding of difficult mathematical techniques and because of a suspicion that they appear to make human behaviour too predictable. The second objection is hardly a good one. The value of a model depends on how well it explains behaviour in the real world not on how it is formally expressed.

Mathematical methods are accepted techniques of advanced economic analysis. The world is a complex place and economists need to work with numerous variables if they are to include interactions between many determinants of behaviour. Verbal argument becomes impossible if we have too many relationships to keep in our heads at the same time. Geometry is ruled out if one needs to work in more than two or three dimensions. When hypotheses are expressed algebraically there is no limit, in principle, to the number of variables that can be included. The better our mathematics and the more sophisticated the computers we have at our disposal, the more complex the situations we can analyse. There can, of course, be dangers in using complex models when the behavioural assumptions are inappropriate. It must not be forgotten that a model is only a model. Hence the importance of comparing the results it gives with those that can be observed in the real world.

MAKING MODELS WORK

We have restricted our use of models so far to examining equilibrium situations. Models can also be made to work, to show the results of any alterations in conditions that might take place. Such a change might occur because of a revision of *ceteris paribus* assumptions made previously. Suppose, for example, that there is a rise in productivity in the ice cream industry, resulting in suppliers being prepared to offer larger numbers of ice creams at every price than they did before.

We can analyse the effect of such a change by means of any of our three methods. Suppose the change in productivity is such that producers offer for sale $3\frac{1}{2}$ times the price of ice creams, rather than $1\frac{1}{2}$ times, as in the previous model. We can either recalculate the new quantities supplied and replace the numbers in the first column of Table 11.1, plot a new supply curve (to the right of the old one) in Figure 11.1, or substitute $Q_s = 3\frac{1}{2}P$ for $Q_s = 1\frac{1}{2}P$ as our supply equation. The new equilibrium conditions can then be found by inspecting the table to find the price at which supply and demand are equal, examining the co-ordinates of the point of intersection of the new supply curve with the old demand curve, or algebraically using the new supply equation instead of the old. The reader is recommended to use all three methods to satisfy himself that the results are identical. The answer is given in a note.[2]

DYNAMIC MODELS

The method of making a model work illustrated in the previous paragraph is one way of analysing what happens when conditions vary over time. It compares two equilibrium situations before and after a change and is known as *comparative statics.* However, we do not always want to contrast equilibrium situations so much as to track the path the economy takes between equilibria.

This may be important when the economy never reaches equlibrium because relationships are such that behaviour continually changes. Suppose, for example, the price of potatoes is relatively low this year because of a bumper crop. The result may induce farmers to plant fewer potatoes now; but when the harvest comes there will then be so few potatoes that the price jumps to a very high level. Farmers are then induced to plant a lot of potatoes and the following year's bumper crop brings the price down again. In other words, there is a time-lag between the reaction of supply to price, which may produce a cycle of disequilibrium prices, high and low, in alternate years without reaching equilibrium at all. To analyse time paths, such as those of prices and quantities, in non-equilibrium situations, economists employ dynamic models. These allow for time-lags and feedbacks and variables have dates attached to them (e.g. P_t and P_{t-1}, to show price in two time periods, t and $t-1$, analysed in a model). Dynamic models are more complicated to analyse than static ones and are beyond the scope of this introductory book.

Stock and flow variables

Before leaving the subject of economic models and moving on to discuss the testing of them, it is worth pointing out that economic behaviour is sometimes related to two distinct kinds of variables: stocks and flows.

For instance, the amount a person spends on consumption may be affected by how much money he has in the bank and also by how much income he earns each year. The former is stock. It is a quantity of money existing at a moment of time. The latter is a flow: income per period of time. Of course, the two may be related. For example, if a burglar steals £1,000 of my stock of savings, I may spend less this year in order to rebuild by assets, even though my annual income is unchanged.

MODEL TESTING

We have repeatedly stressed the need to confront economic models with the evidence of the real world. We now proceed to consider ways in which such testing can be carried out.[3]

The first requirement is to ensure that a model is in a testable form. This will follow if three conditions are satisfied: (1) the model is positively expressed, (2) the terminology is clear and (3) the relationships are preferably quantified.

We have discussed the nature of positive statements in economics earlier. There is no point in seeking evidence with which to confront a theory that income tax is too high, for example. This is a normative statement containing an implicit value judgement and it is not objectively testable. Some such statements may be reformulated by excluding the normative element. For instance, the hypothesis that a rise in the rates of income tax leads to a reduction in the number of hours worked can be tested.

The need for clarity of expression in a model might seem too obvious to be worth mentioning. But language can be a poor vehicle for communication and ambiguities creep in, sometimes, undetected, and cause errors in scientific work. Consider an example from physics. How straight is a straight line? Unless straightness is precisely defined, apparently scientific experiments may give ambiguous or misleading answers. Light travels in waves, which appear only if its path is measured over distances shorter than its wavelength. If observation points are chosen without regard to these, experiments may yield curious and misleading results.

Economics is probably even more susceptible to imprecisions of definition than the physical sciences. Both dependent and independent variables are at risk. For example, if we are testing a theory of unemployment, it may be critical to know the precise meaning of unemployment in the hypothesis and also in the data. Does either refer to frictional, structural, cyclical or total unemployment? Do the statistics used in the test include persons temporarily out of work? What is the cut-off point of days out of work before an individual is regarded as being permanently unemployed? And so on. If there is uncertainty about precisely what the theory is trying to explain, or about the meaning of the data used to test it, there will be doubts about how to interpret the results.

In economics, ambiguities in the meaning of data involved in tests are common. Economists have to work with the best available data, which often do not correspond precisely to what is specified in the model. Proxy (i.e. substitute) variables have to be employed, in the hope that they bear close relationships to those really required. For example, statistical data on the distribution of personal incomes is derived in large part from tax returns. These may under-record some incomes, but be the best at the disposal of the investigator. Provided there is a consistent relationship between the proxy variable and the one that is needed, the results of statistical work may not be seriously affected, though this is not always the case. We may, however, conclude that the clearer the way in which the variables in a model and in data are expressed, the easier it will be to carry out a satisfactory test. One might add at this stage, in anticipation of a later conclusion, that evidence when collected must also be interpreted. A major source of potential disagreement among economists is the interpretations they sometimes give to the results of confronting a model with empirical evidence.

The final requirement for the satisfactory testing of a model is that it should, preferably, be quantified. This need is less vital than that for it to be expressed in clear, positive terms. Nevertheless, there is no doubt that a model which is quantitatively stated may be more useful than one which is put merely qualitatively. For example, we know more about the economy if we can be reasonably confident that price changes are accompanied by, say, 2 per cent changes in the opposite direction in demand, than if we merely know that price changes lead to inverse changes in the quantities demanded. However, many qualitative models may still be useful. Quantification, which raises their value, may come after empirical work has been done by way of testing.

STATISTICAL TESTS

Let us suppose that we are now ready to test the simple model that we examined earlier, that the demand for ice creams was dependent on price. Our object is to see if we can identify an association between the dependent variable, demand, and the independent variable price in a real market situation. We know, of course, that demand is affected by many factors, some of which, such as income, were held constant by the *ceteris paribus* assumptions of the model. If we were testing a hypothesis in the physical sciences, the most effective procedure might be to conduct a laboratory experiment. We could then hold the excluded variables constant while we observed the reactions of those in which we were interested.

Suppose we wanted to find out the determinants of some physical event, for example, what causes a liquid to change into a gas? We know that at least two factors, heat and pressure, are involved. We are able to provide conditions of constant pressure in a laboratory while subjecting a substance to changing heat. We can usually design an experiment to observe the effects of one variable on another, holding other determining variables constant (*ceteris* truly *paribus*). Moreover, we can repeat an experiment over and over again to see whether we get similar results each time. We gain confidence in the results the more often they are confirmed.

Repeated controlled experiments are rarely practised in the social sciences outside psychology. The main reason is that we can rarely hope to simulate, in a laboratory, real conditions that affect the kind of behaviour in which economists are interested. Microeconomic conditions are hard enough. How do you structure an experiment to see how consumers react to changes in the relative prices of goods and services? Experiments with macroeconomic phenomena are inconceivable. No laboratory could encapsulate a world representative enough to test the theory of the multiplier, the quantity theory of money, the Phillips curve or similar relationships between economic aggregates.

The economist is, therefore, denied the advantage of the controlled laboratory experiment. He is forced to turn for evidence to observations of actual behaviour of human beings in an uncontrolled world. The data the economist uses consist largely of statistics which are obtained from public and private sources. The analysis of such data, known as *econometrics*, is a highly specialised task. The statistical tools of the econometrician have to be powerful enough to cope with the complexities found in the real world, when many things are changing at the same time. They must enable him to synthesise the real holding constant of variables in a laboratory in order to isolate relationships between others. They are too technical to describe in any detail here, but we can understand something of the nature of the work of an applied economist by following through the procedure he might adopt in a simple case.

Let us remind ourselves that the econometrician is set the task of testing economic theories which suggest the dependence of some variables upon others; for instance, that the demand for ice creams depends on their price. The method used for testing involves, as a first step, the assembly of data on prices and quantities of ice creams bought, in order to see whether there is a consistent relationship between them. If there is, and if the relationship is thought likely to be a stable one, it might then be possible to express the relationship quantitatively in such a form that would allow reasonable predictions of demand at different prices.

Statistical association

Let us assume that the econometrician has collected data of the quantities of ice creams that were bought at varying prices in the past. His task is to decide whether these two variables show any clear pattern of association with each other. If so, they may be described as being correlated, or it may be said there is some *correlation* between them.

A common and useful first approach is to portray all the observations graphically in the form of what is known as a *scatter diagram.* Each point on the graph represents a particular observation, depicting the quantity bought at a price. The point marked *A* on the graph, for example, shows that when price was 40 pence, sixty ice creams were bought. We can see roughly whether the two variables are correlated by inspection of the diagram. The more scattered they are over the graph the less correlation, and vice versa.

If there is evidence of statistical association between price and quantity, the econometrician can go further and try to establish the quantitative relationship between them. This is done by estimating their average association. We can draw a line on the diagram indicating the average relationship between price and quantity. This is known as 'the line of best fit'. It can be drawn (as we have done) by eye, or by statistical techniques which need not concern us.[4] The line is a straight one (though there is no reason why a curve should not be fitted if the scatter of points suggests it would be a better way of portraying the

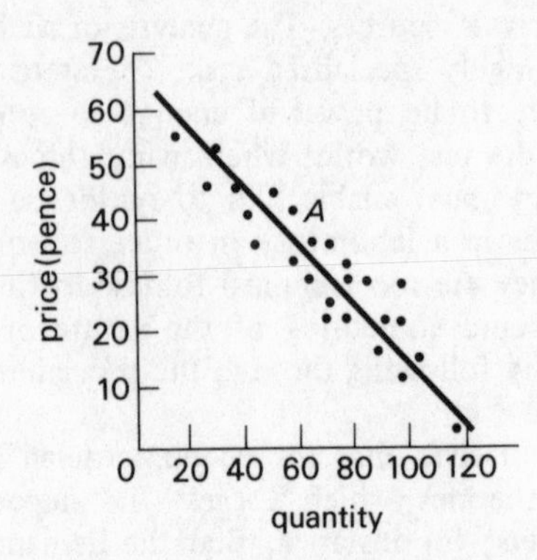

Figure 11.2 *Observations of price–quantity demanded relationships.*

association). The slope of the curve describes the relationship quantitatively. This line has a slope of (–)1. This means that an increase in price of, say, 2 pence would be associated on average with a decrease in demand of two ice creams. A steeper slope would imply a smaller fall in quantity with the same price increase and vice versa.

Statistical reliability

The measure of correlation between price and quantity discussed in the previous section is what is known as a statistical one. It relates to the way in which all the observations are associated and is not intended to apply to each and every situation. How reliable it is as a tool of prediction depends mainly on two factors: the number of observations and their variability. The first of these is only common sense. If we based conclusions on a mere handful of observations of past behaviour we would not think any conclusion as reliable as if we had hundreds or thousands of observed price–quantity relationships at our disposal. Moreover, we ought to expect some observations might be unrepresentative, freak ones. For instance, returning to the ice cream market illustration, there may have been an unseasonal heat wave in February or a couple of bitterly cold summer days when the demand for ice creams was more affected by the weather than by anything else. Such disturbances would make it difficult for us to observe the relationship between price and quantity that we are interested in. It is clear that the probability of a single observation being unrepresentative is greater, the smaller the number of observations. There is always a chance of random errors in any sample set of data, but it is a well-established fact that such errors are more likely to cancel out the larger the sample size, that is, the greater the number of observations.

The confidence that one may have in any apparent association depends not only on the number of observations but on how varied they are. This is best explained in graphical terms as the spread, or scatter, of points around the line of best fit. Figure 11.3 shows two scatter diagrams each of which may be compared with Figure 11.2. The line of best fit in the left-hand graph, Figure 11.3(i), is almost certainly the less reliable of the two because of the wide spread of individual observations. The line in the right-hand diagram, Figure 11.3 (ii), is deserving of less confidence because the number of observations is very small and, even though they lie exactly on a straight line, one would not be happy deriving a general rule from so small a sample.

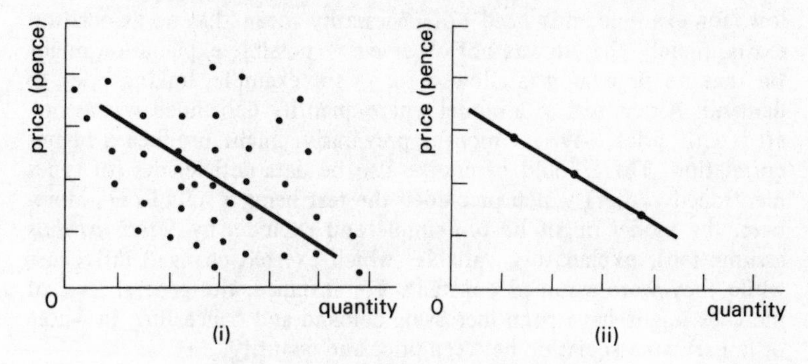

Figure 11.3 *Statistical reliability.*

There is no totally objective way of deciding how far one can rely on a relationship between variables which are statistically correlated. One common method used by statisticians is to consider what the likelihood is that the observed results obtained could have been obtained by chance, that is, without there being any real association between them. With a given scatter and known number of observations, it is possible to estimate the probability of this occurring. By convention, if a relationship is discovered which could have occurred only once in a hundred, or once in twenty, by pure chance, the association is described as being statistically 'significant'. It is important to stress that these are no more than conventional, arbitrary benchmarks which may be helpful in econometric work. Statistical significance is not the same as proof. We may sometimes disregard a statistically significant association, if there are grounds for suspecting that the associated variables may not be correlated.

ASSESSING THE RESULTS OF A TEST

We consider, finally, how to assess the results of confronting an economic model with empirical evidence. Three considerations arise: (1) whether an association has been established, (2) whether it is causal and (3) how general the results are.

(1) Establishing association

In order to decide whether an association between two variables has been found, one must, in the first place, judge the reliability of the correlation, that is, by examining the number of observations and their scatter. One must also look carefully at the way in which the model was formulated and the precise nature of the data used to test it, matters which were discussed earlier. If the correlation appears to be low, for example, this need not necessarily mean that no association exists, merely that it was not observed. A possible explanation might be that no time-lag was allowed for – for example, linking price to demand. A new test of a model where quantity demanded was associated with price, say, six months previously, might produce a higher correlation. There could of course also be data deficiencies (of types mentioned earlier) which precluded the test being a sound one. Moreover, the model might be too simple and exclude, by *ceteris paribus* assumptions, explanatory variables which exerted changed influences while they were assumed constant. For instance, the general level of incomes might have risen increasing demand and concealing, in whole or in part, an association between price and quantity.

The argument in this section warns us not to reject a hypothesis simply because the evidence from a test does not confirm it. The moral should be to subject the model to further tests if there is any reason to believe that it may still be a valid one. Much the same is true of correlations which appear to support a theory. The results are, in principle, just as capable of being due to similar errors. They should be treated with equal caution.[5]

(2) Establishing causality

The most important danger to be avoided in drawing conclusions from statistical evidence is that of assuming that high correlation necessarily means that one variable *causes* changes in another. In the first place, the reason for the high correlation may be that there is an important excluded explanatory variable which is the true cause of the association. For example, there is a high positive correlation between the numbers of suicides and of marriages, but no one seriously believes that the relationship between them is causal. Each happens to be highly correlated with a third variable – the size of the total population, which is increasing. In this case, it is obvious that the correlation is not causal, but by no means all false 'causation' is so obvious as this example. One should add that, sometimes, an incomplete model may nevertheless be useful, as long as it is used with care. For instance, it is said that a better than random way of predicting tomorrow's weather in Britain is to use a model which says that tomorrow's weather will be the same as today's. The predictive value of this hypothesis is apparently good on average. Yet it cannot forecast a single one of the important changes in weather that occur.

There is one other important source of error in inferring causality from statistical association that must be mentioned. It goes under the name of the *post hoc ergo propter hoc* fallacy (after the event, therefore because of it).

Even if a causal link exists between two variables there is still a problem of deciding which is the cause and which the consequence. An example of the way in which controversies can arise over causality in the presence of high statistical association is the question of the relationship between changes in the quantity of money and in the general level of prices. There is no disagreement about the high correlation itself. It will be remembered from Chapter 9, however, that there are two major schools of thought on the nature of the causal nexus. Monetarists believe that the change in the quantity of money causes the change in the general level of prices. Keynesians, in contrast, prefer the explanation of the causal sequence being, at least sometimes, the exact opposite. The statistical association cannot, by itself, prove either of them right or wrong. The importance of this point cannot be overstated. Yet it is all too frequently forgotten. To illustrate, two Cambridge economists discovered that the rate of change in prices in the UK was even more highly correlated with the incidence of dysentry in Scotland than with changes in the money supply! Of course they were not trying to argue a Scottish dysentry theory of inflation, but showing the unjustifiability of inferring causality from mere association, with a suitably absurd example.

(3) Generalising the results

The final matter to consider on drawing together the results of a test is how general they are. This is a vital consideration. If one has discovered a reliable statistical association and is satisfied about the causal chain, it may be used in helping to predict the future. There are two very real dangers to watch for. The first is that of assuming that past behaviour will be repeated, especially if it has persisted for a long time. Circumstances change and unpredictable events can exert new influences, upsetting previously established relationships. The reactions of the community to continuing inflation provide a good illustration. After many years of price stability the first appearance of inflation may not at once change economic behaviour at all. But continuous inflation tends to lead the community to expect it to persist and act accordingly.

The second trap that awaits the unwary observer who is tempted to draw general conclusions from limited data is known as the fallacy of composition. If a statement is correct for each and every member of a population, it is not necessarily correct for the population as a whole. There are many examples of the appearance of this fallacy in economics. For instance, it may easily be established that an individual cereal manufacturer can sell more of his product if he increases expenditure on advertising. But we cannot conclude that, if all cereal manufacturers increase advertising expenditure together, total sales will rise by the sum of the increases by all individual manufacturers. The extra sales of each may be achieved only at the expense of others; total demand for breakfast cereals may be unchanged.[6]

ECONOMIC 'LAWS'

We end this chapter on the methods used by economists to build and test models with an observation concerning the so-called 'economic laws' which may be propounded as a result. We should hardly find it surprising now to learn that economics has not produced as many stable laws as have the physical sciences. The validity of 'economic laws' is, in practice, difficult to establish, and they are perhaps better described as tendencies – the tendency for demand curves to slope downwards, or the tendency for consumption expenditure to increase as income rises. Such 'laws' are useful only in so far as they are supported by evidence. They do not necessarily apply to all individual cases; they may not be reliable in the ever-changing environment of a real economy; and they are in no sense, of course, inviolable.

Predictions concerning economic behaviour are, for the many reasons described in this chapter, liable to error. People sometimes scoff when economists turn out to be wrong, especially when different economists make contradictory predictions. No one should imagine that forecasting is easy, as meteorologists and doctors, for example, may witness. Economics is still a fair distance away from being able to forecast consistently and accurately the course of economic behaviour. It might be a much less interesting subject if it could.

NOTES: CHAPTER 11

1 Models may have more than one solution, e.g. if any of the behavioural relationships are non-linear.

2 The new equation $3\frac{1}{2}P = 80 - \frac{1}{2}P$ has the solution $P = 20$ (pence), i.e. at this price seventy ice creams will be demanded and supplied.

3 For an introduction to the testing of economic models the reader is referred to Haines, B., *An Introduction to Quantitative Economics* (Allen & Unwin, 1978).

4 One of the most common techniques is known as 'least squares'. The line of best fit drawn in such a way is that which minimises the sum of (the squares of) individual deviations from it.

5 Sometimes one can be embarrassed by having too many high correlations for different models all of which purport to explain the same behaviour. Choosing between them may be very difficult.

6 An even more famous example of the fallacy of composition is the Paradox of Thrift (see page 138 above).

Appendix

The Use of Graphs in Economics

Graphs are used in economics to portray the association between observed variables in the real world and also between hypothetical ones used in the construction of economic models.

HOW TO DRAW A GRAPH

A graph represents relationships pictorially. It is drawn on squared paper, on which two vertical lines are drawn, known as axes, which intersect at a point called the origin. Each axis is divided by a scale into units. Along these quantities of a variable are measured.

Figure A.1 is a graph which has been prepared to show the relationship between the price of ice creams and the numbers that are offered

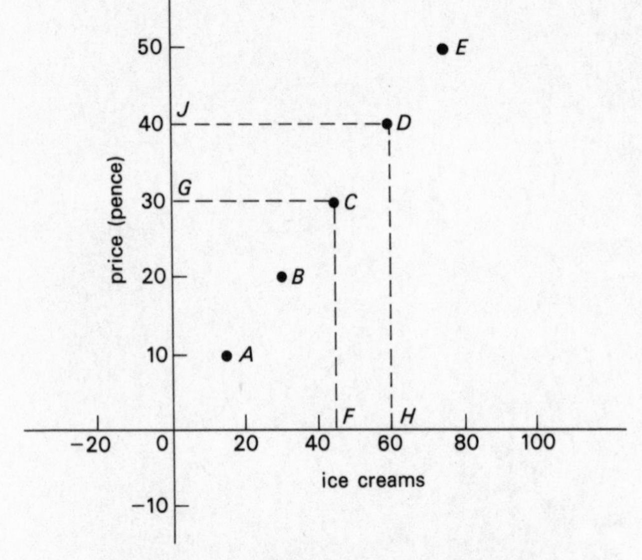

Figure A.1 *Graphing price–supply relationships.*

for sale (i.e. the supply of ice creams). Let us measure price on the vertical axis and numbers of ice creams on the horizontal.[1] (*Never forget to label axes on a graph, and you will be saved from many errors.*)

Next let us set the scales so that 1 cm = 20 ice creams or 10 pence. Then any point on the graph describes one particular quantitative relationship between ice creams and prices. Consider the point marked *D*. To find out what quantities are indicated at *D* we need only drop perpendiculars to each axis. *DJ* and *DH* tell us that the point *D* indicates 40 pence and 60 ice creams. In other words, if we want to convey that 60 ice creams would be offered for sale at a price of 40 pence we could merely stipulate point *D* on the graph.

Similarly, point *C* represents 45 ice creams at a price of 30 pence, point *B* represents 30 ice creams at a price of 20 pence, and so on. All these points are in the 'north-east' quadrant of the graph, where the numbers of ice-creams and prices are positive. Other quadrants refer to cases where one or both variables are negative. They are obviously not relevant here but are sometimes useful.[2]

The data used for the construction of graphs can come from tables setting out the values of the two variables. Figure A.1 is, in fact, based on the numbers contained in Table 11.1 for the supply schedule of ice creams offered for sale at a range of prices. The data could equally have come from an equation. Consider for example the equation

$$Q_s = 1\tfrac{1}{2}P$$

(where Q_s and P are symbols standing for quantity supplied and price). There is sufficient information in the equation to plot the points *A* to *E* on the graph. If we put different values of *P* into it, the equation tells us how many ice creams will be offered for sale in each case. Thus, if we take a price of 20 pence and substitute 20 for *P* in the equation we get

$$Q_s = 1\tfrac{1}{2}(20) = 30$$

This is point *B* on the graph. When $P = 40$, $Q_s = 1\tfrac{1}{2}(40) = 60$, (point *D*), and so on.

Graphs can be used to represent not just a few relationships between variables, but a continuous set. This we do by drawing a line on the graph, such as *AE* in Figure A.2, which is the line that would in fact go through points *A* to *E* in Figure A.1. If the line is continuous, we can infer from it the number of ice creams offered for sale at any price between 10 and 50 pence. The procedure is similar to that described previously and consists of dropping perpendiculars to the horizontal axis. Thus, at a price of 24 pence, 36 ice creams would be supplied (point *K*). Conversely, to find the price at which a given quantity would be supplied, we would drop a perpendicular to the vertical axis. The

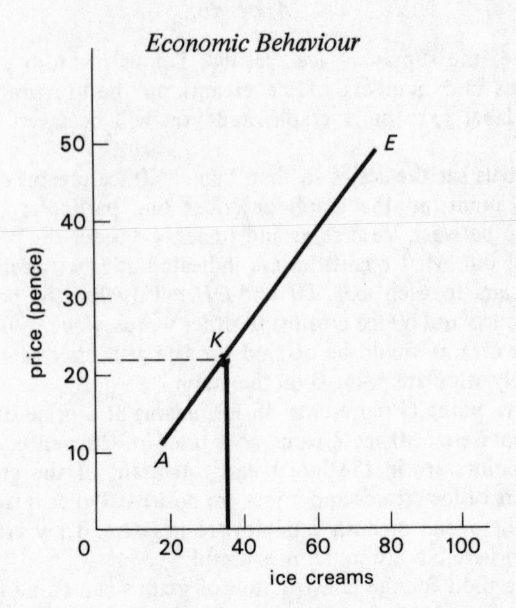

Figure A.2 *The construction of a supply curve.*

line *AE* is then a brief and economical way of describing the full relationship between every single price and quantity depicted by it. We can draw any line on a graph to represent the way in which we believe (or our model assumes) that price and quantity are related. The line *AE* on the graph is said to show a positive *linear relationship.* This means only: (*a*) that when price changes the quantity is assumed to change *in the same direction* as the price (i.e. the association is positive); and (*b*) that when price changes by a given absolute amount from any given starting point, the quantity always changes by a uniform amount (i.e. it is linear).

There is, naturally, no need to make either of these assumptions if they are not true. Negative relationships imply that the two variables are inversely associated, as for example with a downward sloping demand curve, where rises in price induce falls in the quantities demanded.

LINEAR RELATIONSHIPS

The assumption of linearity is often used in economic theory because in many cases it happens to be useful, if only as an approximation. The word linear is self-explanatory, but it is worth trying to understand why a relationship in which changes in one variable always

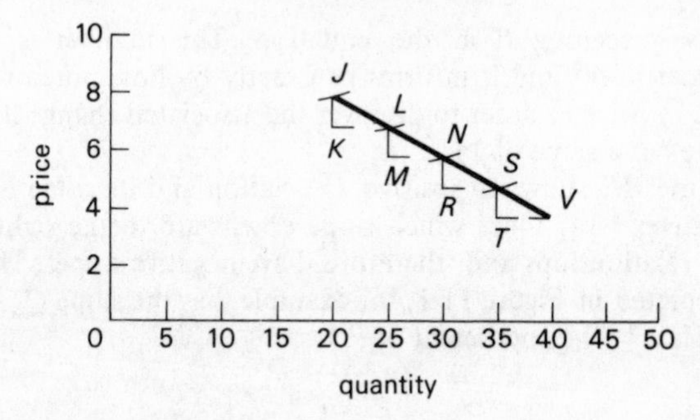

Figure A.3 *Measurement of the slope of a linear demand curve.*

produce uniform changes in the other will obviously be a straight line on a graph.

An intuitive grasp of the reason can be obtained from Figure A.3. We assume that point *I* lies on a line *JV*. This line represents a price–quantity relationship in which a change in price of 1 always leads to a change (in the opposite direction) of 5 in quantity. Let us start from point *J* (price 8 and quantity 20), and move along the line to *L* (price 7 and quantity 25). In other words, we assume price falls from 8 to 7 and quantity rises from 20 to 25.

The movement from *J* to *L* is, in fact, a downhill slide along a hill with a certain slope. To measure this slope, we may imagine that we first descend vertically by *JK* and then move horizontally by *KL*. The relationship between the height *JK* and the length *KL is* the slope.

If price were to continue to fall in steps of one unit (by *LM*, *NR*, *ST*, etc.), exactly the same increase in quantity would recur: 5 units ($= MN = RS = TV$). In other words, the slopes of the line between *L* and *N*, between *N* and *S*, and between *S* and *V* are all the same as the slope between *J* and *L*. This property of common slope of the line *JV* still applies if price falls by 4, from 8 to 4. The quantity rises by 20 (5 times 4) since the slope of *JV* is, of course, the same as the slope of its constituent parts.

You may never have thought that a straight line is one with a constant slope, but a moment's reflection should convince you. If a line starts to bend this means that its slope changes. Hence, the logical conclusion that *JL* has a constant slope really means also that the line is a straight one.

It is possible to infer the slope of a line from the equation describing it without drawing a graph. Consider the equation of the supply curve $Q_s = 1\frac{1}{2}P$, used to construct the first two diagrams. We know that the slope of the line tells us by how much quantity alters with a change in price. But this is precisely the information given by the number, $1\frac{1}{2}$, immediately preceding P in the equation. This number is called the (price) coefficient and it informs us exactly by how much to multiply a change in price in order to discover the associated change in quantity. The curve has a slope of $1\frac{1}{2}$.

The line AE shows a positive association and its slope is therefore also positive, $+1\frac{1}{2}$. Lines which slope downward to the right represent negative relationships and, therefore, have negative slopes. The demand curve depicted in Figure 11.1, for example, has the slope $Q_d = 80 - 1P$. Its slope is $-\frac{1}{2}$, the coefficient of P.[3]

TANGENTS TO CURVES

Sometimes we need to know the slope of a (non-linear) curve, such as AB in Figure A.4. The procedure for finding it is to draw a line tangent to the curve at the point at which the slope is to be measured. The tangent shows the rate at which quantity changes with price.[4] CD has been drawn tangent to AB at W. The slope of CD is the same as that of AB at the point W. Of course, as AB is a true curve its slope varies at differing points along it. At point V, for example, it has the slope of $C'D'$.

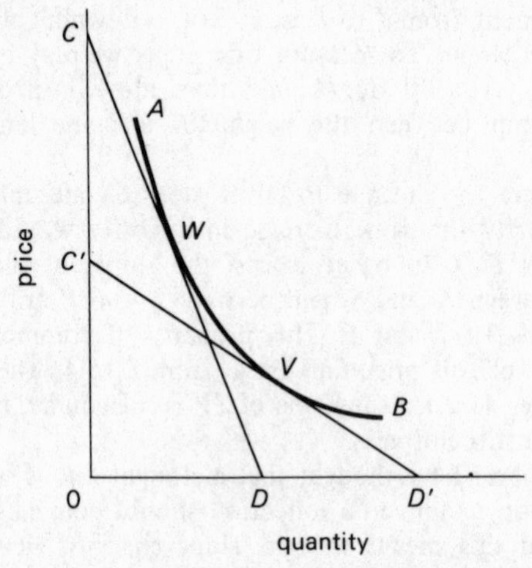

Figure A.4 *Construction of tangents to curves.*

AREAS UNDER CURVES

A final feature of graphs is the meaning to be given to areas bounded by perpendiculars dropped to the two axes from any point on a curve.

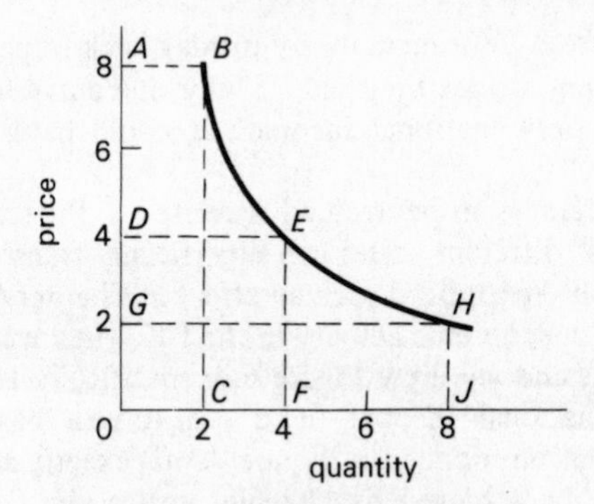

Figure A.5 *A rectangular hyperbola.*

The area of such a rectangle is equal to the length of one of its sides multiplied by that of the other. In Figure A.5, the area *ODEF*, for example, is *OF* times *OD*, i.e. 4 x 4 = 16. Such areas may sometimes have important economic significance. If the curve *BH* is a demand curve, then the axes measure price and quantity demanded. The area *ODEF*, therefore, measures price times quantity, i.e. total outlay by consumers, at the price *OD*. *BH* has in fact been drawn in a particular way, because all rectangles representing total outlay are the same size, irrespective of price. It is a special kind of demand curve. Its peculiar feature is that a given *proportionate* change in price is accompanied by an equal *proportionate* change in quantity demanded. It is known as a rectangular hyperbola. All demand curves of unit elasticity have this property (see above, Chapter 4, page 60).

GRAPHS OF EMPIRICAL DATA

The material in this appendix has so far been restricted to the use of graphs in economic theory. Graphs are, however, extensively employed to depict empirically observed relationships between economic variables in the real world. They must be prepared and interpreted with caution. There are two kinds of danger to be avoided. In the first place attention must be paid to the precise meaning of the statistics used to construct the graph. Consider, for example, a graph depicting the course of national income over a period of years. This can be drawn in two very different ways, one based on statistics of national income at current prices, the other at constant prices. The former shows the trend of nominal national income in money terms, the latter allows for inflation and depicts the course of real national income over the same period. We drew both curves for the UK since 1930 on a single diagram (Figure

6.3). If you refresh your memory by turning back to page 113 you will see what different stories they tell. If only one curve had been shown and labelled simply 'national income', it could have been very misleading.

The second danger to be avoided is related to the scales used on the axes. The use of different scales can superficially transform the picture given by a graph. We noticed such an effect in Chapter 6, when looking at fluctuations in economic activity in the UK. They were barely visible from Figure 6.3 and we drew Figure 6.4, specifically to emphasise the variability of national income on a year-to-year basis. Part of the diagram has been reproduced in Figure A.6(i) exactly as before. But to show what can be achieved by changing scales, the figures have been plotted a second time in Figure A.6(ii) using a larger horizontal and a smaller vertical scale. The effect is to alter the apparent amplitude of the fluctuations quite markedly. Figure A.6(i) gives an impression of great volatility. Figure A.6(ii), in contrast, makes the upswings and downswings look much smaller. And, of course, either or both scales could be further adjusted until they presented any superficial appearance desired.[5] Yet they are all graphic representations of a single set of figures. The moral is that we should always be wary of the impression made by casual inspection of a graph; especially, perhaps, if we know it has been constructed by someone who has an axe to grind and who chooses scales to trap the unwary.[6]

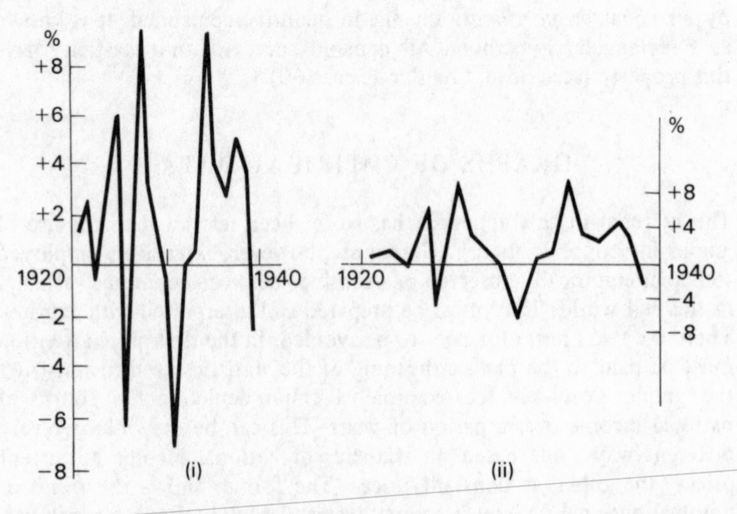

Figure A.6 *Year-to-year changes in national output (per cent), 1921–39, on two scales* (i) and (ii).
Source: as for Figure 6.3.

APPENDIX NOTES:

1 Students of mathematics may be shocked to hear that economists sometimes refer to straight line relationships as demand 'curves', and that the positions of the dependent and independent variables are reversed.

2 For example, saving can be negative at low incomes. Refer back to Figure 7.5.

3 The constant term, 80, in the equation does not affect its slope, which would be the same if the equation were $100-\frac{1}{2}P$, $20-\frac{1}{2}P$, etc. It determines the point of intersection of the line with the axis which is called the *intercept.*

4 For very small (technically infinitesimal) price changes.

5 Omission of the zero point on the scale of a graph can be used with the same effect.

6 For similar reasons we should be wary of descriptions of slopes as steep or gentle without paying attention to the scales on both axes.

Index